Compliments of

The School for Bank Administration
July 24-August 5, 1988
36th Annual Session

MONEY
IN THE
BANK

MONEY
IN THE
BANK

HOW SAFE IS IT?

A. ROBERT ABBOUD
WILLIAM G. SCHOPF
GEOFFREY N. SMITH

BANK ADMINISTRATION INSTITUTE:
ROLLING MEADOWS, ILLINOIS
DOW JONES-IRWIN: HOMEWOOD, ILLINOIS

BANK ADMINISTRATION INSTITUTE

BAI is a unique professional services organization that offers research, information services, and professional development opportunities to bankers worldwide. The Institute's independent, not-for-profit status enables it to serve bankers objectively — as both advisor and analyst.

BAI is a creative partnership, blending the policy-level experience of bankers worldwide with the specialized expertise of its professional staff. These bankers serve on the Institute's board of directors, technical commissions and advisory groups, ensuring that BAI meets changing needs with relevant programs and services.

The Institute presents information across a wide range of critically important areas, including management and administration; strategic planning; accounting, finance and control; audit and tax; corporate financial services; retail financial services; marketing; and operations and technology. This information is conveyed through methods well-suited to the varying needs of banking professionals — ranging from research, technical conferences, and educational programs to a broad and growing array of publications.

Second printing, May 1988
Library of Congress Catalog Card Number: 87-73266

This publication is sold with the understanding that the publisher is not engaged in rendering legal, accounting, or other professional service. If legal advice or other expert assistance is required, the services of a competent professional person should be sought. The opinions expressed in this book are those of the authors, and do not necessarily represent opinions of Bank Administration Institute.

Printed in the United States of America
No. 173   ISBN: 0-01-55520-068-0
2 3 4 5 6 7 8 9 0   9 0 8 9 88

DEDICATION

This book is dedicated to my father, Alfred Abboud, who believed strongly in education and the educational system as the foundation for our country's well-being. He and my mother, Victoria Karam, made the sacrifices and commitment to make possible my own education.

Contents

List of Figures

Foreword

The two questions I am repeatedly asked are: Why are you writing this book and what should I do with my money? The first question is easier to answer than the second, but I shall tackle both.

My purpose is to bring to light some critical issues that, I am afraid, are too frequently misunderstood or neglected in our financial decision-making processes, both personal and public. I use examples from my own experience as a commercial banker to demonstrate that the issues discussed and the decisions made by the leaders of our financial community and by the government officials who regulate them have a very real impact on all of us, and on our entire society. I would like to share some insights into the banking industry whose everyday workings need to be better understood and better policed by the enforcers of public policy.

Our money is the product of our labor. It constitutes our savings and our future security. Our money can only be as safe as the economy which backs the nation's currency. The currency, in turn, is only as safe as the banks and thrift institutions that hold it and invest it. The banks and thrifts are only as safe as the quality of their managers and the principles that guide them. The principles and the competencies of those who direct our banks and thrift institutions are a direct reflection of the standards of our citizens. If the general public sets high standards, the institutions will be governed in accordance with these standards. Conversely, if the public prefers to keep its hands off of policy, the institutions will be subject to repeated boom-and-bust cycles. The resulting instability will damage the banking system and, in turn, the economy. This can cause us to lose our jobs, our savings, and ultimately our society.

Our system of money and banking is, to use a popular banking term, highly *leveraged*, and in three ways. First, the U.S. Government issues currency, only a fraction of it backed by gold. The currency does have the "full faith and credit" of the U.S. Government, but as we know, governments sometimes go broke. The U.S. Government publishes income statements that are consistently in deficit and balance sheets that show a negative net worth of approximately four trillion dollars, hardly a rousing endorsement for either "faith" or "credit."

The private banking system, in its turn, takes the currency issued by the U.S. Government and creates more money (i.e., deposits) in a second round of leverage. The banks and thrifts create a third round of leverage by engaging in activities not subject to reserve requirements or regulatory controls. These activities give rise to more liabilities, both actual and contingent.

I ask you to keep this triple-leverage pyramid of money creation in mind as you read and study the following pages. The possibilities of miscalculation and the dangers of error are omnipresent, their consequences impossible to measure.

Do I see storm clouds hovering above? I'd have to be blind not to see them. However, my purpose is not to preach doom and gloom. Rather it is to demonstrate that the system is workable if we, as voters, establish standards to keep it working properly and to keep it from being abused. But, we have to take the time and effort to learn about it, and too few of us do.

As to my second question, "What should I do with my money?"...

No one answer can be right for everyone. Each individual or family situation must be considered in terms of its needs and priorities. This is why it is important to have a competent source of financial advice and counsel. Such services should be available as a public service of all depository institutions.

Furthermore, a prudent financial program is defined by how you view the present and the future. For example, if you believe that inflation is coming, then one set of investments may be appropriate. If you believe recession or depression is coming, or if both inflation and recession are on the way, then other strategies are appropriate. Your freedom to match an investment approach to your convictions and beliefs is the foundation of our free market system.

I personally believe major challenges and hard times lie ahead. I think the regulatory environment governing our money and banking system needs major attention. And I believe our money is not now safe and will not be safe in the future unless we allow the marketplace to be the ultimate disciplinarian.

I certainly do not believe it prudent to put all of one's eggs in one basket, one type of investment, or even one institution. There are just too many variables at work to be certain of anything these days. I have always advocated owning a little gold or silver or precious minerals or stones. For those who can afford it, owning some art can also be an anchor of stability. As for bonds, I like short-term Government bonds (inflation could hurt the long-term bonds) and U.S. Government savings bonds, as long as they carry the floating interest rate. I also like short-term, high-grade insured municipal bonds.

Corporate bonds are another story. I would certainly lean toward highly rated bonds and floating-rate bonds versus those with fixed rates. I also prefer bonds with equity kickers and/or conversion rights. Equities or stocks of high-grade companies that earn a better than 12 percent after-tax return on their equity and pay a decent and ever-increasing dividend are also good investments. Bondholders in companies that decide to do so-called "leveraged buyouts" are often disadvantaged unless they have equity kickers or conversion rights. So, watch out! I don't like companies that take on a lot of debt and then do not take action to reduce that debt quickly.

As for stocks of companies that earn less than a 12 percent after-tax return on their equity and/or do not pay a dividend, I'd rather have their senior bonds, where I get a cumulative contractual rate of return of 10 percent or better with covenants fixing penalties in case of default. I also prefer, when available, equity kickers such as warrants or rights and/or conversion privileges. I don't care if these are labeled "junk bonds." I'll pick them on a case-by-case basis.

Real estate, particularly real estate that yields a positive return or that is a home, farm, or vacation home, is always a good investment. Don't let anyone tell you otherwise.

Savings programs or certificates at banks and savings and loans that carry U.S. Government insurance are also sound investments, provided your institution is well managed and safe, gives you the same investment options at the retail level that it gives the "big guys" at the wholesale level, and publishes full particulars on the market value of its asset portfolio together with its capital and reserve accounts.

I am assuming in all of this that investment in U.S. dollar instruments is, in and of itself, a prudent thing to do, although foreign currency investments are available as are municipal bonds denominated in non-U.S. currencies. This assumption is based on my optimism that in order to keep the currency safe and sound, the public at large will exercise its political will over the U.S. Government and force it to stop incurring deficits at all levels. I am also assuming that the public at large will demand and receive an acceptable standard of business and political morality. Sharpening the dialogue in this area is what this book is about.

The book is not a guide to investments, nor is it a manual for portfolio management. The above recitation of my personal investing preferences is simply to bare my biases and to demonstrate my willingness to expose my personal judgments as directly and candidly as I know how. You may disagree with some of my judgments. Wonderful! And, I may be wrong at times. But what I think or believe is not as important as what the voting public thinks and believes and the consensus that develops. Through this book, I simply want to contribute to that consensus-building process, drawing from my own experiences both inside and outside the money and banking system.

ACKNOWLEDGMENTS

In grateful acknowledgment to my wife, Joan, my daughter Katherine, and my family, my sister, Mona, and my niece, Ashley, for their support, to my staff for their tireless efforts in research, ordering of materials, and endless typing. . . Miss Rose Marie Loparco, Mrs. Joy Throssell and Mrs. Susanne Williams. Grateful acknowledgment is also made to my daughter, Jeanne (Mrs. Paul Harrison), who designed this book and to my son, Robert, for his assistance in the many computer applications. My thanks also to those many friends and associates who responded to my inquiries for information.

ONE

We're Only Human

We Americans are truly blessed. We have a great country with plenty of room, fertile land, abundant supplies of water, mountains, coastline, climate, and natural resources beyond measure. We also have a talented, creative population with proportionately high rates of literacy and education. Put all of this together and we have the most productive economy the world has ever known.

However, we cannot seem to avoid having recurrent financial crises.

In the 1950s, the Marshall Plan, despite its good intentions of reviving the war torn economies of Western Europe and Japan, created severe payments imbalances in those parts of the world.

In the 1960s, it was our growing military involvement in South Vietnam, in the midst of an expansionary domestic social policy, that spawned deficits in the national accounts of the United States from which we have never completely recovered.

In the late 1960s and early 1970s, it was the gold crisis. Mounting U.S. payment deficits caused the U.S. dollar to become progressively overvalued relative to gold (the price of which had been pegged at \$35 per ounce since 1944) and relative to other currencies. The result was a run on the gold stock in the U.S. Treasury. In 1971, the United States ended the convertibility of gold into dollars, and thus ushered in the era of freely floating— and often volatile—foreign currency exchange rates. Subsequently, there was the Real Estate Investment Trust crisis, which led to a collapse in the real estate market of the early to mid-1970s.

Then, in the mid-1970s, following the oil embargo and skyrocketing prices of commodities in general, came the energy crisis.

By the early 1980s, as oil prices began to fall sharply, the oil industry fell on hard times. International payments problems in South America had evolved into a full-fledged debt crisis with the looming possibility of country defaults. The rapid deregulation of key industries such as telecommunications, air travel, and gas pipelines caused disturbing economic disruptions. A takeover wave swept the corporate world, loading balance sheets with debt and inhibiting productive capital investments. Meanwhile, our overvalued dollar brought on a surge of imports that crippled domestic manufacturing to such an extent that a large part of the country came to be called the "Rust Belt." Washington was unable to cut spending, which, in concert with the trade deficit, led to the budget deficit crisis.

These were real crises. They affected each and every one of us in individual ways. To some it meant substantial losses when institutions or businesses failed or lost value. Of course, to others it meant a loss of jobs. To still others, it provided opportunities to speculate and make a lot of money.

Strangely enough, it is we who cause these crises. Just as it is we who feel the consequences.

Each of us is a player in the economic system. Labor and management, professional and nonprofessional, white collar and blue collar, the saver and the borrower, the lender and the securities broker, the insurance man and the tax collector, the bond dealer and the corporation, the regulator and the retiree—every man, woman, and child, every corporation and every governmental agency—all are players.

It is our ball, our bat, our playing field, and we make the rules. Yet, most people view the financial system of which we are all a part with the same awe as they view the mysteries of the universe. We sometimes act as if the system were thrust upon us by some superior force from above and we are merely victims with no choice but to endure it. When big busts occur among brokers, or banks, or savings and loan institutions, the explanations are phrased in terms of cosmic mystery, as if we were victims of forces beyond anyone's control. The terminology makes everybody seem blameless. To the contrary, whatever happened, we allowed it to happen.

One problem is that nobody bothers to tell us what went wrong with the financial system in simple terms so that we might all understand and take prompt and effective corrective action. As a result, we accept the *status quo*, not realizing that we are setting ourselves up for a repeat performance.

In every case with which I am familiar, the reason something went wrong was because people erred. They were greedy and trying to make a killing, or they wanted power or psychic income, or their reasoning power was overtaken by adherence to blind ideology, or they were in the wrong business and didn't know any better, or they were too smart for their own and everyone else's good. They thought they had new answers to old questions and didn't have to play by the rules.

All this is simply human nature. One of the first accounts of the recurrent financial crises caused by the follies and greed of human nature was penned back in 1841 by a Scotsman named Charles Mackay. It is entitled, rather grandly, *Extraordinary Popular Delusions and the Madness of Crowds*. It is a delightfully ironic and learned dissertation on how ordinary human foibles led to such well-known scams as the South Sea Bubble, the tulip bulb mania, and a Mississippi variant of Florida land frauds, not to mention the Crusades. For those who want to learn more about these legendary frauds, I recommend Mackay's book. Each incident is one of investor psychology run wild, mass hysteria in the financial markets.

What makes Mackay's account so contemporary is his quiet reminders of how the scoundrels of yesterday were able to succeed. He describes John Law's outrageous Mississippi scam. In the Paris of Louis XV in 1717, he notes "Amid the intoxication of success, both John Law and the regent, Louis XV, forgot the maxim so loudly proclaimed by the former that a banker deserved death who made issues of paper without the necessary funds to provide for them." That is: they printed paper money without gold or something similar in value to back it. John Law, a giant in the history of economics, preached that whoever did such a heinous thing deserved death. Yet, in the end, he too was an offender.

We might think death a bit too harsh a penalty, but understanding the system and fixing accountability is at least as critical today as we issue paper money without gold or other tangible backing. The economy, on which we all depend, can prosper only if it is fueled by a healthy financial system whose backbone is banking. Banking is based on trust. Break the trust and you break the bank. Break the bank and you weaken or cripple the economy.

Corrupt the financial system and you corrupt everybody!

The implications are clear. A country that lacks the will to keep a close watch on its purse strings is doomed to lose its purse. A country that lacks the enterprise to learn about banking and finance is doomed to be betrayed by it. The financial system, its impact and interrelationship with the economy, is everyone's business.

My intent in *Money in the Bank* is to explain, as best I can, in everyday English, what banking is all about and the difference between good banking and bad banking.

I was a banker for 22 years, all of those years at The First National Bank of Chicago. As chairman and chief executive from 1975 to 1980, I did my very best not to betray duty or trust. What made that particularly challenging was the need for courage to

4

do the right thing and still communicate fully in an industry that traditionally had argued that too much disclosure and too much openness could damage public confidence and thereby weaken individual banks in the system.

In my judgment, this lack of openness was dangerous and totally unnecessary. The money and banking system of this country is a man-made system. To an extent, it's like a sporting event. It has rules, scorekeeping, umpires, established time periods, penalties, winners and losers, and columnists and reporters to tell us about them. The only difference between a sporting event and an economic event is that there are pure spectators in the first, but not in the U.S. economy. None of us can avoid being players unless we become wards of the state.

In the following chapters, I will try to explain the rules of the game as I understand and have experienced them. I will describe some of the key players with whom I have dealt and give you my own highly personal, subjective view of where we are and where I believe we are vulnerable.

It is essentially a story about people—their ambitions and their self-discipline. There are no heroes and no villians, just ordinary people playing the game with varying degrees of skill and daring and with varying perceptions of obligation and duty.

There is no intent to embarrass or offend anyone. If I have caused anyone discomfort, I apologize with all my heart. Personal references are used solely to describe real situations, involving real people, in the context of policies that worked and policies that didn't work between the 1920s and the present.

TWO

Learning the Hard Way

Some of my ideas may be accepted for their perceived validity. The acceptability of other ideas, I believe, will depend in large measure on the reader's confidence in my credibility and experience. It is for that reason that I digress into my personal circumstances—to establish my credibility to discuss the subject at hand.

I am a proud member of that happy group whose families had the drive and courage to leave their ancestral homes and settle in the United States. My family came from Lebanon, an unusual qualification for the boardroom of The First National Bank of Chicago. When I was hired in 1958 by the then General Vice President Gaylord Freeman, I was told, very supportively and sympathetically, that I could never hope to be chairman of the bank because I was not Anglo Saxon, six feet tall, and fair complexioned. It is a tribute to Mr. Freeman and others of his generation that, under their leadership, all that is past. In fact, ethnic groups have proved to be a fertile source for the current generation of business leaders. We are, of course, a country of immigrants.

I am convinced that this aspect of my experience was critical to whatever successes I achieved and ultimately to my qualifications for putting forth my ideas in this book.

I completed my high school education at Roxbury Latin School, in Boston, just as World War II ended. I entered Harvard University on a Naval R.O.T.C. scholarship. I was much more interested in the philosophical speculations passed down by the ancient Greeks and Romans than I was in officers' training. However, my military training at Harvard proved invaluable. Graduation coincided with the outbreak of the Korean War. I put my Harvard education to good use, spending two years in the United States Marine Corps as a platoon leader and then company commander in Korea. I might note that I received a considerably different reception on my next visit to that part of the world when I began negotiations that ultimately resulted in the establishment of a full correspondent banking relationship between The First National Bank of Chicago and the Bank of China, the first such relationship between an American bank and the official overseas bank for the People's Republic of China.

With the war behind me, I went back to Harvard to the Law School. After receiving my degree, I stayed on at the Harvard Business School, pursuing a course of study leading to a business degree. I married Joan Grover. We have three children— Robert Grover, Jeanne Frances, and Katherine Jane.

With business and law degrees in hand, and a newborn son, Robert, I had to get a job as we were flat broke. I had had little experience with banking and most of that was bad. I thought of banks as bloodless institutions of the type that put my father out of business during the Great Depression of the 1930s. Bankers were humorless, low paid and invisible. I had something quite different from banking in mind, at least until I met Gaylord Freeman, then general vice president and later the chairman and chief executive officer of The First National Bank of Chicago. Mr. Freeman looked like he came right out of central casting. He was tall, urbane, every inch the patrician. He painted a picture of banking, and particularly his bank, as exciting, vital, important, and lucrative.

I would not have chosen the same adjectives to describe the mailroom of The First National Bank of Chicago when I arrived in 1958. All trainees started in the mailroom, working their way through all the major operating departments for about 18 months. I kept detailed notes, which later were invaluable when I was sent to Frankfurt, Germany to open our branch there. From the start I was interested in international banking and First Chicago appeared to be the most opportune place to enter. First Chicago had pioneered international banking among American banks during the late 1880s. But, from the 1930s on, it had all but given up. It stood to reason that with its tradition and former orientation, it would once again seek to achieve an important international role.

I wanted to be part of rebuilding the tradition and, as promised at the time of my hiring, I was transferred to the Foreign Banking Department in late 1959. I soon became interested in a new area for banks—Eurodollars. An article I wrote, "The Significance of Eurodollars in Today's World Markets," (*Banker's Monthly*, 15 February 1964, 28-40) was noticed by Gaylord Freeman. The article also generated interest and brought me recognition outside the bank. I was in the right place at the right time.

International banking was growing exponentially, and First Chicago was growing with it. In 1963, I was assigned to open an international subsidiary, called an Edge Act bank, in New York City. (The Edge Act was a 1919 law sponsored by Senator Walter Edge. It permitted domestic banks to open offices in other states to do foreign business.) In 1966, I was sent to Frankfurt, Germany to open a branch there. A year later, I opened a Middle East subsidiary in Beirut, Lebanon. In 1968, I returned to head the International Banking Division and presided over First Chicago's dramatic worldwide growth in that area with more than a score of branches and offices in as many countries. In this assignment I met with commercial and central bankers all over the world and participated in many U.S. and foreign banking

9

organizations, including the Bankers' Association for Foreign Trade. It was a heady experience during a period of growth and expansion.

In 1971, Gaylord Freeman, then chairman and CEO, elevated me to head all the bank's domestic and commercial banking activities. The charge was to expand the domestic bank with the same vigor we brought to the international bank. But I soon discovered a difference. In the international bank we knew we could not outrun our capacity to fund ourselves—we could not overextend our resources to make loans—because we had been told not to count on Chicago for funding. No similar discipline existed in the domestic bank. Prior to Mr. Freeman's rise to the top, funding at First Chicago was the province of the chairman, Homer Livingston, and the sound and conservative president, Herbert Prochnow, Sr. These men kept us safe and solvent. Gaylord Freeman, in contrast, was the builder, the leader of the marketing charge. He gave "go-go" banking genuine meaning, and his quote, published in *Business Week,* that the bank "runs on the feet of its lending officers" became the rallying cry.

When I took over as head of commercial banking, both domestic and foreign, I discovered that the bank had embarked upon an aggressive program to increase earnings and the price of its stock by dramatically increasing the size of its domestic loan portfolio. Gaylord Freeman's April 1972 directive to me and the lending officers was: ". . . we can take as much in the way of additional commercial loans as that department can develop." Mr. Freeman was explicit in telling us his strategy: ". . . in any event we have to have far more commercial loans, and to obtain these, of the rate and quality that we want, means that the Domestic Banking Section is going to have to be far more aggressive than it has been."

By late 1972, I began to speak out against this lending juggernaut. I was concerned by a memorandum of November 6, 1972, explaining a decision to raise the bank's maximum commitment to real estate investment trusts by 50 percent—from $400 million to $600 million. I am loyal by nature and I know there can only be one boss. But, as an officer of the bank, I also had a duty to the depositors and the shareholders to object when I thought a policy was incorrect. I advised Mr. Freeman, "I cannot in good conscience recommend that we move from $400 million to $600 million in commitments to REITs." Mr. Freeman backed my position as head of domestic and international lending but soon reassigned me to the newly established position of chairman of the Asset and Liability Management Committee, which went by the acronym ALCO. He said I was too conservative and he wanted more asset growth. With my reassignment, First Chicago moved to $600 million and more in commitments to REITs, while I continued to speak out and lean against the winds of growth from my new position as chairman of ALCO. The ensuing collapse of REITs, needless to say, proved me right.

This is not to say that Mr. Freeman and my other colleagues were irrational. This aggressive growth strategy would have been sound if Mr. Freeman had been correct in assuming that the Federal Reserve Bank would provide First Chicago with enough liquidity to fund those loan commitments, and that because the bank had prudent lending officers, only quality loans would be made.

My attitude and stubbornness in the face of what everyone felt was great success were not popular. I was kicked upstairs. In April 1973, I was promoted to vice chairman of the bank, with responsibility for the Bond, Trust, Personal Banking, and Executive Departments. Significantly, I no longer had responsibility for domestic and commercial banking, but I did remain chairman of ALCO. However, I was not gone for long.

By early 1974, Mr. Freeman's aggressive increase in outstanding loans and commitments came home to roost. That spring, our REIT customers had not yet gone into default, but their worsening financial conditions required them to draw upon loan commitments that we had made previously. This massive call on commitments caused a liquidity crisis at the bank—a great shock to us back in 1974.

Mr. Freeman, perhaps realizing that I was right to be worried all along, promoted me to the newly created position of deputy chairman of the bank and holding company. He looked to me for a solution to this crisis.

First, I turned to the asset side of the balance sheet. At a May 1974 ALCO meeting, I demanded and received agreement to put strict limits on new loans, with a virtual freeze on growth for a period of time. Worried about the steadfastness of my colleagues, I wrote a June 12, 1974 memorandum to all of the top executives, asking each of them to initial our agreement. On July 19, 1974, I wrote Mr. Freeman, saying our near-term objectives were to restrict loan growth severely and work out troubled credits.

I also looked at the funding, or liability side, of the balance sheet. In 1974 and 1975 we often considered making a public securities offering to raise capital but just as often rejected it. We decided that high interest rates would have made an offering too expensive, and we would have had to disclose information that would not have reflected well on the bank's condition.

I had to face a potential inability to meet the bank's clearing obligations overseas. If we failed to make payments we owed to other international banks, there could have been a disastrous domino effect of bank failures. Fortunately, I had long been building up a reservoir of trust in my counterparts abroad. This allowed me to engage in foreign exchange swaps to cover our interbank clearings overseas. A foreign exchange swap is an agreement with another institution, usually a foreign bank, to take immediate delivery of a foreign currency in return for spot dollars or a promise to deliver dollars at some point in the future. Thus, when nervous foreign investors sought to withdraw their funds from our overseas branches, I was able to meet those demands for funds in their local currencies. My ability to execute those transactions, and avoid borrowing from the Fed, was the only way to stave off the adverse publicity that always risks a crisis of confidence and possible run on a bank.

In spite of our efforts, rumors about First Chicago's soundness began to circulate, and the bank's board of directors got nervous. We made a presentation to the board. We prepared slides that listed 15 rumors ranging from "...we are having trouble selling our CDs and commercial paper..." to "...we are too highly leveraged..." Minutes of one senior staff meeting on June 12, 1974 recorded:

> ...we cannot sell our certificates of deposit as fast as they are maturing, we have some problems in marketing commercial paper, and we are trying to go as far out as possible on Eurodollars. We could get into a position where we would be unable to fund ourselves and would have to go to the Fed, which would create real problems.

By October of that year we found ourselves paying 30 to 50 basis points more than the New York banks to obtain CDs. (A basis point is .01 percent; 100 basis points equals one full percentage point.) By December, there were rumors that the Federal Government was concerned about three major banks in the country. Of the three, we were the only money center bank and the most heavily dependent on volatile purchased money—the sizable amounts of Eurodollars and other Eurocurrencies that we bought to fund our growing loan portfolio.

In January 1975 the board of the bank, contemplating the future, announced that I would succeed Mr. Freeman as chairman in December 1975. To say the least, the challenge ahead was formidable. The overhang of commitments was rapidly being converted into loans outstanding as customers experiencing liquidity problems drew down their lines of credit. It always works this way. In tough times, companies that are good credit risks don't borrow, because they want to preserve and protect their liquidity. The troubled companies draw down every dollar available because they need it. Our mistake was making too many commitments in order to increase earnings by collecting commitment fees. My job was to apply the brakes to a vehicle traveling at very high speed and careening downhill.

Soon after, I informed the board that it would take three to five years to clear up the classified loans and that, in the meantime, the loan ceiling I imposed in 1974 would stay in place.

Twice a month our Worldwide Loan Administration & Review Group prepared a review of the entire loan portfolio, with particular concentration on problem loans. Those loans were listed by each division along with their current classification and status. The first two pages of the document also provided certain analyses in the form of financial ratios that were particularly useful in obtaining a quick, photographic summary of the condition of the bank. It also provided a two-year history of those ratios. When I think back on my inheritance from Gaylord Freeman, I remember the November 28, 1975 bimonthly review of the loan portfolio.

Looking at that document, we see that on November 30, 1973, problem loans were 7.9 percent of total loans and 61.5 percent of the bank's capital. A year later, those ratios had grown to 20.2 percent of total loans and 183.1 percent of capital. At the dawn of my tenure as chairman, November 28 1975, problem loans stood at 34.1 percent of our total loans and 256 percent of capital. It was clear that if I had to write off as little as 40 percent of those problem loans, we would be out of capital and out of business.

Particularly painful were our loans to REITs. Where I had sought to limit *total* REIT commitments to $400 million, by year-end 1975 we had over that amount of *bad* REIT loans. Additional commitments, of course, were much higher.

I not only had to take charge of a terrible and frightening loan portfolio, but I also had to change the corporate culture and practices that had placed us in this situation. Even while Gaylord Freeman was still my boss and my chairmanship was in the future, I wrote to him on December 26, 1974 and described it bluntly:

> The administration of the corporate banking department has been poor, not only in terms of personnel and salary control, but more importantly with regard to controls for credit submission. Throughout most of the year we were catching up on old commitments which were not submitted in timely fashion.

The following May, I wrote to Mr. Freeman commenting on the growth of the corporate banking department and observed that "one result of this proliferation was loss of control and the first order of business in the reorganization was to re-establish control of the decision-making processes."

Upon taking the reins as chairman, one of my first duties was (fully) to inform the board of the situation. My February 1976 presentation was diplomatic, but it contained very strong medicine for my blue-ribbon collection of movers and shakers. I reported to them the concerns about the adequacy of the bank's capital in light of the level of classified assets.

Worse, I told them that the quality of the loan portfolio was continuing to deteriorate. My exact words were recorded:

> In a sense, the tide continues to run from good, to not so good, to worse. And I cannot honestly tell you that the tide has turned even now. Although, almost daily, we have a series of little victories, some recoveries, and some improvements, we continue to be buffeted by movement of loans previously unclassified or lightly classified moving into the heavier classifications of doubtful and loss. And the loans so moving are individually so large that they continue to obscure the myriad small recoveries and modest upgradings.

I finished this grim scenario by informing them that there was a serious impairment in the bank's capital position, possibly preventing us from paying dividends. Fortunately, we decided in favor of paying the dividend that year. We did not wish to worsen public concern about our condition, which would have aggravated our already sensitive funding position.

Having told the board the previous summer that it would take three to five years to clear away the classified loans, I now confirmed that our strategy would be no-growth, that we would not further leverage the corporation, and that we would concentrate on rebuilding the level of capital. Procedures and controls would be tightened and we would weather the storm.

We overcame our loan and capital problems. (See Figure 2.1.) In 1978, First Chicago Corporation, the parent holding company, reported earnings before securities transactions of $131 million, an all-time record. The 1979 earnings of $115.4 million were the second best in the corporation's history. Cumulative earnings per share and dividends during the five years I signed the annual report as CEO were greater than in any prior consecutive five years in the corporation's history, despite the record provisions for bad loans and writeoffs of loans no longer deemed collectible. Earnings also compare favorably with any consecutive five-year period following my departure when adjustment is made for the special credit resulting from termination of the surplus in the pension plan, a surplus created over many decades. (See Figures 2.2 and 2.3.)

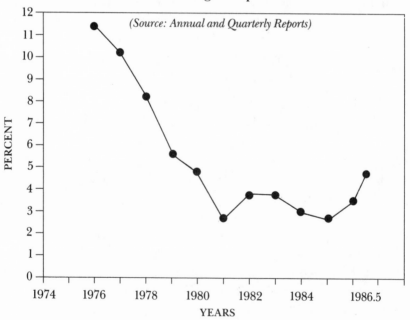

FIGURE 2.1: NONPERFORMING ASSETS AS % OF LOANS & ORE
First Chicago Corporation

FIGURE 2.2: EARNINGS PER SHARE*
First Chicago Corporation

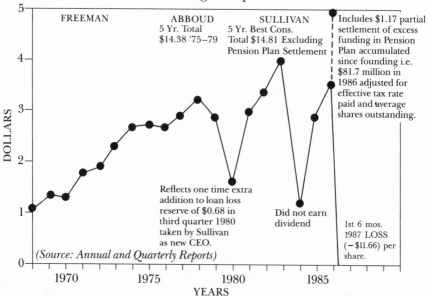

FREEMAN

ABBOUD
5 Yr. Total
$14.38 '75–79

SULLIVAN
5 Yr. Best Cons.
Total $14.81 Excluding
Pension Plan Settlement

Includes $1.17 partial settlement of excess funding in Pension Plan accumulated since founding i.e. $81.7 million in 1986 adjusted for effective tax rate paid and average shares outstanding.

Reflects one time extra addition to loan loss reserve of $0.68 in third quarter 1980 taken by Sullivan as new CEO.

Did not earn dividend

1st 6 mos. 1987 LOSS (–$11.66) per share.

(Source: Annual and Quarterly Reports)

DOLLARS

YEARS

*Earnings per common and common equivalent share would have been $4.17 for 1986, $2.58 for 1985, and unchanged for 1984, had common stock been issued at the year-end market value to satisfy the requirements of the agreements under which the equity commitment and equity contract notes were issued. *(Source: 1986 Annual Report p.47)*

FIGURE 2.3: COMMON DIVIDENDS
First Chicago Corporation

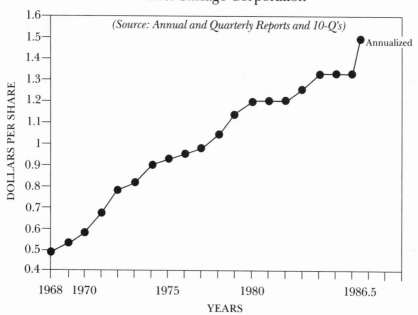

(Source: Annual and Quarterly Reports and 10-Q's)

Annualized

DOLLARS PER SHARE

YEARS

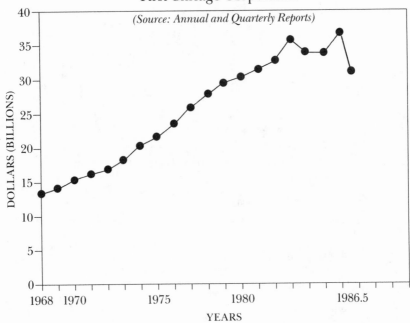

FIGURE 2.4: BOOK VALUE PER COMMON SHARE
First Chicago Corporation

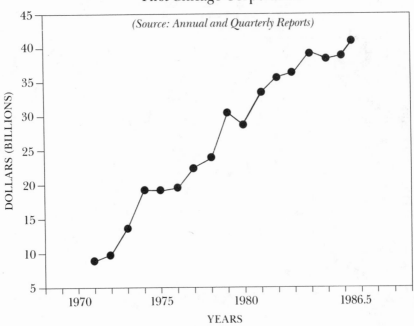

FIGURE 2.5: TOTAL ASSETS
First Chicago Corporation

The balance sheet improved similarly. Total capital increased by one third, from $886 million at the end of 1975 to $1.187 billion at the close of 1979 with commensurate increase in book value per common share. (See Figure 2.4.) More than that, the nominal capital became good, hard capital because of the overall improvement in the quality of assets. While our closest competitor, the Continental Illinois National Bank and Trust Company of Chicago, was establishing its reputation as a creative lender, First Chicago was being criticized as too stodgy, too conservative, and too tightly controlled. But, tightly controlled or not, the record shows that during this period, assets grew by 57 percent to $30 billion and deposits grew by 48 percent to $21.1 billion. (See Figure 2.5.) I was obviously pleased with these results, but criticism continued that they were not enough. I did not take off the brakes.

There was a stark contrast in management philosophy between Continental Illinois and First Chicago. Continental was expansive, creative, and freewheeling. It was named by *Dun's Review* as the nation's best managed bank. Conversely, First Chicago was considered dull, uncreative, and preoccupied with capital and balance-sheet ratios. Media attention focused on me as a martinet who kept the bank on a close leash and thereby caused discontent and dissent among some of my officers because they could not compete on equal footing with their Continental Illinois counterparts.

Chicago has a close-knit business community. Most of the board members of First Chicago were on a first-name basis with most of the board members of Continental. My board was constantly confronted with comparisons between the two big banks. In view of Continental's astonishing growth in size and earnings, people were decidedly unimpressed with the conservative course I charted after the "go-go" years of Gaylord Freeman. My board appeared to forget quickly the experience of the middle 1970s. I reminded them that the history of competition between the two banks had been one of repeated booms and busts. Each bank seemed to take turns overheating and then trying to get over the resulting trauma.

The pattern of First Chicago and then Continental getting into trouble started in the mid 1860s, soon after The First National Bank of Chicago was founded. It repeated itself at the turn of the 20th century, when to repair First Chicago's wounded loan portfolio, James B. Forgan installed the divisional system so that loans to an industry could be made and supervised by specialists in that field. The rise and retreat of the two banks in alternating order reoccurred in the 1920s and 1930s, and again in the 1970s and 1980s.

I had read and reread this history. I told my board that we should continue to build strength so as to be able to take advantage of Continental's inevitable downfall. It was a little like trying to persuade hedonists to forgo earthly pleasures and wait for their reward in the hereafter.

Ultimately, I refused to chase after Continental. The differences with some of my senior officers and some of my board members heightened, which resulted in my early retirement in August 1980. Mr. A. N. Pritzker, investor in Hyatt Corporation and other well known companies, was quoted as saying that he engineered my demise (Jon Anderson, "Pritzker on Pritzker," *Chicago Tribune*, 24 November 1985). With all due respect to Mr. Pritzker's formidable influence, the issue was deeper than just his view of a few credits in which he was interested. It went to the heart of how conservatively a bank should be managed.

For a full year after I departed, the prevailing wisdom was that Continental Illinois and its chairman, Roger Anderson, were in the right and Abboud was the fuddy duddy tyrant hobbling First Chicago's ability to be in the thick of the race. My successor, Barry Sullivan, was brought in with the mandate to put First Chicago back in competition. The checks and balances and credit restraints I had laboriously installed were summarily dismantled. The charge was sounded and loans spurted in a crescendo reminiscent of the early 1970s. First Chicago paid the price in large writeoffs. Fortunately, I had left First Chicago strong enough to weather the new round of losses stemming from the new emphasis on loan growth.

Then the far worse difficulties within Continental Illinois came to the public's attention. Less than three years after, the *American Banker's*, Sanford Rose had characterized me as the "banker who contributed most to Continental Illinois' success" (presumably because my conservatism allowed them to increase their loan growth dramatically), Continental was being bailed out by the Federal Government and its board was asked to resign.

As always, there was small consolation in being able to say "I told you so." But from a banker's and businessman's perspective, this experience left me more convinced than ever of the need for a broader understanding of the interplay of economic forces and personalities in our financial system.

If nothing else, perhaps we might temper the mistakes we seem to make over and over again. Whether I happen to be right or wrong on particular issues is probably unimportant as long as the issues are openly discussed. I have been fortunate to have had the opportunity to sit in many chairs: most of the line banking positions, president of the American Bankers Association Commercial Lending Division, director of the Association of Reserve City Bankers, director of the International Monetary Conference, member of the Bankers Association for Foreign Trade, director of the Seventh District Federal Reserve Bank, witness before the Joint Economic Committee of the U.S. Congress, director of a publicly traded savings and loan, outside director of a publicly traded bank holding company, successful bidder with the FDIC to lead a major Texas bank recapitalization, author, and guest lecturer on banking. I have risen from trainee to chairman and chief executive of a great money center bank—a bank, I might add, that is greater than any individual who has had the honor and privilege to lead it for any period of time. I love banking and finance. I believe there is no more honorable profession in the world. And I believe that being a banker carries with it duties and responsibilities of great import.

THREE

The Origins of Money and Banking

E ver since the first hungry man swapped an animal hide for a meal, people have been trading goods to improve their lot in life. Nearly 3,000 years ago, my own forebears, the Phoenicians, became the merchants of the Mediterranean, using their fast little ships to barter one country's products for another's. In time, Phoenicia became an important crossroads where the caravans from the Orient exchanged goods with the caravans from Europe.

Understandably, the traders, with their small ships, favored the smallest, lightest, and most universally valuable items as cargo. Pots and pans and tools and weapons became their standard merchandise. Such goods became a kind of surrogate money. These readily transportable things that everyone wanted served as a crude measure of worth, store of value, and medium of exchange. In other countries, all sorts of commodities ranging from slaves or furs to olive oil and cattle (the Latin derivation of both *chattel* and *capital*) served as media of exchange. The Phoenicians came up with a rare purple dye produced from snails off the coast of

Tyre which did not fade and could not be reproduced. Eventually cloth dyed with it came to be thought of as "royal purple" because its scarcity and cost made it a valuable emblem of power and status to the royalty of each land the Phoenicians visited. Caravans from the Orient traded in spices for the same purpose. Caravans from the West carried jewelry and small artifacts of gold.

Around 600 or 700 B.C., the Lydians introduced coins: standard, premeasured units of a gold and silver amalgam. They were even lighter and more transportable than previous currencies, were more widely desired, and obviously helped to solve the basic problem with barter: what to do when two strangers want to exchange goods of greatly different value but lack something to make up the difference. Coins of fixed value were a convenient way to "make change." So convenient were they that the practice rapidly spread. Not long thereafter, the Greeks introduced the drachma and the Romans the denarius (silver) and the aureus (gold).

Aristotle himself saw fit to explain the practical advantages of this new thing called "money." He wrote that men could not easily carry the goods they used in everyday life (presumably to trade for barter with peoples in distant lands). Therefore, they substituted something intrinsically valuable, such as iron, silver, or gold. Value was at first measured by the weight. Later, for convenience and to fix the value, men designed shapes and stamped the weight on the face, creating coins.

Once the world started using money, job specialization became possible on a mass scale. Specialization was the crucial foundation for the enormous increase in global prosperity that was to follow. Prior to the widespread use of money, job specialization outside of farming was only possible through patronage under the feudal system. Enlightened feudal courts supported huge coteries of artisans, painters, writers, musicians, politicians, lobbyists, soldiers, and poseurs who exchanged their services for support and protection.

Money gradually changed all that. Little by little wealth came to mean more than ownership of land. Wealth also meant ownership of money. In the cities, at least, one could amass some money through the intelligent choice of a job specialty. Money, by allowing the human mind to concentrate on what it does best, sealed the fate of feudalism.

Metallic money continued to be the principal means of exchange and served the world of commerce well for more than 1,000 years. Gold remained by far the preferred medium because of its unique properties and its scarcity. The alchemists, try as they might, could not duplicate it. Even with the discoveries in the Spanish colonies of South America and centuries later in California and South Africa, the world supply of gold remained extremely limited. Even today, the world's entire gold supply can be stored in a space the size of a football field 300 feet high.

Silver, too, remained in demand because of relative scarcity and beauty. Somewhat more plentiful than gold, silver was useful for money of smaller denominations. And silver had an important added advantage: When fashioned into eating utensils it would discolor when dipped in poison, thus prolonging the life of the owner!

Not surprisingly, the process of stamping and marking coins, i.e., the power to create this new source of power called money, was soon co-opted by the sovereigns, whose power had been based on control of the only previous source of wealth: ownership of land. Once money started flowing through royal treasuries in the normal course of commerce, rulers quickly discovered that they could make extra money by cheating a little bit—by literally shaving the coins at the edges, by punching holes in the middle, or by sanding them all over to collect dust. The extra money thereby obtained helped finance the royal courts and the military forces. It became a form of hidden taxation. Since the coins continued to have the same face value, though they purchased less, this practice produced an early form of inflation.

All kinds of techniques were employed to assure the public that a government wasn't debasing the currency by "clipping" their coins. Coins were issued with serrated edges as proof that they had not been shaved. The ruler's profile was stamped on the coin to show that it had not been sanded or hole-punched. But rulers will be rulers. Soon governments simply changed the metallic content of the coins, using less valuable fillers. They are still doing it. Americans remember that, prior to 1965, quarters were not merely silver-coated copper and zinc, but silver. Debasing has been going on for nearly 2,000 years, because the reality of all human experience is that governments tend to spend more money than the tax base will support. Once they do that, they must either borrow money, thus putting the burden on future generations, or debase the currency, thus putting the burden on the current generation—or both, as we are seeing today.

Eventually the public catches on, giving rise to a phenomenon known as "Gresham's Law": Bad money drives out good. People with two coins in their pocket, both stamped as having equivalent weight and equivalent nominal value, will spend the lighter coin (i.e., the one shaved or punched) and keep for their permanent savings the heavier coin (i.e., the untampered one). The lighter the coins, the faster they are circulated; and the heavier the coins, the more carefully they are hoarded. Perhaps that is why "junk bonds" are so popular today, as we shall discuss later. Any coin or stamp collector will act the same way. If a hot new issue is minted or printed, as the case may be, those coins or stamps are seldom used in everyday commerce but are tucked away in a vault to appreciate in value.

Both inflationary devices, borrowing and debasing the currency, reached their fullest flowering with the widespread introduction of paper money in the 17th and 18th centuries. Folklore has it that the Chinese invented paper currency and Marco Polo introduced it to the Western World. It started out innocently enough. In an increasingly complex world economy, the sheer volume of gold and silver being exchanged had become burdensome and unreliable, if only because of the constant risk of theft. So merchants and bankers began issuing their personal IOUs which promised to deliver to the recipient or bearer a certain amount of gold or silver or coins. This was, in a sense, merely an extension of a practice that had begun in medieval cities where goldsmiths and jewelers, dealing as they did in relatively large amounts of such precious materials, were forced to trust each other's written receipts or risk theft daily. Goldsmiths accepted the receipts as proof that the gold had reached its intended destination safely, that a transfer of value had occurred. Those paper receipts became literally "good as gold." Over time, paper receipts, or certificates of deposit, became money for the average person on the presumption that the gold backing these paper documents was stored in a safe place, a bank. So began a tradition of trust on which all modern economies are based.

While not all merchants or bankers issuing the notes were equally credible (credibility often diminished with distance in those days), paper money increasingly supplanted coinage because of convenience. Bankers with offices in different cities or countries began to offer depositors the convenience of making payments by drafts, or *checks* as we now know them. The word *check* is derived from the French, meaning counterfoil (presumably against forgery or tampering) by using a checkerboard pattern. An English merchant importing French wine could pay his banker in London in English currency. The banker would notify his Paris office that payment had been received, whereupon the London merchant's Paris supplier would be paid in French francs. From these modest beginnings sprang such instruments of modern banking as letters of credit, collections (drawing a draft on someone who owes you money and asking the bank to present it for collection and credit to your account), share drafts (a draft drawn on one's share of a purse, a common fund, or profits), travelers checks, and credit cards. In each case, the banker in one location is telling the banker in another location to pay on order of the customer up to a specified amount.

Today the 14,500 banks and 3,500 thrift institutions in the United States perform the same historical function of providing a safe place to keep money in deposits payable on demand in coins, paper currency, or checks. (By the way, that's the basic definition of money that economists call "M1," which the Federal Reserve Board uses to measure and manage the money supply.)

The depository institutions promise to pay money out as we instruct with checks drawn on our accounts. They also pay us interest for money we promise to leave with them for longer periods of time. These are called savings deposits and certificates of deposit, "M2" to economists. Throw in government bonds and you have "M3." Thereafter, there is a whole series of "M"s, each adding a new layer of near-money or available credit.

Banks provide a very necessary public service, but they are also in business to make a profit. So they take some of our money and lend it out to others for a fee or invest it in government or municipal bonds. There's little danger in doing that because under normal conditions, most of us don't write checks for all the money we deposit in banks. Indeed, on any given day, only a small fraction, say two percent, of all the money deposited in banks will be required by depositors. So banks have the use of substantial amounts of other people's money most of the time. They either invest in bonds or lend it to others for a fee. That means that the overwhelming majority of money in circulation at any moment is money that started out being borrowed from others. In other words, when banks make loans they are actually creating money. Almost all of our money is created in this manner.

No government would trust such enormous power to bankers without also imposing stern safeguards on how they use it. In addition to the obvious need to guard against unsafe practices that would lead to bank failures, there is the need to keep control of the nation's money supply. Too much money chasing too few goods results in inflation, with soaring prices and sharp depreciation of the currency value. Too little money in circulation means demand will fall off as people spend less, which results in a business contraction or deflation. As a result, the banking system in any country is closely regulated.

What governments seek to do is to keep things in balance— not too much money around, and not too little. Our own central bank, the Federal Reserve System, regulates the U.S. money supply in three different ways: 1) by buying or selling government bonds on the open market, 2) by raising or lowering the "discount rate" charged on money loaned to member commercial banks, or 3) by changing the amount of money commercial banks are legally required to keep in reserves.

By far the most important of these techniques is the buying or selling of government bonds, which either expands or contracts the so-called "multiplier" in the money system — probably the world's most efficient chain letter.

Here's how the multiplier works. For the sake of simplicity (and also because it's not far off) let's say banks are required by law to hold 10 percent of every deposit they receive in reserve. They can invest or loan out the other 90 percent.

Here's what happens when you deposit $100 in your bank. The bank loans out $90 and holds the remaining $10 in reserve. The borrower then goes to his bank and deposits $90. His bank holds back $9 in reserve and loans out $81. That borrower deposits that amount in his bank, which holds back $8.10 in reserves and loans out the balance, etc. If you could trace that original $100 through the entire U.S. banking system, you'd find that $900 worth of new loans or investments had been made, and $1,000 of new deposits had been recorded. Against that, banks would have set aside only $100 worth of reserves.

Now suppose the Fed thinks money is too "easy"— that is, there's too much of it around. The Fed can fix that by simply selling U.S. Government savings bonds. You buy a $100 bond by withdrawing $100 from your bank. The bank has only $10 in reserve against that deposit. It needs $90. So the next $100 deposit it gets it puts entirely into reserve, making no loans or investments. The multiplier stops dead in its tracks. The reverse, (when you sell your bond back to the government) expands the money supply. The Fed might want this to happen in a recession. You deposit the cash in your bank and the 10-fold multiplier is off and running.

It sounds like an easy system for the Fed to administer. If too much money, then sell bonds; too little money, then buy bonds. Sounds simple, but it isn't. The problem is in accurately measuring the "money supply," a task that is more art than science because of a variable called velocity. Velocity is the speed with which you and I spend our money, and, collectively, we can be most unpredictable. Figuring this all out and then buying or selling the proper amount of bonds to keep the system in balance is the judgment call of the Open Market Committee of the Federal Reserve System. Its job is to keep the various "M"s, M-1, M-2, M-3, and so forth, within certain limits even though it is exceedingly difficult to measure the "M"s with precision. So, from week to week, the members of the Open Market Committee guess and adjust and readjust. On the whole, they do pretty well most of the time.

That's the way we've all learned that the U.S. banking system is supposed to work. Unfortunately, in the real world things don't always work quite as smoothly as they're supposed to in theory.

The system is delicate and easily corruptible. The only true safeguard is for the public at large to be the watchdog. And why not? After all, it is your money!

FOUR

How Banks Get Into Trouble

In 1984, the man who headed the agency responsible for insuring banks became concerned that the money center banks—the big multinationals in New York, Chicago, and California—were allowing the quality of their loan portfolios to deteriorate too far. In the view of the chairman of the Federal Deposit Insurance Corporation, at the time William M. Isaacs, the bankers were more concerned with reporting record profits to their shareholders than with clearing their bad loans off the books. Mr. Isaacs began lecturing the banks in public about the need to clean up their ailing loans first, and to worry about outdoing each other on the profit statements later.

Mr. Isaacs was right, of course. But you wouldn't think he would have to make public announcements to be sure that his point sank in with the money center bankers.

Mr. Isaacs' former agency, the FDIC, is one of three federal bodies that share responsibility for overseeing the nation's 14,500 commercial banks and ensuring their safe and sound operation in the public interest. The Comptroller of the Currency regulates national banks; the Federal Reserve Board, which also runs the central bank, watches bank holding companies and state-chartered banks that choose the Fed as their regulator; and the Federal Deposit Insurance Corporation monitors other state-chartered banks while maintaining the fund that insures all bank deposits up to $100,000.

The simple fact is that these regulators cannot be expected to impose the needed discipline on every bank in the country, any more than our police forces can be expected to prevent every crime before it occurs.

Bankers, as well as their counterparts in the savings and loan industry, suffer from the common human foible of believing that they live in a new era, that the problems and opportunities they face have never happened before, that old rules of prudence and caution no longer apply.

The banker is in some respects, just like any other businessman whose principal task is to maximize income. But Mr. Freeman compared banking's return on capital with that of other industries and found banking to be a far worse business than most. So, to earn more money, he believed bankers should take more risk by leveraging more—by expanding their assets faster than their capital. On banks' balance sheets, the primary method of expanding assets is to make more loans. The more loans they make, the more risk they take.

At Harvard Business School they teach the risk/reward ratio: The greater the risk, the greater the potential reward should be.

The banker's top priority is to ensure the safety of depositors' money. If depositors wanted their bankers to take significant risks, they would put their money into venture capital funds. The banker's job is that of financial intermediary, taking deposits and investing them so prudently that the depositors need not worry about the safety and availability of their funds. Bankers forget this, when they think their performance is measured by the same standards as their customers': earnings growth, profitability, and size.

None of this has changed over the years, yet bankers come and go and whole banking institutions come and go. Those who leave the scene are usually those who manage poorly and make disproportionate numbers of bad loans and investments. They are the ones likely to proclaim that they live in a new era, that basic principles of caution no longer apply, that business cycles have been abolished.

Business cycle theory may be inexact, but no student of economic history denies their existence. I find that there are cycles that recur every 30 to 35 years in the banking industry—dependable boom-and-bust patterns that last about as long as it takes for a new generation of bankers to rise to power.

Congressional testimony from the late 1960s, just before the real estate investment trust debacle, included bankers saying that theirs was a totally new era, that past experience offered no relevant guidelines because of all the changes that had occurred.

If you go back to the 1890s, just before the Panic of 1900, the bankers of that time denied that there were patterns. They sounded very much like my predecessor at First Chicago. "This is a new era," they said. "We have to do things differently."

Bankers were saying the same things in the late 1920s, just before the crash. By "ordinary standards" they looked healthy enough. But many of the banks that failed in the 1930s were the ones that had reported the most profits or had the highest stated book ratios of capital to assets—in other words, the banks that looked good on paper because of accounting treatment that failed to give proper recognition of asset erosion but, in fact, had taken the biggest risks. Many of the failed banks of the 1930s had more than adequate book capital as recorded in their published statements. But most bank failures do not occur due to lack of reported book capital. Failures generally are caused by inflated assets (bad loans that aren't recorded on the balance sheet at their true value) and lack of liquidity. Liquidity is as much a function of "asset structuring" (the soundness and saleability of loans and investments) as it is of gaining and maintaining acceptance by depositors and the money markets.

The simple, inescapable fact is that, whenever there is an economic bust or debacle, it's the depository institutions that always pay. Every time there is an economic shakeup, the financial institutions end up with the bad assets and the big losses.

All of this suggests that the time for bankers to put on the brakes is just when they're really starting to grow and make money—just when their loan officers are beginning to feel their oats.

When I was running First Chicago, one reason it appeared as if our competitor, the Continental, was doing much better than we were was the fact that Continental loan officers could write loans on the spot. They weaned a lot of business away from us, which disturbed our directors.

Our lending officers had to wait for documentation so that their requests could be reviewed. That review occurs in what most banks call the Credit Review, or Loan Committee. If approved, the documentation is then reviewed for sufficiency and completeness by the so-called "Discount Department" before disbursement can be made. That's the final checkpoint before the loan goes to the board of directors for final approval, if necessary, and then gets paid into the customer's account. And make no mistake, the board of directors is charged with the responsibility of approving the specific loans, not just the policy. The one function for which board members can legitimately be held accountable is that of the Discount Department. Every loan must specify what documents the loan officer has to present to get the money. The documentation may represent collateral, or resolutions by corporate borrowers containing authorization by their boards of directors, or stock powers, or any other document that is deemed a necessary guarantee.

It's only natural that loan officers tend to think this paperwork a diminution of their status. When they are approving the loan, they see themselves as the ultimate authority. They relish this power and confidential knowledge. But when the loan officers come to the Discount Department to get the money, they are just perceived as representatives of one customer in a highly institu-tionalized process.

When a bank starts pulling away from the rest of the pack in terms of growth or profitability, the organization starts to out-strip some of its critical support activities—such as the Discount Department. Loan officers will start demanding the money even before documentation is complete. It's very hard for Discount Department personnel to stand up to that kind of pressure when times are good. That's why I think it's critical that the Discount Department have at least some direct communication with the chief executive officer of the bank so the CEO can protect them if they encounter that kind of pressure. I would say the same for the general auditor.

There's another familiar symptom of trouble: Banks and sav-ings institutions that are beginning to get into difficulty will produce reams and reams of paper. That information goes to a lot of people, but nobody reacts to it. Nobody is reading the material.

There may be a simple reason for this lack of internal discipline. Sometimes large volumes of data are produced as a protective device by a lending officer who knows or suspects that all is not well with his or her client. The material is generally of little managerial value, and so is not studied to indicate whether in fact the loan conforms to the bank's overall lending policy. A good bank will want the information compressed into a few pages of very descriptive material. Then, the top people can reasonably be expected to spot trouble if it exists.

This is also a duty of the board of directors. Board members should insist that they not be inundated with reams of paper but be given well organized, intelligible summary reports with am-ple time to discuss them in detail at board meetings. It is the CEO's responsibility to make certain that the business of the bank is accurately summarized in reports received by the board. To fulfill this responsibility, the CEO, personally or through trusted associates, must be knowledgeable about everything that goes on at all levels. Notice that this accountability is far greater in a highly leveraged depository institution than it is in an industrial corporation because the margin for error is far thinner.

It is also the board's responsibility to know about troubled loans in some detail. I used to present the Executive Committee of the board, which met weekly, with a bi-weekly report on the status of all troubled credits. Examining these reports line by line is tedious and a source of discomfort to bank officers, who may be called in to discuss particular credits in detail. But it builds confidence in the integrity of the system. It is particularly important if the institution has suffered an embarrassment. And, if it is not done, then I believe the board, not just the management, is culpable for any losses or embarrassments that ensue.

Barry Sullivan, who came to First Chicago from Chase Manhattan Bank in New York, replaced my management approach with a matrix management structure. This means that individual accounts became the responsibility of a group of officers with varied functional skills, not just of one principal account officer as in the past. This caused a rapid buildup of loans at First Chicago. Credit review procedures laboriously installed after the 1974-1976 debacle appeared to have been loosened or abolished. These checks and balances were eliminated amid much fanfare about delegation and matrix involvement dubbed "The First Team" and were not replaced with comparable safeguards. It appears no controls in key areas were set up. This has resulted in unprecedented losses and writeoffs over the past five years (see Figure 4.1) and depressed the price of the common stock in comparison to stock price performance by First Chicago's more successful competitors. (See Figure 4.2.)

Whose responsibility is it? Until we collectively answer this question and firmly affix accountability, we will not safeguard our depository institutions.

This is not to say that I did not make mistakes during my stewardship. Of course, I did. But my mistakes tended to be of commission, rather than of omission. Some say I was too conservative and that the system of controls I instituted stunted the

FIGURE 4.1: ANNUAL PROVISION FOR LOAN LOSSES
First Chicago Corporation

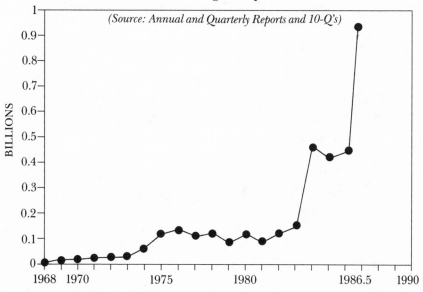

FIGURE 4.2: STOCK PRICE COMPARISON

	June 1980	Splits & Stock Divs.	Price June 30, 1987	Percent Increase
First Chicago	15	0	29½	197%
Bankers Trust	12	2 for 1—1981	51	425%
		2 for 1—1986		
Wells Fargo	14.5	2 for 1—1986	54⅜	375%
Security Pacific	12	20% div.—1983	42	350%
		2 for 1—1985		
Morgan J.P.	12	2 for 1—1985	47⅞	399%
		2 for 1—1987		
Chemical N.Y.	18	50% div. —1982	42	233%
		3 for 2—1984		
Chase Manhattan	23	2 for 1—1986	41¼	179%
First Interstate	33	0	59¾	181%
Citicorp	23	0	59	257%
Bank America	25	0	11½	(−58%)
Manufacturers Hanover	36	0	44⅝	124%

Reprinted with permission from Value Line Investment Survey

organization's creativity. Perhaps so, but the growth in loans was adequate by any historic standards except when compared with First Chicago's growth in the early 1970s or Continental Illinois' growth in the latter 1970s. That was deliberate. First Chicago did not have the balance sheet or the reserves or the unencumbered capital to compete on these terms even if I had wanted to do so.

First Chicago's loans had grown from $196 million in 1934 to $304 million in 1940, $963 million in 1950, $1.7 billion in 1960, and $4.2 billion in 1969. Then they skyrocketed to $12.4 billion by 1974, dropped to $11.7 billion from 1974 to 1976 with the writeoffs and losses, and rose under my administration to $17.0 billion by 1980. Following my departure, loans grew almost 20 percent to $20.2 billion during 1981, then moderated to a more normal rate of growth, ending up at $25.3 billion by year-end 1984. As the inevitable workouts and consolidations took place, loans fell back to $23.6 billion at the end of 1985 — a repeat of the 1974-76 pattern. (See Figure 4.3.)

In compound annual percentages, First Chicago's loans grew by about seven percent from 1934 to 1940, 12 percent from 1940 to 1950, six percent from 1950 to 1960, 11 percent from 1960 to 1969, and 24 percent from 1969 to 1974. They retreated three percent from 1974 to 1976, resumed their growth at about a 10 percent rate from 1976 to 1980, grew 20 percent from 1980 to 1981 and then at a more modest eight percent rate from 1981 to 1984. Because of bad loans, they dropped seven percent in 1985.

Two lessons jump out. The first is that if loan growth exceeds 10 percent on a compound annual basis over any extended period, trouble is sure to follow. Twenty percent and over for any length of time is sure-fire disaster. First Chicago had 12 percent growth during the 1940s and experienced some loan problems despite the availability of government guaranties for defense loans. Mr. Freeman's "go-go" period was almost matched by the 20 percent growth of 1981.

The second lesson is that periods of rapid loan growth will almost surely be followed by a period of actual loan decline, as

FIGURE 4.3: LOANS
First Chicago Corporation

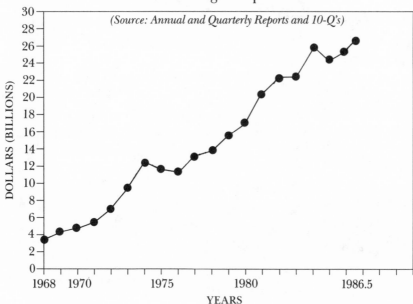

(Source: Annual and Quarterly Reports and 10-Q's)

happened at First Chicago in 1974-1976 and again in 1984-1985 under Mr. Sullivan.

The Continental experience teaches us the same lessons. If big losses are to be avoided, loan growth must be watched and monitored all the time with checks and balances and control procedures that are enforced and comprehensive. Continental's rates of growth in the late 1970s and early 1980s were a mirror image of First Chicago's growth from 1969 to 1974. (See Figure 4.4.)

Phillip L. Zweig, detailed the demise of the Continental Illinois Bank in his 1985 book *Belly Up*. It is an interesting report of a moving sequence of events. It is a moving picture, a chronology of the notorious 1982 failure of Penn Square Bank, an energy lender in Oklahoma that exhibited all the symptoms of banks that get into trouble. The main theme of *Belly Up* appears to be that Penn Square Bank's failure, and energy loans in general,

FIGURE 4.4: LOANS
Continental Bank

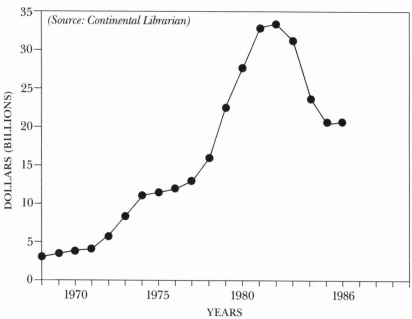

(Source: Continental Librarian)

DOLLARS (BILLIONS)

YEARS

brought down the Continental Illinois and Seattle-First Banks and caused considerable trauma to others such as Chase.[1]

The fact is that the trouble was not just in the Penn Square energy loan portfolio. The problem was extensive across a broad front, and it wasn't just documentation, at least in the credits I had the opportunity to review. It was bad lending, lending too much to nonqualified borrowers with too little analysis and too little verification of what the borrower was representing as the asset and income base against which the loan was made.

Extreme care must be taken in bank lending. A wise banker once told me, "The best that can happen with a bank loan is that the bank gets paid back at par with interest. It goes downhill from there."

---

[1]Phillip L. Zweig. *Belly Up.* New York, New York: Crown Publishers, Inc., 1985.

So, the bank cannot afford to take chances. The collateral and income must be adequate, must be verified, and must be available exclusively to service the loan. The credit review must be thorough and the systems to record and monitor the progress of the borrower must be exemplary.

Mr. Zweig also got some of his facts wrong in describing how First Chicago fared during Continental's rapid growth leading up to its debacle. His most glowing misstatement was that the First lost such key customers as John Deere, Inland Steel, and the Pritzker family holdings. Internally, bank officers accused me of losing the lead bank and possibly the entire relationship with the Hunts.

The fact is that the First lost none of these accounts. I am now and was then on the board of Inland Steel and a member of the Finance Committee of the board. Mr. Jaicks, then chief executive officer of Inland Steel, was on my board at the First. Two of our senior directors were board members of Deere. The Pritzker family holdings remained as one of the most significant single concentrations of business.

What did change was the nature and primacy of the Inland relationship.

With Inland, the question was whether we were going to be able to sustain our newly adopted 15 and 5 deposit requirements or, in the alternative, the "facility fee" introduced by Citicorp, which we had followed. The 15 and 5 deposit requirement stipulated that the customer would maintain 15 percent of the approved credit line in compensating balances if the line was unutilized and 20 percent of the amount of the line which was drawn down and utilized. In the alternative, the customer could pay a "facility fee," which amounted to about the same net cost as the 15 and 5 requirement (perhaps a little more).

At the time, the First was undergoing a liquidity crisis brought on by the love affair-gone-sour with REITs. What was not known was the depth of problems with loans other than REITs. These non-REIT troubled credits aggregated as much as the troubled REIT loans.

The problem in the loan portfolio, however, was not the primary concern. Liquidity was. We were experiencing problems in the money markets satisfying our requirements for purchased money at a time when committed but unutilized lines of credit were being drawn down, primarily by customers facing liquidity problems of their own. There was no way to repudiate these commitments without unpredictable consequences. At the same time, I had given instructions to the money market desk not to borrow a penny from the Federal Reserve Bank, even overnight. My purpose was to convince the market that we had plenty of excess liquidity and that we were in a position to place deposits with other banks in the interbank market. The only way to get that liquidity was to reduce the outstandings of the prime borrowers, who had the ability to repay, while not signaling any sign of distress. The answer was to follow the lead of Citicorp with the facility fee or, in the alternative, the 15 and 5 on compensating balances. For my purposes, I preferred the compensating balances because I wanted the cash in the bank.

The maneuver worked. Inland chose Continental to be the lead bank on the new revolving credit line, a position the First had historically enjoyed. For the First, it meant loss of prestige and a smaller share of the credit.

Deere sent us a clear signal that it disapproved of our pricing policy by allocating a smaller share in its new credit than the lead bank, although we were not traditionally Deere's lead bank.

Other prime customers also sent us a signal by paying down their loans.

The net result saved the bank. We did not go into the Fed, except by accident, on infrequent occasions, and then for only very small amounts that represented miscalculations in computing the reserve requirements for the week. More than that, we became aggressive placers of deposits in the interbank money market, a market in which the big money center banks must roll over billions and billions of dollars every day. The First was a net taker of funds in the billion dollar-plus range, as were the other money center banks.

Time for healing was important to the success of this maneuver. Let them attack our pricing policies but avoid any discussion of liquidity or the extent and depth of trouble in the loan portfolio. Once liquidity was assured, the necessary repairs to the loan portfolio could progress in an orderly fashion over time. Obviously, the marketing thrust would also have to be reinvigorated, and this, too, would take both time and effort.

With the Pritzker and the Hunt families' relationships with First Chicago, the situation was different and the timing of the period of tension was much later.

The issue in both cases was a question of concentration of exposure. Even though the controlling family operates through separate, self-standing businesses, how much total exposure should the bank have to a combination of entities controlled by a single source? Additionally, with the Pritzkers, there were certain special arrangements with particular workout credits arranged by my predecessor, Gale Freeman, that I preferred, as a policy matter, to unwind.

But, the central issue was concentration of exposure. This question was subjected to considerable study on a case-by-case basis. A policy was formulated establishing limits, presented to the Executive Committee of the board for approval, and then implemented. It frankly meant, as A.N. Pritzker stated in a *Chicago Tribune* interview, that the First could no longer be his family's sole bank. I personally visited with A.N. about this decision, and offered to lead a bank syndicate to accommodate the exposure, but after that meeting our relations were never again the same. In fact, as mentioned previously, he is quoted as saying that he and the family engineered my demise. I choose not to believe it, but perhaps it is true, since reporters have told me such was the case. Nonetheless, feelings within the family against me did run deep and, with the power and influence of the family, this was no small burden to carry.

The Hunt situation was also an issue of concentration. The Comptroller of the Currency makes rules regarding concentration of credit to a single borrower, but these rules are subject to broad interpretation. The key rule is found in the National Banking Act, which prescribes the legal lending limit for national banks and assesses director liability for breach of this limit. However, most of the cases interpreting the rule occurred in the 1930s, and there are no cases embracing the current structure of bank holding companies. The challenge, therefore, was to interpret the "do's and don'ts." This task was assigned to Ken Arnesen, who later became the First's general counsel.

The policy approved on family concentrations was put into effect and communicated. I heard no dissent from any of the Hunts. In fact, the opposite occurred. Both Herbert and Bunker told me that they viewed us as "big boys," that we should assess the credit on its own merits and make our own decisions. I took them at their word.

The situation at the time of the silver crisis in 1980 was very specific and quite different.

We were operating meticulously within our policies. Bunker, Herbert, and Lamar were buying silver, I am firmly convinced, because they believed that inflation would erode the value of the U.S. currency. As we were lending against collateral, I encouraged them to take delivery and we stored the silver bullion in the bank. In this regard, the insistence on taking delivery became the subject of investigation by the Commodity Futures Trading Commission. Some argue that the insistence on taking delivery inhibits the smooth operations of the futures market. After all, these same people say, the futures market is primarily intended to be paper transaction against paper transaction and actual delivery in the normal course is not contemplated. Yet, there is direct linkage with the banking system because bankers are lending money on the premise that their loans are collateralized. In my opinion, there is a regulatory void in this area. The futures markets for commodities or financial instruments are directly linked with day to day lending transactions, and the rules for delivery, title, and margin requirements must be compatible or there will be trouble, just as there was trouble in the stock market crash of October 1987. It was precisely for these reasons that I encouraged the Hunts to take physical delivery of the silver. My concern was purely and simply protection for our loans and advances. So they took delivery. In fact, I was worried at one point that the weight on one of the floors of the bank would buckle the structure. When we reached the limits established by our policy, I said, "No more." The pressure to increase the limit was tremendous.

While I was on a business trip to New York, the Credit Policy Committee convened and approved an increase with then Deputy Chairman, Harvey Kapnick, presiding. One of our executive vice presidents telephoned me and gave me the news. I asked if the decision had been communicated to the customer. He said no. I told him to inform Mr. Kapnick and the Credit Policy Committee that the decision was reversed. He did and it was.

However, howls of protest greeted me upon my return. "The collateral coverage," I was told, "was more than adequate to support the extra borrowings." I reminded everyone that this request had been considered at a previous meeting of the Credit Policy Committee, at which I had presided and the decision rendered was clear. "Yes," I was told, "but our whole relationship is at stake." I reminded everyone that the ground rules had been clearly established and we had abided by our end. We expected the customer to do the same.

Subsequently, Herbert Hunt telephoned me and asked if we would be willing to transfer the excess collateral to another bank and, thereby, support additional borrowings. I told him that we would transfer the collateral only if the silver loan were paid off in full because I feared that such a move could jeopardize our legal position in the remaining collateral if anything happened. There is a rule in bankruptcy called "preference" that prevents lenders from taking collateral or changing collateral or perfecting their position within months of a bankruptcy. The only way to avoid such a result is to stand still on a perfected position and not change. Thus, it was essential that the loan be paid off in full before any of the collateral could be moved.

Herbert said okay. The loan was paid off in full, the collateral was moved, and another bank was selected to be the lead bank in putting together a multibank credit. Chairman Volcker of the Federal Reserve met with a group of the Association of Reserve City Bankers, mostly leaders of big banks, to tell them how important it was to provide support so that the silver market did not collapse to everyone's detriment.

I was obviously not in good graces with our customers, Bunker, Herbert, and Lamar, nor with my own senior officers. I had personally "ruined" an old and highly valued relationship. Moreover, I was told, I had single-handedly endangered the whole economy. How flattering! I knew this latter compliment was nonsense. In fact, the market had worked the way it was supposed to work; and unless we all abided by the rules, the economy would indeed be endangered.

The next thing I knew, our stock price plummeted on the New York Stock Exchange from about $15 per share to a brief low of about $11 per share! No one could explain what happened. Gradually, the story began to unfold. One million First Chicago shares which, unbeknownst to me, were owned by the Hunt's but used as collateral for other borrowings, about 2.5 percent of our total outstandings, were thrown on the market in block. No one had called me or warned me.

Obviously, in situations like this, a courtesy call to the chief executive is in order to determine if the stock can be privately placed so as not to disrupt the market. It was put directly on the market by the broker and, I was later told by Herbert Hunt, was sold without specific direction from the Hunts and without their knowledge. What I do know is that the precipitous drop in the price of the stock was used as a club against me internally. It was a temporary thing, as the price of the stock climbed back to about $15 per share by the end of July of that year, when I left. However, the drop in the price of the stock just before the annual meeting in April was a formidable weapon.

Later, after I left, the relationship between First Chicago and the Hunt brothers was reinstituted and expanded. Harvey Kapnick, who was a great proponent of the relationship, was also gone. But, the prime sponsor of the relationship, President Richard

Thomas of First Chicago, not only remained but was given more power in the hierarchy. It was a new day with a new beginning. . .which has now deteriorated into a bitter lawsuit.

Although I am not privy to the agreements and understandings entered into after I left the bank, I can be specific about my discussions with the Hunts. I never discussed the matter with Lamar, but both Bunker and Herbert told me on several occasions that each borrowing stood solely on the creditworthiness of the particular borrower. There never was any intent of a moral commitment or a crossover or pooling of assets. This is what First Chicago and possibly other banks now appear to be claiming. And, this is how banks get into trouble. The lesson is simple. Don't be afraid to ask the fundamental questions and, above all, take to heart what you hear.

All of this will be settled by the courts. My point is simply to relate my own direct experiences and to state that the Hunts did exactly what they told me they would do, no more and no less. I was not afraid to ask and I listened carefully. Bunker and Herbert Hunt, with whom I dealt directly, are zealous about keeping their word and insistent that the parties with whom they deal keep theirs. I did not deal directly with Lamar but, since he too was a party to some of the transactions, I must conclude that he shares the same values. In my judgment, these are honorable people.

Mr. Zweig makes other charges. In *Belly Up,* he says that I "put in strict lending controls which made the loan approval process unwieldy and time consuming for customers." I plead guilty as charged. Yet Mr. Zweig in a prior paragraph quotes a former Continental officer as stating, "Loan operations have been screwed up (at Continental) for as long as I can remember. It was an antiquated system." Then Mr. Zweig writes, "To be sure, Continental's biggest competitor, First National Bank of Chicago, was screwing up and screwing up royally." He quotes a former officer at First Chicago as stating, "Continental just started to do things better." How was better defined? The author tells us ". . .Continental was showing impressive growth in earnings, profitability, and loan volume. It had become the darling of Wall Street and the financial press... *Dun's Review* rewarded success by naming it one of the nation's five best managed companies..." So, "Continental Illinois National Bank and Trust Company of Chicago could do no wrong" while First Chicago was "screwing up and screwing up royally." But, shortly after I left First Chicago, Continental Illinois began coming apart at the seams and eventually was taken over by the FDIC in the biggest banking bailout in history. Some screw up—only it wasn't First Chicago, it was Continental.

The point is simply that the financial press, which is a key player in maintaining the integrity of the system, was frankly not doing its job. It was taken in by slick public relations, it was not all that well schooled in the intricacies of banking (one publisher told me "banks are all a faceless, impersonal mystery behind that facade"), and it was not privy to the type of disclosure that is so important to make informed judgments.

I am not blaming Mr. Zweig. I am merely responding to the charge that I "screwed up" First Chicago by instituting strict lending controls that made the loan approval process more unwieldy and time-consuming for customers. I think his logic is screwed up. First Chicago didn't fail. Continental failed. And Continental failed because there were no lending controls, strict or otherwise, just as there were lenient credit controls at First Chicago in the early 1970s.

Successful lending is a team effort. It requires liquidity derived from good liability management. It requires good account officers supported by a good lending staff with knowledge of the industry being serviced. It requires good policies and procedures codified into a manual, with a watchdog surveillance from a strong Credit Policy Committee. It requires good operational backup with superior control and accounting systems. More than that, it requires acceptance and adherence to those principles at all levels with respect accorded to the Discount Department charged with responsibility for assuring proper documentation before a loan is disbursed. And, the pace of the organization cannot exceed the weakest link in this chain without inviting trouble.

Continental had none of these checks and balances. It had a cadre of bright, aggressive officers on an ego trip, bound and determined to rub salt in the hurt pride of its principal city rival by making deals across the board, committing on the spot in a show of flamboyance, and disbursing funds before the documentation was complete. Did this capture the notice of our customers? Of course, it did. Did it capture the notice of Wall Street and the financial press? Of course, it did. Continental could do no wrong. Or as one director whispered to me on one occasion, "How can the whole world be wrong? They must have something."

Having pointed out Continental's structural mistakes, let me now point out one of ours to which Mr. Zweig alluded. He writes, "Continental had also thrown money in REITs, but through a series of imaginative 'asset swaps' arranged by the bank's real estate czar, James Harper, it managed to escape a major bruising. And when the crush came, it proved itself more adept at pulling out of bad deals than First Chicago."

I want to point out a fact not mentioned. Continental had its own REIT and did much of its real estate lending through this vehicle, just as Chase and others had done. This created a separate and additional layer of capital to take some of the charge-offs that were necessary in swaps. Moreover, the bank–sponsored REITs to which First Chicago was a lender, negotiated concessionary interest rates on those loans so that the carrying costs of the non-performing real estate was considerably less painful. I never thought I would see the day when a bank would dishonor an obligation of a subsidiary that carried its name, but Continental did and there were others.

First Chicago had no such luxury. Dick Thomas had persuaded Gale Freeman that we did not need to set up a separate REIT because there was no point in sharing all those "good assets" with another group of shareholders. We would keep them all to ourselves and avoid any potential conflict of interest. Because of this decision, our team had a much tougher burden to overcome with fewer tools.

Mr. Zweig charged that 200 officers left us over a period of years and the recruiting program was scaled back. Again I plead guilty in part. During the early 1970s, First Chicago was growing at a compound rate of nearly 25 percent per annum. The policy was to overstock the personnel roster by 20 to 25 percent to support the continuation of this growth. First Chicago and its subsidiaries at the time had approximately 1,000 officers and assistants to officers. When the liquidity crisis struck in 1974 and the loan challenges began to emerge in 1975, it became obvious that, with the capital constraints and the writeoffs and the interest reversals and the tight funding, First Chicago had to pull in its belt, curtail growth, mend its wounds, and above all, cut expenses. From that point forward, First Chicago, for at least a five-year run, would have to be lean and cost sensitive. I note with great empathy the pain and suffering that so many banking institutions are undergoing today, confronted with the reality of dashed dreams and the necessity to survive. It is no fun. The Bank of America is undergoing the trauma at this very moment. Having lived through it, I witness the unfolding story with the same pain as a bamboo shoot under the fingernail. Unfortunately, it is a time for banks and thrifts to slim down, cut out the frills, adjust to new realities. Because of circumstances, I was forced to begin 10 years ahead of the pack. But, wouldn't it have been so much less painful for all if the whole industry had started earlier as well?

I don't know where the figure of 200 officers came from in describing the employee turnover during my four-and-one-half-year tenure as chief executive. Our turnover rate did jump from about nine percent per annum to 12 percent per annum for a brief period to adjust for the need to change direction. However, in the context of today's realities with banking institutions, even a 12 percent turnover rate appears tame.

The whole economy, including banking, is in a state of transition and, unfortunately, turnover always accompanies a major change in direction. That's the way the "culture" gets changed in a big institution.

Yes, we curtailed recruiting for the same reasons, cut it in half or less. But we did keep our First Scholar program, a program instituted by Gale Freeman, who was the best breeder of talent First Chicago ever had. I understand it is no longer operative. I also understand that the turnover rate among official personnel at First Chicago and elsewhere is today greater than anything I ever experienced. I say this with sadness as a commentary on our times. Money, rather than allegiance to an institution, appears to be the prime motivator, and the introduction of investment banking objectives and reward systems is running the risk of endangering the safety of the banking system. For a fiduciary institution lending depositors' money, this is a precursor of trouble, possibly big trouble. And where are the directors? Who is to be held accountable?

FIVE

Politics, Internal and External

I made my share of mistakes—of commission. When I reassigned, from Asset and Liability Management to Commercial Lending, the responsibility for setting limits on fixed-rate
loans in late 1978 and early 1979, it was tantamount to putting
the proverbial fox in the chicken coop. Commercial Lending was
committed first and foremost to putting loans on the books. The
structure of the balance sheet was only a secondary concern. Before I could put the genie back in the bottle, we had exceeded
the prescribed limits set by the Asset and Liability Committee
by nearly half again as much. As interest rates on purchased
money to fund these loans began to escalate, the interest rate
spread—the banker's profit—got squeezed. The antidote, of
course, was to get more inexpensive retail deposits (they were subject to legal interest rate ceilings) to fund these loans. Since our
retail program was well established and led by very talented
officers, the imbalance could soon be redressed.

I did not realize until later, however, how much it irked the
corporate lenders that retail banking had gained new status in

the hierarchy equal to their own. The corporate lenders had accorded themselves unique and singular status as "Princes of the Church," and they resented the attentions I gave the retail operations. Privately they called me a "populist," which, I suppose, is the opposite of elitist.

In any event, I was convinced that the retail operation had been neglected for too long. If the bank was to be stable, we had to build our own personal savings and checking deposits. I felt strongly that we could not make a living by purchasing money, "buying" it on the certificates of deposit market, taking Eurodollar deposits, or making foreign exchange swaps. So I pushed branch banking, retail outlets, credit cards (First Chicago was the first in the country to impose the now common annual fee on bank credit cards, thus making that activity profitable), travelers checks, automated teller machines, retail bankers acceptances, passbook accounts for gold and silver bullion, Individual Retirement Accounts (IRAs), high-net-worth banking, and a host of other innovative services. I was determined that we were going to build our retail business just as we had built our international foundation for growth.

In the late 1970s, I became convinced that large-scale international lending was heading into trouble, and I ordered cutbacks. Mostly I was worried about the very large sovereign loans that were being proposed at very low spreads. I formed an International Advisory Committee of the Board, chaired by Mr. Freeman, and at the quarterly meetings had presentations of current and future cash flows for individual nations around the world. This effort was pioneered by Edwin Yeo, a former undersecretary of the Treasury for monetary affairs and a brilliant tactician. It was the same type of credit analysis that we would perform on a domestic corporate customer. The exercise demonstrated that some countries were borrowing too much and that they could not possibly repay.

I was trying to show the directors why I had curbed First Chicago's appetite for foreign-country loans, even though my primary background was international banking and even though most banks, including our competitor, Continental, extolled such credits as great earning assets. I thought it prudent to lean against the wind, but the resistance from some of my senior officers was extreme and pressures mounted to relax the restraints.

In the late 1970s, foreign lending was the big growth area for U.S. banks. Rising energy costs and rising interest rates required many countries to increase their overall borrowings dramatically. The dollars per loan transaction were large, the fees for syndicating the loans to other lenders were attractive, and the risk was considered nominal because the central bank of the borrowing country generally guaranteed the loan. I still didn't like it because our analyses clearly revealed that the countries' debt service coverage was inadequate. I kept the restrictions on sovereign loans in place until I left the bank.

I erred in late 1979 and early 1980 in overbuilding the investment portfolio and the *due from deposit* accounts (i.e., cash placed on deposit with other banks). The International Monetary Fund meetings had just been held in Yugoslavia. Chairman Volcker of the Federal Reserve, with whom I had visited at the meetings, announced a fundamental change in the Fed's monetary policy, away from managing interest rates (i.e., the Fed funds rate) to directly managing the money supply. Interest rates were thus set free to escalate rapidly. I feared a recurrence of the funding crises we experienced in 1974 and 1975. I wanted to take all the money we could lay our hands on to build up First Chicago's approved borrowing limits with corporate depositors (corporations and banks typically set limits on how much exposure they will take with any one institution) and money market lenders. This strategy hurt First Chicago's earnings, however, and, in retrospect, it was a mistake. With 20/20 hindsight, I would have tempered the move. But, the direction was correct. It was an insurance policy, easily corrected in 90 or 180 days.

I wanted to limit our exposure to Real Estate Investment Trusts but was unable to get the rest of the bank to agree. That was in 1971 and 1972 when I was in charge of both international and domestic lending. All I knew was that the REITs were highly leveraged and that heads of REITs were paid a percentage of gross assets. This is like letting the salesman double as the credit manager. He had no incentive to apply strict credit standards on the deals he agreed to book. I also remembered two old banking adages: First, if everyone is doing it, be careful; and second, too much of a good thing, even ice cream, can give you indigestion.

With nothing more scientific than that, I decided to limit our commitments to REITs to $400 million, about two times our legal limit to any one customer. There was a lot of friction. Other banks were competing vigorously for the business. Some banks, including Continental and Chase, formed their own bank-sponsored REITs, which carried their names. We chose not to do this because we did not want to share those good assets with a different base of shareholders, i.e., the shareholders of the REIT, some of whom might not be shareholders of the bank. Why should we deprive our own shareholders of any of the goodies? Paradoxically, this is what saved Continental and Chase and others from taking as large a writeoff as First Chicago. Of course, no one at the time believed for a minute that a first-class bank would default on an obligation of an institution it managed and sponsored, especially if it had its name on the door. But, *astonishingly*, it happened.

Soon I was moved over to the funding side of the bank with the explanation that I was too conservative to produce the growth that Mr. Freeman believed we needed. A large part of the record growth from 1972 to 1974 came from renewed investment in REITs and other real estate. REIT outstandings climbed to more than $900 million. Then, the dam broke in the fall of 1974.

Tight monetary policy at the Fed, together with the "voluntary credit restraints" imposed by the Committee on Interest and Dividends led by Chairman Burns, brought a superheated U.S. economy to an abrupt halt. Real estate liquidity all but disappeared. The banks that were the recognized leaders in real estate lending, particularly in lending to the REITs, were singled out for criticism by the financial press, with First Chicago featured prominently. We began to have problems in rolling over deposits on the money desk. All money center banks are required to buy substantial sums in the money markets every day, and First Chicago at the time was buying proportionately more than its peers because of its rapid growth, its heavy backlog of undrawn commitments that were now being utilized, and its location in a unit banking state that did not permit the branch banking that would have enabled us to accumulate retail deposits. We experienced three severe liquidity crunches, in May 1974, in September 1974, and in December 1974.

The directors discovered that the bank was in trouble. So they turned to me and asked me to take over. It was a job I never would have inherited if the bank hadn't been in trouble. I didn't fit the mold in terms of appearance or background. But there was a problem, and the situation called for the toughness I was perceived to have exhibited.

I felt sympathy for my predecessor at that point. It is very difficult for any banker to resist the call of additional business and pay attention to basics. It really is. There are times when, like Ulysses, the banker must tie himself to the mast—or the rulebook—to avoid following the siren songs to certain shipwreck. And who are the sirens? They are his customers, his loan officers, even his own directors. Which is why it is so often true that a bank that starts outperforming other banks by a wide margin is really in trouble without knowing it . . . as Continental was when it had to be bailed out by the Federal Deposit Insurance Corporation in 1984.

Also, the symptoms of the disease are subtle. They masquerade as understaffing, a sudden crush of business. Nobody thinks he or she has time to read those reports, or attend to that documentation. It all seems so mundane. The unspoken logic is that nobody can fail in the prevailing business environment.

I understand how this happens. The current crop of loan officers from the 1960s and 1970s have never been schooled in the operational back office, the mechanics of the system. All they know how to do is to talk to the customer, hopefully to say "yes" and to put new business on the books, and to read analysts' reports. Up through the 1950s the banks were run by people who had come through the Depression, and served their apprenticeship in the operational departments of the banks, and their whole temperament was forged in the banking crisis of the 1930s. That situation is now changing. Credit training, with sophisticated computer applications, is now being given to entry-level and mid-level lending officers.

With the end of the 1950s, however, a number of changes were taking place in banking, on a global scale. Foreign creditors had to be paid. Either we were going to give them gold, and thereby deplete our gold reserves, or give them dollars which would export our inflation to others, or give them an IOU that could somehow be sterilized and remain outside our own monetary base. The last alternative is what we tried to do with the Roosa bonds, i.e., an IOU of the U.S. Government to its foreign creditors, bearing interest, but not freely negotiable. They were named for Robert Roosa, an investment banker at Brown Brothers Harriman & Company. It was a good try, but it didn't completely work as planned because the result was indirectly to increase the U.S. money supply.

Second, there was the increased use in the 1960s of Eurodollars, which probably started around 1953. Some say that the two Russian banks in Western Europe, Moscow Narodny Bank, Ltd., London and Banque Commerciale pour l'Europe du Nord, S.A., Paris, opened the Eurodollar market to find a use for temporary surplus dollars emanating from gold sales, and additionally to finance imports. Others say that the London merchant banks started it to attract the large dollar balances previously maintained with the big British clearing banks at little or no interest. Most of the evidence points to Brown Shipley & Co. Ltd., a London merchant bank. However it began, it was clear to me that the Eurodollar Market could become quite dangerous.

In "The Significance of Eurodollars in Today's World Markets," (*Bankers Monthly*, 28-40) I predicted the evolution of a truly international money market of which the Eurodollar was the harbinger. That market developed. Trading of Eurodollar deposits in London and other foreign money centers soon gave rise to a whole new source of liquidity. No reserve requirements were imposed on Eurodollar deposits, so the expansion of credit was theoretically infinite, with clear implications for the condition of international banks participating in the boom.

Third, in 1963, there was the introduction of certificates of deposit (CDs). Were they deposits? Or was the bank really borrowing the money from its customers? It was an important question. If they were classified as borrowings, the banker would be required under federal and state laws to limit CDs to a certain percentage of capital. But if they were considered deposits, there was a much more liberal limit on the extent to which the bank could theoretically increase its liabilities.

The traditional wisdom in the 1960s had been that the ratio of a bank's loans to deposits (total loans are the biggest item on the asset side of the balance sheet; total deposits the biggest item on the liability side) should not exceed 70 percent. That was considered very venturesome "go-go" banking at the time. Conservative banks were reporting 50 percent to 60 percent loan to deposit ratios. This placed an automatic brake on the banking system. Regulations limited the rate of money creation. They stipulated a 17.5 percent reserve requirement on demand deposits, which limited the multiplier of these funds to around five; and a three percent reserve requirement on savings, which limited the multiplier on those deposits to around 30. Remember, the multiplier is the maximum the banking system can expand, since the total volume of loans, and hence deposits, that can be created is the volume of reserves in the banking system times the number needed to multiply the reserve requirement and reach 100 percent. For example, if the reserve requirement were 20 percent, then the multiplier would be five.

Once you introduce the idea that freewheeling Eurodollars and certificates of deposit can be treated as regular deposits, an idea that was pushed primarily by New York's Citibank, the multiplier can become almost endless. It gave bank managements the ability to control their own balance sheets. It untied Ulysses from the mast while the sirens were singing.

But then it got worse.

In the late 1960s, bank common stocks were not listed or traded on the New York or American Stock Exchanges, and NASDAQ had not yet been formed. Banks could maintain hidden reserves and manage their earnings. In bad years, they invaded those reserves. In good years, in theory at least, they built them up. Banks encouraged the public perception that, if you only knew the size of the secret reserve, you would never have any concern. All of that was really a result of the 1930s Depression. Bankers wanted to recreate confidence in the banking system by being conservative.

It is quite interesting that the one bank that created a little flutter during this period was none other than solid, conservative Morgan Guaranty, in 1965-1966. Basically, it had inflated its balance sheet to the point where it ran into liquidity problems. I know that sounds like anathema today. But it happened. And that's the point: It can happen to any bank.

Subsequently, the Morgan senior management "took a blood oath" that they would never again allow the bank to get into that condition. Consequently, during the late 1960s and early 1970s, when other banks were rapidly expanding, Morgan adopted a very conservative course. Analysts looked disparagingly on Morgan as a laggard and as a bank losing position to more aggressive competitors, like First Chicago, which in the early 1970s was expanding proportionately more rapidly than anyone. But with the collapse of Real Estate Investment Trusts in 1974, Morgan catapulted from the bottom to the top because of its conservative base. Those who had been "go-go" dropped from top to bottom.

Finally, in the late 1960s, the Bank Holding Company Act was enacted and companies could list their securities on the major stock exchanges of the world. Bank managements viewed the public listing of their securities as an opportunity to get higher multiples on the stock and to make stock options more valuable. There was also the publicly proclaimed reason of greater flexibility to engage in new activities, hitherto closed to banking. The hold-ing company was not a depository institution and therefore could be granted broader powers to enter more risky businesses since, if the holding company suffered losses, there would be no adverse impact on the subsidiary bank. That was the theory at the time and is currently being advanced as the theory justifying holding company subsidiaries performing investment banking functions.

The net result of all these changes was to alter dramatically the culture of the business. Business school graduates of the time thought this was a whole new world. And indeed it was.

In this new banking environment, the general public percep-tion does not provide a reward for the banker who accepts the responsibility of resisting the prevailing orthodoxy. Indeed, he is sharply criticized for doing it. Moreover, there do not appear to be penalties for directors who permit their managements to go with the tide to the detriment of the bank.

That, perhaps, is the Achilles heel in the whole system.

Again, let me cite from my own experience to illustrate the point.

I had to make a decision in 1976, when First Chicago's non-performing assets equalled 11.5 percent of total loans and other real estate owned, whether to acknowledge the problem publicly by taking a huge writeoff or to make the appropriate disclosure but tough it out by taking the writeoffs over a period of years. At least one director urged me to accept the necessity of a mas-sive writeoff. I chose not to do that because the writeoff would have been too big. The bank's capital would have been virtually wiped out, and the confidence of the money markets would have been shattered.

There was only one thing to do to avert a crisis of confidence: make appropriate disclosure in the footnotes of the official pub-lications (in banking jargon), be seen everywhere in public, smile a lot, cut back on the loans to create liquidity, liquidate invest-ments when and where possible but not noticeably, and above all, never, never go to the Fed's discount window for temporary borrowings, no matter how normal and legitimate the transaction. Moreover, there had to be a credible explanation to the public as to why loan growth was being cut back.

I had a strategy to solve the liquidity crisis and spread the writeoffs over a period of years. But how to get it done?

The Board of Governors of the Federal Reserve System gave me an unintended cue. Since 1973, certain Fed Governors (notably Robert Holland) had persuasively argued that banks were not levying commitment fees, not demanding sufficient compensating balances, not pricing their loans adequately, and were too free with commitments that were seldom used in good times but which hung like the sword of Damocles over the system when the markets tightened. Whether these concerns were appropriate for the times or not, I'll leave for you to judge. For me, it was a superb excuse. This is what the Fed wanted the banking system to do and we, First Chicago, were determined to be the star pupil. Those policies were adopted over the protests of some of our less discerning officers. Loan growth gradually halted during 1975, then declined slightly in 1976. Thanks to that, we weathered the worst of the storm. There was still a long way to go in working out the bad loans, but the liquidity crunch was behind us. What remained was the job of maximizing recoveries from the more than two billion dollars of troubled credits and making certain that the new business was sound.

Very few of First Chicago's management saw the entire picture during this period. Some of those who did see chose not to believe it since the troubled assets were of their own creation. But the directors knew, because I told them and the national bank examiners told them.

In retrospect, my strategy to tough it out proved to be correct. Nonperforming loans were brought down from over one billion to roughly $400 million by July 1980, when I left. They continued to trend down throughout 1980 until the new "matrix" management reversed the process again. (See Figure 5-1.)

The point of the story is that we have not clearly delineated the duty and responsibilities of the analyst community in the

FIGURE 5.1: NONACCRUAL LOANS
First Chicago Corporation

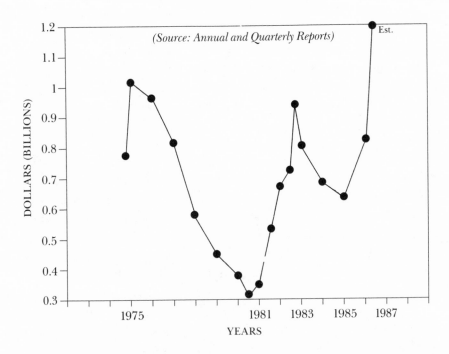

YEARS

whole financial system as the watchdog to ferret out the real truth and either to sound the warning signal or to give credit as events unfold. There appear to be no penalties for directors who permit their managements to go with the tide and then get into trouble. Similarly, there does not appear to be any way to provide reinforcement to the banker who resists the prevailing orthodoxy and turns out to be right.

Here was a case where First Chicago led the pack in the early 1970s and experienced difficulty. There was great acclaim for First Chicago at the time because it was clearly out in front and leading the prevailing orthodoxy during the "go-go" period. It was just as clearly out of fashion during the healing period and was criticized for being a laggard. The directors were uncomfortable with being labeled a laggard. Many of them were the same ones who permitted the excessive expansion during the "go-go" years. Those same directors decided to reject the process in 1981 and 1982 and First Chicago subsequently suffered massive writeoffs once again.

Where was the system of checks and balances? It certainly is not the regulators. Under our system, the regulators only take action after the difficulties are known and pronounced. There is some monitoring on a concurrent basis but the laws make it very difficult for a regulator to have real influence until the damage has occurred.

The only real disciplinarian is the marketplace. Analysis, scrutiny and public disclosure are the only real protection. Let us have more disclosure. If the disclosure is bad, then deposits will decline and stock prices will drop. This is the medicine to keep directors and managements on course.

The banking system in the United States is unique in this respect. The Japanese, for example, have difficulty with the concept. I know this from my experience with First City Bancorporation of Texas, Inc. in Houston. First City is a bank holding company that was required to undergo a forced recapitalization. In the process, the creditors of the holding company, together with preferred stockholders and common shareholders, were required to accept large discounts on the values of their securities as part of the recapitalization. The Japanese holders of First City Bancorporation senior notes could not understand how the United States banking authorities could allow holders of such securities, particularly foreign bank holders of the senior debt, to take losses. Moreover, they could not understand why holders of junior debt or preferred stockholders or even common shareholders would get anything as long as they were required to accept losses on their senior securities. I was told that such a thing would never be permitted in Japan and that the precedent in the United States would surely damage the credibility of United States bank holding companies in the eyes of foreigners.

The confusion is understandable because our system is different. Banking institutions in the United States are indeed run by the directors of those institutions, and the stockholders are responsible for electing the right directors. Moreover, there are differing rights and obligations that attach to these shareholders based on the state laws where the holding companies are incorporated.

The point is clear and simple. In the United States, the free market is the ultimate disciplinarian. For the market to work efficiently, there needs to be information available to the market on each institution on a timely basis and penetrating critical analysis of that information by analysts and media commentators. The public, shareholders and depositors alike, are expected to take action based on their judgments which flow from the receipt of the analysts' reports. This is the only way to hold managements and boards of directors accountable. Only with such accountability, imposed and enforced by the public at large, will the United States banking system be safe and sound.

SIX

The Regulatory Mess

I t's no secret that a number of things are seriously wrong with the way the U.S. Government regulates financial institutions. Our elected representatives know it and the regulators themselves know it. But true reform never seems to get accomplished.

As recently as 1983, sweeping changes in bank regulation were recommended by a blue-ribbon study group that included men such as then Federal Reserve Chairman Paul Volcker, then Chairman of the Council of Economic Advisors Martin Feldstein, then Treasury Secretary Donald Regan, and then Budget Director David Stockman. The group's chairman was Vice President George Bush.

That very sensible report was ignored, as was the so-called FINE study (Financial Institutions in the Nation's Economy) commissioned by the House of Representatives in 1975. Like the Bush report, it recommended consolidation of financial regulators. The same thing happened to the Hunt Commission report of 1971, and the Hoover Commission report of 1949.

Let's face it: The reform of bank regulation, necessary as it is, is a topic generally thought to have very little voter appeal. What legislator would want to launch a campaign for grass-roots support on so seemingly complex a topic? Let the next congressman deal with it. The trouble is, by then it could be too late.

The problem, simply put, is that there are too many regulatory agencies, and their responsibilities overlap. Worse, some agencies do not have their sights set on the right objectives. Still worse, some regulators are too closely allied with the industries they oversee.

The union between the Federal Reserve and the commercial banks is necessarily tightly knit. The problem foreign-country loans, the problem energy loans, and the problem farm loans have made the interests of regulator and regulated one and the same. Their common interest is to save the banks, particularly the big banks. That is why the spread between the prime rate and the inflation rate (that is, the real rate of interest) remains unprecedentedly wide. The U.S. economy is paying an invisible tax to pay for the bad loans. In fact, the sluggish domestic economy is a direct consequence of this policy. This is pure, out-and-out subsidy, and it was never intended as one of the Fed's missions. Quite the contrary! The Fed's role is to ensure the adequacy of credit needed to maintain a strong, vigorous economy. Levying an invisible tax on interest rates is not one of the intended tools to achieve that goal.

The heads of state bank and savings and loan regulatory agencies are political appointees, and the institutions they regulate are notoriously large contributors to state political campaigns.

The Federal Home Loan Bank Board (FHLBB) is a flagrant example of regulatory interconnection. The Federal Savings and Loan Insurance Corporation (FSLIC) is an even more flagrant example. The close tie between the FSLIC, the FHLBB and the thrifts they regulate was underscored by no less an authoritative source than Peter Stearns, who was reported to have resigned as director of the FSLIC in 1986 over this very issue.

Mr. Stearns told the *Wall Street Journal* that the Bank Board "unlike the very 'independent, very tough,' Securities and Exchange Commission, 'doesn't regulate anything unless the U.S. League (of Savings Institutions)—the principal trade association for the nation's thrifts—and the top S&Ls agree.' "[2]

American bankers and thrift executives in the United States are not alone in wanting sympathetic colleagues in the regulatory chairs. No less venerable a group than the Swiss bankers expressed discomfort when it became known that Paolo Bernasconi, a former state attorney of the canton of Ticino and one of Switzerland's more famous fighters of white-collar crime, emerged as a candidate for the Swiss Banking Commission. Swiss bankers were quoted as saying they would be happier with someone more willing to negotiate and compromise.

This is not to say that the present system has not served us well. It certainly has. But 50 years after our Depression-era patchwork system was thrown together in fear and haste, it badly needs streamlining and updating. After all, financial institutions and financial instruments have changed dramatically.

Up until just before World War I, we took an Adam Smith *laissez faire* attitude toward banking in this country. For most of that time, commercial banks issued their own currency. There was no central bank. The Treasury Department, thanks to Andrew Jackson's Independent Treasury Act of 1840, had had no dealings with commercial banks whatsoever until the second decade of the 20th century.

The financial markets started misbehaving in the latter part of the 19th century. Burdened with the Civil War debt, our existing financial system seemed powerless to prevent financial panics, which occurred in 1866, 1873, 1884, 1893, and 1907. With the wisdom of hindsight, many now blame that pattern on adherence to the gold standard—the convertibility of dollars into fixed amounts of gold. Nonsense! The blame rests squarely on

---

[2] Leon E. Wynter, "Bank Board Impedes FSLIC Aid, Its Ex-Chief Claims," *Wall Street Journal*, 10 April 1986.

the bankers who made bad loans and who issued IOUs (scrip) without liquid assets on hand to back up those IOUs. Remember John Law's maxim: those who did such a heinous thing deserved death.

Any currency needs backing, and the traditional backing throughout history has been gold. Hence the gold standard. All the gold standard did was to curb the rate of inflation and to bring on a day of reckoning for excessive speculation. And what is wrong with that? We are desperately searching for a smoother braking mechanism today. Some say the gold standard is too harsh. Perhaps so. But, again, let us not forget history: Every sovereign power has seized every available opportunity to inflate the currency. Gold was always the antidote to this penchant.

We have never been comfortable with a simple, inanimate, non-judgmental metallic standard like gold. Attempt after attempt has been made to replace gold with judgments of some watchdog group or to temper the abrupt dislocations that rigid adherence to the discipline of gold often causes. The trouble is that no judgmental standard or watchdog group has ever been consistently successful over any extended period of time. When the value of the U.S. dollar drops, as it did in 1987, and prospects for inflation rise again, gold inevitably acquires an aura of new respectability. The on-again, off-again love affair with gold has played an important role in U.S. banking history. That love affair appears to be warming up again with Secretary of the Treasury Baker's suggestion of a basket of commodities, including gold, to be used as a reference in establishing a proper exchange rate for the dollar.

Modern monetary history began in this country in 1913. As the economic boom-and-bust cycles that usually accompany war seemed likely to recur in Europe, Congress set up the Federal Reserve System with the twin objectives of creating a "flexible currency" attuned to seasonal changes in the demand for money, and—with the world still on a gold standard—of safeguarding the nation's gold reserve.

With 12 co-equal branches and one governing board, the Federal Reserve System was supposed to be a central bank peculiarly sensitive to regional economies. As originally conceived, the Fed would invest in commercial bank loans of up to five years. This was meant to provide additional liquidity for private enterprise where such liquidity was unavailable because of seasonal agricultural demands. That function was quickly forgotten, however. The U.S. Government realized that the Fed, then run by the Secretary of the Treasury, was a money machine to which it could sell government bonds. Once the Fed got hooked into financing World War I, it was stuck with federal debt from that point forward. So the Fed's central banking role was subverted right from the outset. The regional Fed banks, left with little to do, became virtually powerless, except as gatherers of information for transmittal to Washington and for execution and implementation of policies established by the board in Washington and its principal agent, the Federal Reserve Bank of New York.

Never having financed a war effort before, the Fed made a few mistakes. The board didn't realize, for example, that the early buyers of government bonds would be unfairly penalized by subsequent war-induced inflation as successive new bond issues came out at ever higher rates of interest.

After the end of World War I, the Fed was too late by over a year in tightening credit — largely because the Treasury wanted to be sure it could pay all its bills. Powered by all that wartime liquidity, too much money chased too few goods in an economy slow to readjust to peacetime conditions. By early 1920, prices were double their prewar levels.

The leading central banks around the world slammed on the brakes. There was a sudden, sharp slump in world commodity prices as people cut back spending. Many American farmers, accustomed to inflated wartime prices, had over-mortgaged farms. The fledgling Fed was roundly accused of being out to get American farmers. Bank failures in farming communities reached alarming levels. One wonders why the Fed, at that time, did not perform one of the primary functions for which it was founded:

i.e., to invest in five-year commercial loans at a time when liquidity was curtailed. Indeed, one wonders why the Fed does not do so today. It need not buy into the inflated values that existed when the loans were made, but it surely can invest in loans at their current values.

In its 1921 annual report, the Fed published some wise observations:

> ...the Federal Reserve System should not be expected to accomplish the impossible. It cannot control individual judgment or action. It is not a panacea for all economic and financial ills, and it cannot, however skillful its administration may be, prevent periods of depression, although it can do much to modify them.

These words of wisdom should have been read and reread by the Fed Board of Governors during the early 1930s. Perhaps today's Board of Governors should also reread them as it struggles to cope with the farm and foreign debt crises.

With economic recovery in 1923, the Fed learned another important lesson. Its massive open market sales and purchases of U.S. Government debt were an important tool for influencing the national economy. Since it could determine how much U.S. Government debt commercial banks had to hold at any time as security for their loan portfolios, the more Federal bonds it bought, the easier the money supply became. The more Federal bonds it sold, the tighter the money supply became. This process has been refined to an arcane art and is today the province of the Fed's Open Market Committee.

Given its Wall Street location, the Federal Reserve Bank of New York became first among equals, coordinating the purchases and sales of Federal securities by its constituents. As originally conceived, the New York Fed was not accorded a position of primacy relative to the other 11 Federal Reserve banks. It gradually acquired it because of the need to manage the growing government debt and the burgeoning U.S. involvement in international economics and finance.

In 1924, with the ravages of World War I safely past, the countries of the world went back on the gold standard. Great Britain announced that the pound sterling was again convertible to gold at its prewar rates. In retrospect, the price was probably far too low for a permanently changed world. Be that as it may, the Fed cooperated by easing credit in the United States to avoid luring all those British reserves to our relatively higher interest rates. That, in turn, meant that the New York Fed bought large amounts of U.S. Government bonds from commercial banks. The banks dutifully paid down their debts to the Fed banks and expanded their lending—especially to people who wanted to speculate in the stock market.

Several years later, as a consequence of its decision to go back on the gold standard, Britain was in a major depression and bleeding sterling reserves to higher interest rates prevailing elsewhere, particularly in the United States. Spotting an opportunity to shore up its own currency, France wanted to go on the gold standard, but it too worried about losing reserves to the growing U.S. economy. Again the Fed came to the rescue by easing up on credit, thereby lowering interest rates. Such international coordination was the precursor of modern-day cooperation among central banks to harmonize interest rates globally, and it makes a mockery of those who argue that the central banks are just now learning how to work together. We saw it in the 1920s and again in 1944 when the Bretton Woods agreements were adopted, the framework for more than 20 years of global prosperity.

With the easing of credit by the Fed to accommodate Britain and France in the 1920s, speculation soared in the United States. Wild, unrestrained investments in the the stock market and in land were made with what seemed to be cheap and plentiful, borrowed money. This was clearly a mistake. The Chicago Federal Reserve, to its credit, protested strongly that, at least in its region, the policy seemed unwarranted. But the Chicago Fed was overruled because cheap credit did serve the short-term national political goal of brightening a depressing economic picture. The Fed Board of Governors asserted its veto power over the Chicago Fed and thus sealed any future prospect of independence for the regional banks. The heady environment of the 1920s became even headier when the Board of Governors eased credit at a time when it should have done the exact opposite. The Chicago Federal Reserve again objected and was overruled. We all know what happened next, as speculative fever seized the country. The board became justifiably concerned about the huge demand for bank loans secured by common stocks, which kept interest rates high. With the cost of money rising steadily, corporations deferred their spending plans. The economy began to stagnate and contracted.

But the Fed was not through. In 1928 it really swung into action. First came an announcement by the Fed that securities-backed loans were excessive. Second, the Fed raised the rate of interest it charged commercial banks to borrow reserves. But it was too late to ration credit because the U.S. economy was already stagnant. The Fed was tightening credit when such action was bound to bring on a general economic downturn. Strangely enough, the policy was applauded by the regional Fed banks, who were alarmed at the buildup of securities loans. The regional banks saw tight money as a way to curb the feverish speculation in the stock market.

Then the Board of Governors made the mistake that pushed the economy over the brink. The Fed announced that commercial banks could not borrow reserves from the central bank for stock market loans. The squeeze was on. Liquidity dried up.

The *coup de grace* occurred in August 1929, when the Fed decided to tighten money further by raising the discount rate on money it loaned to commercial banks. The wobbly financial markets were pushed beyond any possible recovery. In October, the stock market collapsed, leading to a full-scale financial panic.

Imagine the shock of the crash to the recently inaugurated President, Herbert Hoover. One wonders whether he had any idea of the power of the Fed and of how the money and banking system would almost single-handedly seal the fate of his administration.

The 1929 securities market panic in the United States turned into a worldwide depression that lasted more than a decade—until military spending in the years leading up to World War II stimulated economic recovery. That the impact of the Crash of '29 was so severe suggests that there must have been other forces at work besides speculative excess in land and securities. And indeed there were.

To begin with, like Japan today, the United States in the 1920s exported far more than it imported. It practiced what the history books used to call a "beggar-thy-neighbor" policy in foreign trade. Perhaps Washington bureaucrats had been frightened by the experience of being a debtor nation for many years following the Civil War. But, by holding back the prosperity of our European trading partners, that policy backfired badly when we ourselves needed help.

Second, most U.S. corporations were hopelessly in debt. The end stages of any financial fashion always produce excesses, and we may be seeing it again in the 1980s. The substitution of debt for equity is just such a fashion; and, if history is any guide, we will once again pay dearly for the excesses.

Third, *laissez faire* banking as had been practiced for a century and a half turned out to be a disaster. In the four years between 1929 and 1933, almost 10,000 banks in the United States failed. That put the fear of God into surviving banks and thrifts. They became overly cautious, which obviously made economic recovery more difficult in the years that followed.

Had the Fed continued to be the lender of last resort on some categories of stock market call loans, instead of excluding such loans in 1928, the worst of the panic might have been avoided. But, since all the loans were being called at the same time, the Fed could not have averted the crash. There is no way the Fed could have provided that much liquidity, any more than it could provide all the necessary liquidity today should there be a sudden rash of failures. This is why the current Fed's interests and the interests of the banks they regulate are hopelessly intertwined. It is also why I suggest that any bank that breaches its fiduciary responsibilities for safety and liquidity should be allowed to fail or be forcibly recapitalized. If it fails or is forcibly recapitalized before the industry gets in so deep, the impact could be cushioned and the marketplace would become the disciplinarian. In 1933, it took a three-day bank holiday and an emergency infusion of $1.3 billion in bank liquidity from the new Reconstruction Finance Corporation plus another $900 million from the Fed to stop the panic.

In fairness, I think we have to say the Depression generation did pretty well in coming to grips with these frighteningly new and complex problems. Landmark legislation, such as the Banking Acts of 1933 and 1935, the Securities Acts of 1933 and 1934, and the Glass-Steagall Act of 1933, did much to correct the situation. Today's legislators should take note that such reform had great voter appeal.

The Securities and Exchange Act of 1933 created the Securities and Exchange Commission, which has given us the most intelligently regulated and, consequently, the most efficient stock markets in the world. The U.S. capital markets are the envy of free economies everywhere. The basic ingredients are disclosure and factual financial reporting.

Similarly, the Glass-Steagall Act of 1933 sought to put a "Chinese wall" between the entrepreneurial function of investment banking and the fiduciary function of commercial banking by forbidding commercial banks to own investment banking operations in the United States. Accordingly, the investment banking arm of Morgan Guaranty was split off to become a separate company called Morgan Stanley, and so forth. It was a good law, and there were very sound reasons for its enactment. Back in the 1920s, a bank lending officer might feel obliged to extend credit to a company whose common stock the bank's investment bankers had just underwritten. If that lending officer later had reservations about the company's ability to repay, he might be tempted to ask the investment banking side of the bank to bail the company out with a new issue of common stock, which was then purchased largely by the bank's own trust department. Would you expect that same bank in the meantime to be entirely disinterested in offering investment advice to customers about that company? The conflicts that arise when a bank is both an owner and a lender are not simply hypothetical. The November 7, 1987 *Chicago Tribune* reports that the Comptroller of the Currency's Office stated that Continental Illinois National Bank and Trust Co. of Chicago ignored its warnings against lending too much money to First Options of Chicago Inc. (wholly owned by the bank holding company) during the stock market crash of October 1987. First Options is reported to have suffered a 90 million dollar loss during the crash. Yet, this is precisely the type of business Continental Illinois intends to pursue and emphasize. I don't necessarily disagree. I merely point out the conflicts, pressures, and dangers.

Today, many large commercial banks are putting together leveraged buyouts and merging their commercial banking departments with investment advisory services, raising exactly the danger Glass-Steagall sought to prevent. If investment banking is ultimately to be made a permitted activity for commercial banks, there needs to be an impenetrable Chinese wall between the subsidiary engaged in such activities and commercial banking. The drive to modify or repeal the Glass-Steagall Act has considerable support. I would simply urge careful deliberation and proper caution. To a large extent, the investment banking community has invited this thrust by the commercial banking community because of the large fees and charges they have successfully imposed. Their own actions in this regard not only invite but, indeed, necessitate effective competition. The commercial banks are not going to stand by quietly while the investment bankers milk the market when, in reality, it is the loans and other credit facilities provided by the banks that make the deals put together by the investment bankers possible.

Bankers Trust Company in New York has been at the forefront of this movement. After a recent reorganization, Bankers Trust stepped up its efforts to take equity positions in certain client companies. These opportunities often arise through the bank's involvement in mergers and acquisitions, leveraged buyouts, and venture capital financing. George Vojta, Bankers Trust's executive vice president, told the *Wall Street Journal* that Bankers Trust "thought about" creating an arbitrage operation that would speculate in the stocks of takeover candidates. "We may do it later, we aren't going to do it now." The Journal article noted that, under existing bank regulations, a bank may generally own as much as just under five percent of a nonbanking company.[3]

J.P. Morgan & Co., the commercial banking survivor of the 1930s breakup of the Morgan empire, joined Bankers Trust in the new drive into investment banking. It sought to remove legal barriers to underwriting corporate securities. Morgan Bank's 1985 noninterest income — an approximate indication of what it earns from investment banking — equaled 33 percent of total income, up from 27 percent in 1983.

A Morgan spokesman told the *Wall Street Journal* that it considered giving up its bank charter if barriers against investment banking were not relaxed (Phillip L. Zweig, "J.P. Morgan Is Expected to Reorganize, Reflecting Investment Banking Growth," *Wall Street Journal*, 12 February 1986). Bankers Trust too had explored that option but rejected it because management believed that Congress will eventually pass legislation granting underwriting powers to banks.

In 1986, the Federal Reserve Board gave Britain's giant National Westminster Bank approval to combine brokerage activities and investment advice in one subsidiary, an important step in the steady erosion of the Glass-Steagall "Chinese wall." Meanwhile, many major money center banks have full-scale investment banking operations in London and other overseas locations. Back home, many have at least venture capital departments, which, in function, come very close to violating the spirit of the Glass-Steagall Act.

The evolution has already blurred the distinction between the banker as conservative intermediary and as entrepreneur. The

---

[3] Phillip L. Zweig "Bankers Trust Merges Three Divisions into Single Groups," *Wall Street Journal*, 23 April 1986.

banker can be a lender and a principal, using depositor's money as chips in the game. Why are the bankers doing it? To make more money, to pay bonuses, and to justify the payment of higher salaries.

"There's no ceiling on what I can make," David Dougherty, senior vice president in charge of Bankers Trust Company's merger and acquisition department, said in the *Wall Street Journal* (Phillip L. Zweig, "Commercial Banks Beef Up Merger Arms," *Wall Street Journal*, 9 April 1986). Commercial bankers are well aware that top Wall Street investment bankers earn well over one million dollars annually, which is two to three times what a senior commercial bank specialist makes. The commercial bankers say that, as their volume increases, their compensation should approach the level of their investment banking counterparts.

Chase Manhattan Securities, a subsidiary of Chase Manhattan Corp., acquired two London stock brokerage firms. Not long thereafter, some of its London employees made a quick profit by purchasing shares in a public offering Chase managed, then quickly selling in the first few days of trading, a practice known as "stagging." While this is not illegal, it is at best an "error in judgment," as Chase itself characterized the event. The motive was obviously to make a quick profit in securities trading, which is what the firm does every day. So, why not the employees, too?

In a free-enterprise system, these are laudable motivations, ones to be encouraged. The issue is simply whether such activities are compatible with the fiduciary responsibilities of a depository institution. When the banks engaged in these activities before, they ran into trouble. Regulatory reform in the 1930s got them out of it. With the passage of time they are getting back in. We can expect more trouble in the future.

I think it would be a great mistake to scrap the Glass-Steagall barriers totally, as some bankers and legislators would like to do. How many times do we have to make the same mistake? Bankers cannot be deal makers, investors, and fiduciaries lending depositors' money, all at the same time. There needs to be some demarcation.

Specifically, the prohibition should continue as to underwriting and investing in equity securities. On the other hand, there should be no prohibition on securitization of debt by a bank, which I view as an extension and modernization of a traditional banking function. Where a bank is currently authorized to make a particular loan or buy a particular bond, it should also be allowed to securitize that loan or bond, i.e. to package it in small units and market it to the public. In so doing, a bank is engaged in its traditional function of providing credit and at the same time it will be able to provide itself liquidity from the asset side of the balance sheet as well as providing the small investor with a new investment product. The Chinese wall must be built to keep depository institutions from underwriting or investing in straight equities because there is a difference between debt and equity. The only exception should be equities acquired in a venture capital subsidiary. This, in part, at least as I understand it, is the position advocated by Federal Reserve Board Chairman Alan Greenspan—and I agree.

Concurrent with Glass-Steagall in 1933, the Federal Deposit Insurance Corporation (FDIC) was created to guarantee deposits up to a certain fixed amount ($100,000 per account today). The purpose was to restore confidence and to assure depositors they would be paid even if their banks failed. While state-chartered commercial banks do have the option not to join the FDIC if they choose, almost all of them do because of the obvious appeal of FDIC insurance to depositors.

But not everything enacted during the 1930s has endured the test of time. Even with all the regulations and safeguards in place, no one regulatory body has sufficient authority to do the job that has to be done. The Federal Deposit Insurance Corporation supervises all FDIC-insured banks. The Fed supervises all Federal Reserve member banks. The Office of the Comptroller of the Currency, in the U.S. Treasury Department, supervises all nationally chartered banks. State banking departments supervise state-chartered banks. If the bank is owned by a bank holding company, as the larger ones are these days, the holding company is in turn regulated by the Federal Reserve Board and the Securities and Exchange Commission. The latter requires that its financial statements be audited by certified public accountants in conformity with generally accepted accounting principles.

Therefore, most banks in the United States are regulated by more than one of the supervisory authorities, whose jurisdictions overlap. All state-chartered banks are examined by the various state banking departments. If they are not members of the Federal Reserve System, they are also examined by examiners from the FDIC. If they are members of the Federal Reserve they are examined separately by Fed representatives.

National banks get a break. They get examined by the employees of the Comptroller of the Currency, who sends copies of their reports to the Fed and to the FDIC, which accept them in lieu of their own examinations. The thrift institutions have their own regulators and insurance corporation to deal with.

Despite these armies of examiners poring over bank books, banks still get into trouble without warning. One reason is that bank examiners are there mainly to see that banking laws and regulations are being followed and that the institutions are fundamentally sound. They are not there to look for fraud; and they seem incapable of warning against the kinds of imprudent banking that nearly caused both of Chicago's biggest banks—First Chicago and Continental—to fail in recent years.

While the books of bank holding companies are scrutinized by outside auditors, those auditors provide no meaningful safety net either. By their own standards, they are not there to warn of fraud or grossly imprudent banking, although their Financial Accounting Standards Board is now suggesting that such risk assessments be made. The accountants have not satisfactorily addressed the sorry state of financial reporting in the banking industry, despite years of trying. The composition of loan portfolios, for example—how much has been loaned to which companies and countries—remains a mystery to bank shareholders to this day. Yet those numbers are the most important ones in the bank.

When trouble finally becomes obvious to the Federal regulators, the fragmented responsibilities in this patchwork system begin to work against each other. Even the Fed has limited power to enforce its will, given the political reality that depository institutions have strong constituencies who promote their interests at home and in Washington.

In 1973 and 1974, Federal Reserve Chairman Arthur Burns was trying to tighten the money supply and saw that First Chicago's liberal lending policy was working against him. I remember being summoned to Burns' chamber and being taken out to the woodshed for a licking. "You stop it out in Chicago," he said. "Your loans are no good. I don't like it. You are getting into trouble." It was a very stern talk. As a matter of fact, the Fed was taking measures against us at that very time by not approving our applications for foreign branches. Chairman Burns was using every device he could to rap us across the knuckles.

It didn't work. Mr. Freeman told me, "No! We'll call an analysts' meeting and I'll make a speech that it's the role of the Fed to guarantee the liquidity of the bank. It's not up to them to tell us what to do. It's up to them to provide us with enough money to fund what we are going to do, because there is no conceivable way for us to cover our obligations if there is a real demand for money." Those were his very words.

If leaders of depository institutions feel they are being pressured by the "common enemy" in Washington, it is easy to mobilize support. The trade associations jump into the fray. Local congressmen and senators also help. Important customers are asked to telephone Washington. The pressure is formidable.

The local Federal Reserve Bank, as a member of the same club, may try to persuade the banks in its district from the inside. A quiet, informal visit by the president of the local Fed with the CEO of the errant bank sometimes does the trick. I remember several such visits. But, sometimes the warnings fall on deaf ears. Local Feds are like the clergyman to the flock. In my experience, they have never been empowered to be real regulators, with "teeth."

Surely the most celebrated example of bank regulatory agencies openly contradicting each other occurred in January 1986. The Supreme Court ruled 8-0 that the Federal Reserve Board had exceeded its legal authority in 1983 when it asserted control over limited-service banks. These "nonbank banks," which either make loans or accept deposits, but not both, thereby avoid the legal definition of a bank and, hence, regulation by the Fed. Nonbank banks neatly skirt Federal prohibitions against interstate banking and against commercial companies' ownership of banks. Applications for permission to form some 300 limited-service banks from insurance companies such as CIGNA, conglomerates such as ITT, Sears Roebuck & Co., and money center banks seeking to cross state lines were granted preliminary approval by the Comptroller of the Currency, but the Fed demurred, took their case to the courts, and lost.

The unhappy British experience with such nonbank banks, which have figured prominently in numerous banking crises there, suggests strongly that the Federal Reserve Board was entirely correct in its attempt to assert control over them. Instead, the Fed wound up having its authority diminished and its influence seriously tarnished. What was lost in the process is the reality that an institution, chartered by the Federal Government to take public deposits, is viewed by the saving public as subject to regulation and thereby safeguarded. The use of the name bank is enough by itself to create this perception. So is the use of the word deposit.

The judgment by the Supreme Court, which is undoubtedly technically correct under existing legislation, clearly reflected the mood of the moment. Only one month before, Fed Chairman Paul Volcker's move to limit the use of high-interest, high-risk "junk bonds" in certain hostile takeovers was also criticized as overstepping the bounds of Federal Reserve authority. . . in words reminiscent of the high-flying late 1920s. I am, in no way, opposed to hostile takeovers. Takeovers are a healthy cleansing mechanism that eliminates managements that take advantage of shareholders and depress the values of their securities. The issue is not whether hostile takeovers are good or bad. The issue is simply the quality of the instruments that banks and thrifts are permitted to purchase with depositors' money, particularly when the Government is ultimately responsible for those investments through the FDIC or the FSLIC. I also do not subscribe to the broad appellation, "junk bond," which was the target of Mr. Volcker's ire. Some high-yield bonds are good and some are bad. It is simply a question of prudent selection. This is the message that Mr. Volcker was trying to deliver, and there is nothing wrong with that. The point is that there is no easy, mechanical way to invest depositors' funds prudently. Those entrusted with the responsibility, institution by institution, must monitor the assets in their care continuously and scrupulously.

I sympathize with both the Administration and the Federal Reserve in their attempt to invigorate an economy that has been growing at a mere two percent to three percent in recent years despite a massive infusion of foreign savings, and that sustains a stubborn six percent unemployment level we used to regard as intolerable and dangerous. The Administration, however, wants lending for anything and everything to build values in order to stimulate new capital formation. The Fed, with its responsibility to oversee the safety and soundness of banks, is frustrated to see scarce savings being deflected into unproductive takeover financings by business and increased consumption by individuals.

Currently, the Fed, the Comptroller, and the FDIC are all concerned with how to measure the risk in bank loan portfolios. This may be a highly theoretical question to the accounting profession; but to government officials worried about their responsibilities and mandates, it is a very pragmatic question indeed. For the FDIC it is a question of survival. How do you set up a radar system that will warn of an impending Continental Illinois crisis before it happens?

At the moment, the amount of reserves a bank is required to keep is determined by its assets, that is, the size of its loan portfolio. So the Federal Reserve recently segregated troubled bank assets into four separate categories of risk, with proportionately higher reserves as the degree of risk rises. The Federal Home Loan

Bank Board is reported to have explored a similar concept for thrifts. The Comptroller of the Currency is working on the same approach. It is difficult to obtain information on the implementation of these programs, despite the fact that such disclosures (i.e., that a bank has a higher reserve on its assets) are a critical determinant of a bank's market value.

The FDIC, as the agency that has to pick up the pieces of banks that fail, came up with the most imaginative and controversial proposals. One was a subjective assessment of a bank's portfolio risk by the FDIC's own inspectors. That produced such howls of protest from the banking community that it was quickly, but temporarily, replaced by a statistical formula. Meanwhile, the FDIC staff says it's hard at work trying to come up with another way to measure portfolio risk so as to be able to charge member banks a risk-based insurance premium. The irrefutable test, it seems to me, is imposed by the marketplace. Take a statistical sample of the portfolio, say one percent or two percent, and require a bank's or thrift's management to resell it. If the market takes the loans at par, that is their value. If, on the other hand, the market discounts them for reasons of risk, then the required reserves must go up accordingly. Tough medicine? Of course! But, we need tough medicine when we are talking about safeguarding the nation's savings. The argument advanced against this approach is that another lender will always discount a loan below par if the loan is made by someone else. So, the market test may, in reality, be skewed against the seller and, thus, too harsh a test. Perhaps so initially, but, in my opinion, such would not be the case once the practice is established.

I like the concept that the riskier a bank's loan portfolio looks to disinterested observers, the more the bank should pay to the deposit insurance corporation. The added insurance premium puts an additional brake on bankers' natural tendency to lend their way out of trouble with risky rollover loans—critically important as they often are. For another, it provides a warning signal that the bank is getting too loose with the depositors' money.

Bankers have a point, I think, when they object to a snapshot risk assessment of their portfolio that is not periodically updated to reflect changes in creditworthiness. Even the best loans can look risky at some stages of their life. This can be remedied via the market mechanism. Once the market accepts the participation at par, the premium can be lowered.

Loans and investments are not the only areas that require surveillance, disclosure, and some form of market check. There is also the trading of securities and foreign exchange. For the large money center banks and thrifts, these are high-volume activities with the potential for substantial risk.

Then there is the whole question of liquidity. When the Comptroller of the Currency decided to treat money market certificates of deposit (i.e., purchased money) as true deposits with reserve requirements approximating the low reserves on savings deposits, it opened new challenges for measuring and monitoring bank liquidity. It was a whole new ball game without new rules to match. More leverage of assets meant lower pricing. Lower pricing meant more affordability for borrowers, and the inflationary furnace was stoked. These forces contributed to the economic pressure cooker of the late 1960s and early 1970s, yet another example of human miscalculation with profound impact on the economy.

Although it may not sound that way, I do not believe we need more regulation or more regulators. I believe we should unleash the most unerring regulator of all, the marketplace. Make the market the test. If banks and thrifts are run badly, let them fail, or be forcibly recapitalized, and let the consequences fall to those who direct and administer them. If the institutions desire insurance, let them pay market rates and let the commercial market be the arbiter of what those market rates should be. Let rules and regulations for loans and investments apply only to those financed by insured deposits. Insured deposits, only up to $100,000 per account, constitute only a small fraction of a large institution's liabilities and generally not all of even the smallest institution's liabilities. Since the Government guarantees these deposits and must pay promptly at all costs, investment rules are appropriate. These are the only assets that regulators need examine. As for the rest, let the market be the disciplinarian. It will be an efficient disciplinarian. A whole new private industry will emerge to rate banks and thrifts and to grade their portfolios. The basic health of the economy is everyone's business and concern. Why shouldn't it be the subject of informed discussion in the daily business journals?

One promising solution emerges from the growing tendency of big banks to swap loans. A big New York bank with too many Argentine loans, for example, may wish to trade some of them for Brazilian loans or Turkish loans that other banks hold. An eager market has sprung up that permits them to swap loans anonymously. When such swaps occur, a market value is inevitably assigned, perhaps 70 cents or less per dollar on Latin American loans, for example. In this case, the regulators should require banks to increase their reserves to make up for the market's decision that the particular loan has deteriorated in value. Outside auditors should require those writedowns to be made in the form of reserve additions, which are deducted from earnings. This will prevent publication of misleading earnings reports and capital ratios. Citicorp took such a step in May 1987, initiating a trend that the rest of the industry rightly followed.

The trouble with loan swaps as an alternative to reserve additions, I fear, is that it may encourage banks to swap their best loans—not their worst ones. So the loan portfolios of money center banks could, if deceptively administered, deteriorate. First Chicago refused this temptation in the mid-1970s when good real estate loans could have been sold in order to report big reductions in overall real estate loans, since the market was viewing real estate loans negatively at the time. I instituted a policy to sell only poorer quality credits, because the objective was purely to upgrade the overall portfolio. The temptation to do otherwise certainly exists. My proposal to allow the regulators to select a statistical sample of the entire portfolio for sale in order to measure its overall quality would obviate this risk.

What is to be done about this mess? Congress must address the entire issue of bank regulation as soon as possible. The Bush task force has already set forth some common-sense guidelines on which I think key constituencies can agree. Here they are:

1. *Let each regulator be responsible for supervising specific functions, no matter who performs them.* In other words, let the SEC deal with the topic of junk bonds, whoever holds them, and leave the Federal Reserve Board out of it.

2. *Merge the thrift regulatory agencies and insurance corporation and the commercial bank regulatory agencies and insurance corporation.* If there is going to be very little significant difference between what thrifts can do and what commercial banks can do, then having two separate regulatory bodies is clearly redundant. Once the huge losses of the FSLIC have been disposed of, then merger with the FDIC would also make for more efficient regulation.

3. *Set up one bank superagency with one chairman to coordinate all bank regulatory efforts.* If we are intent on limiting the powers of the Federal Reserve, then merging the FDIC and the Office of the Comptroller with the Fed is probably not feasible. Each performs a useful and important function and serves as a counterbalance to the other. The objectives of the U.S. Treasury in seeking to finance the budget deficit may conflict with the monetary policy objectives of the Federal Reserve. But a coordinating superagency would clearly be helpful in avoiding duplication of effort and in resolving conflicting objectives.

4. *It is an imperative of national policy to guarantee deposits of the general public, at least up to $100,000.* It is not critical to guarantee large commercial deposits; the large depositors can pay for the analysis to determine whether the banks to which they entrust their money are sound and prudently managed. The big depositors would exert a marketplace discipline on the depository institutions seeking their business. As I personally experienced in 1974 and 1975, when General Motors tells you that it is reducing the amount of money it is prepared to leave in your bank, it is a powerful incentive to make things right fast.

Small savers and depositors need to be protected. The U.S. taxpayer foots the bill for the excesses of poorly managed depository institutions. There is no clearer example than the 1987 recapitalization of the Federal Savings and Loan Insurance Corporation, with $10.8 billion in borrowing authority. The U.S. Government had to bail out the FSLIC because the agency got too close to the thrifts it regulated. It viewed itself more as a fraternal trade association than a regulator and thus was lax in its supervision. FSLIC inherited the industry's problems and undermined its insurance fund. The only feasible remedy was a federal bailout; and, in everyday terms, that means the U.S. taxpayer.

Knowing what we know about how banks get into trouble, and keeping in mind the Bush task force recommendations, I would ask that three broad principles guide the future regulatory structure:

1. *A fiduciary entity like a commercial bank must not be entrepreneurial because its primary responsibility is to preserve depositors' capital.* A.N. Pritzker once remarked about First Chicago (Anderson, "Pritzker v. Pritzker," p. 4): "We were practically running that bank." That, of course, was precisely the problem. No bank can be run solely for the benefit of its biggest commercial borrowers. It does not receive an adequate reward for undertaking such risk, nor do its depositors. More to the point, its depositors do not wish or expect it to take such risks with their money. In other words, to let some customers run the bank violates a bank's fiduciary responsibilities to its other depositors and the community it serves.

2. *Bank regulators are there to guarantee the preservation of depositor funds, and in order to do that effectively, they must allow banks to fail, or be forcibly recapitalized, as a discipline for the others.* If the Federal Government is going to underwrite the mistakes of all commercial banks, then commercial banks should be nationalized. That at least would be honest. Since most of us believe that private-enterprise banking is more effective than nationalized

banking—precisely because the industry is at risk, and therefore more careful—then it follows that private-enterprise bankers who violate their fiduciary trust must be allowed to fail, or accept recapitalization, as a warning to banks who indulge in dangerous entrepreneurial banking. We had such an experience between 1929 and 1933, when nearly half the banks in the country failed. They had participated in, and become party to, the rampant securities speculation of the time. They did not lean against the wind, despite overt signals and exhortations from the Board of Governors of the Federal Reserve to do so. They viewed themselves as businessmen instead of bankers, and their failures brought on the economic consequences that followed. They also brought on new regulation and new safeguards, which are now in danger of being eroded.

3. *The free market has to be the arbiter of what bank risk is acceptable and what is not.* The only truly disinterested yardstick against which to measure the acceptability of bank portfolio risk is the free market. Any attempt to legislate or regulate acceptable risk is doomed to fail, since the market keeps changing, often quite dramatically. Laws and regulations only set up challenges for bankers to try to get around. They just don't work and never have.

The marketplace will determine whether the institutions in question are deserving of confidence. If they fail, let them fail, or let them accept the penalties of forced recapitalization. Investors who entrusted resources to them did so at their own peril. However, there needs to be a clear demarcation between these unregulated activities and the activities that house insured deposits. Two clearly separate entities are required. Once the two are intermingled, it is like an egg that is scrambled. And when the egg is scrambled and there is trouble, it becomes very difficult, if not impossible, for the regulators to isolate those activities that need to be protected with government funds and those activities that should properly be allowed to fail. This is why investment banking was originally separated from commercial banking. That lesson is as relevant today as it was in 1933. The two activities must be physically separated. The management must be separated and the resources must be separated. If combined within the same holding company, then the Chinese wall between the subsidiaries must be secure.

During the Continental Illinois Bank crisis in 1984, the word was widely circulated that the FDIC would not let any of the top 20 banks fail. This may or may not have been actual policy, although the alleged deferential treatment of big banks compared with small banks generated considerable rancor at the time. If such a policy were ever carried out, the taxpayer could never have afforded multiple bailouts of the scale of Continental. In the future, saving the big banks, should that ever be necessary, is not the answer. The answer is to carve out the part with the insured small deposits, examine that part for compliance with well-defined rules, and let the market and individual managements take care of the rest. Forced recapitalization with attendant losses to shareholders and creditors is a good middle ground because it achieves the desired result. At the same time, it protects depositors, customers, the communities served, and the staff. It also saves the resources of the insurance fund. New legislation is needed to make forced recapitalization an effective tool which can be quickly and effectively applied.

SEVEN

Cleaning Up the Boardroom

Understaffed as they may be, the banking regulators have a duty to perform. They have laws to enforce; and when laws are broken, someone must be held accountable.

On December 1, 1984, the Federal Deposit Insurance Corporation demanded the resignations of 10 directors of the Continental Illinois National Bank and Trust Company. They were the cream of the Chicago business community. They were to be held accountable for what happened on their watch.

Many in Chicago criticized the FDIC for taking action that embarrassed those involved. Yet, the FDIC was making a valid statement.

Being elected to the board of directors of the local bank is not just another of the perquisites that come with success. Unlike what happens when you go on the board of directors of any other type of corporation, you have to take an oath as a director of a national bank. You must pledge before a notary public to "diligently and honestly administer the affairs of the bank and not knowingly violate or willingly permit to be violated any provisions of the bank laws." Directors of most state-chartered banks are required to take similar oaths.

In the primer for bank directors, *Responsibilities and Liabilities of Bank Holding Company Directors*, Robert E. Barnett lists 10 different counts on which the directors of a failed bank have been successfully sued: They engaged in self-dealing; they approved excessive or imprudent loans; they failed to correct problems spotted by regulatory bodies; they failed to provide proper guidance for management; they failed to make sure that proper audits were conducted; they didn't insist on good internal controls; they permitted the bank to become illiquid; they didn't go to enough meetings; they didn't insist on enough diversity in the loan portfolio; they failed to exercise independent judgment. Mr. Barnett's book is now supplemented by a new book issued by Comptroller of the Currency Robert Clarke entitled *The Role of a National Bank Director.*

But care in these areas is not enough. You also have to know the business and you have to pay attention. Being a bank director has special responsibilities. Too often bank boards become little more than frequent-flyer clubs, a little bonus for the best customers. In my experience, the principal concern of most bank managements when a board meeting is coming up is how to get the directors to feel upbeat. The idea is to entertain them so they won't get bored, to make them feel it's worthwhile for them to come, but not to have them get down to the nitty-gritty. Usually you parade your senior officers before the board, assigning each of them a subject for presentation. Each has a bunch of slick slides and handouts. Each has been well rehearsed.

Now the director who is listening to all this and who has the regulator's examination report in front of him may lean across the table and say with great wisdom, "Well now, I understand there is some concern being expressed here by the Comptroller of the Currency. Is that concern valid? What does that really mean, Mr. Chairman?"

The chairman will look over to one of his officers and say, "Well, let's let Joe deal with that because he is the one who has had in-depth conversations with those people when they were here."

Joe, who has rehearsed the answer to that question until he could say it in his sleep, says, "I'm glad you asked that question." There is another presentation. He trots out a new bunch of slides. Then everybody settles back, lights up cigars and agrees, "Wonderful, things are great."

There are warning signs for which bank directors ought to be on the lookout, signs that suggest a bank is really heading for difficulty. Even something as seemingly trivial as the decibel level of money desk conversation (which should be reported by a competent officer at each meeting) should be looked into if it's significantly higher than normal. In the bond department, where huge amounts of trades and underwritings are done, directors should ask if the transfer powers are in the files. Is there a disproportionate number of "fails" (securities deliveries that don't occur on time)? Is collateral sufficient to secure the day loans (loans made to brokers against the securities they hold in inventory)? On broker dealer loans, where the bank is lending on a secured basis against depository receipts or against securities in portfolio, the auditors should be sent out from time to time to determine whether the control systems of those brokers are adequate.

The officers in charge of important functions—asset and liability management, operations, credit—and the chief executive officer should be board members so that other directors are informed and have direct access to the key people. In addition to these day-to-day responsibilities and their accessibility to the other directors, officers on the board should recognize their independent fiduciary duty to the depository institution and to their fellow directors.

No one should be a bank director unless he or she knows how to mind the store. Of course, if directors ask questions in sufficient depth, they will be assured that the necessary controls and procedures are in place and that the bank has the best people monitoring them. Directors must put management to the test.

Directors, by law, cannot accept superficial answers to responsible, reasonable questions.

If, before the bailout, Continental directors had asked the proper questions about energy loans and if they had been given complete answers by management, they would have discovered that, in some instances, there were no reserve reports and no evaluations by independent engineers of the value of the properties. They had no operating reports as to what energy production was expected to be. They had no reservoir reports. It was unbelievable that a bank would lend money like that. There didn't even appear to be a credit policy committee. As bad as it was thought to be at the time the FDIC took control, the new management at Continental discovered to its dismay that the situation was even worse.

Once directors determine that their bank is in trouble, decisive action has to be taken quickly. This is where I fault the Continental directors, who probably should have removed the top officers right then and there. The new management has to shrink the bank drastically, which is hard to do because a bank is geared for growth. It must reduce staff, turn customers away, go against the grain of everything a banker has been trained to do. It must attack vested interests, which is not going to be popular with the customers or with the bank staff. The only favorable comment the new management is going to get for carrying out conservative policies will come from the federal and state regulators. But I'm afraid the directors won't be too impressed by it.

The trouble is, I would venture to say, that not only most directors but also most senior bank officers don't know how to ask the questions I am talking about. Most bank officers haven't grown up on the operations side of the bank, and they are not in tune with systems and controls. That's why I'm convinced that one of the top three officers of the bank who sits on the board— whether it be the chairman, president, or vice chairman—ought to be an expert in operations.

I also think it would be constructive if the federal bank regulators were to publish guidelines for bank directors that stressed the importance of monitoring internal controls. You don't let airline pilots sit in the cockpit of a 747 unless they can pass certain tests. A bank or a thrift is not a 747, but its crash could be just as catastrophic in a different way.

It's nice for the pillars of the community to have a place to meet. It undoubtedly builds morale. But, in my opinion, the local titans of business are already country-clubbed and Union Clubbed to death. They don't need the bank's boardroom too. They are there to safeguard the institution, and if it gets into trouble, particularly by making bad loans or investments, they should be held accountable for not doing their job.

If the directors are among the bank's best customers, I would argue that they could potentially be problem directors if their own businesses or the businesses they manage get into trouble. I can hear the protests now. How can these business leaders, who give jobs to thousands and are busy building prosperity for everyone, possibly be excluded from the bank's board? They can because they have a conflict of interest the size of their companies.. Do you really think that they will be motivated to caution a bank chief executive against being too aggressive in his or her loan policies if their own company is a customer, is in trouble, and is anxious for a rollover loan? The answer is far from academic. I lived it and will describe the pressures that were brought to bear.

First Chicago had made a nonrecourse real estate loan to Marshall Field's company, Field Enterprises, which caused the bank some loss. Because Mr. Field was a director of First Chicago and I was a director of Field Enterprises, the matter was fully described in the First Chicago proxy statement and was the subject of discussion at one of our annual meetings, with appropriate notice in the media. Mr. Field insisted that Field Enterprises would not go beyond its technical, legal obligations on the loan. I said, "Marshall, the bank will honor its nonrecourse commitment, but, as a director of the bank, you have special responsibilities. You must seriously consider whether you are subject to a higher standard."

I was, frankly, at fault not to have resigned as a director of Field Enterprises right then and there. But I thought that to call attention in this way to a major disagreement at a time when the bank needed all the support it could get would have been counterproductive. This was obviously a rationalization. The fact is I was wrong not to resign. The letter of agreement was non-recourse and the rate charged was for a nonrecourse loan. The bank made a deal and it would keep its end of the bargain. Suffice it to say, however, if a director was going to insist that a loan gone sour to his company was going to be honored by the letter of the agreement, then that was going to set a precedent for all transactions with that director and his company.

The supposed clubbiness of the boardroom dissipated amid the unpleasantness involving the bank and Field Enterprises.

On August 4, 1980, *Business Week* reported that Field Enterprises paid off a $35 million loan three years early because First Chicago was allowed to reprice the loan if Field bought or sold properties without the bank's approval. "They were technically within their rights," Marshall Field said of our loan. "But not within the spirit of the loan covenants," he added.[4] *Euromoney* magazine, in March 1981, brought First Chicago's "retrenchment" into wider focus, discussing the delicate balance in maintaining relationships with valued customers who also happen to be directors.

"Abboud introduced a policy of having a high compensating balance deposited with the bank when the loan agreement was made, with a further balance deposited when the funds were drawn down," *Euromoney* reported. "Some customers weren't used to, and didn't accept, that normal banking practice."[5]

The directors wanted special treatment, which tipped the delicate balance between keeping customers satisfied and protecting the institution. Directors must find a way to play the appropriate role at the appropriate time. If directors are going to do business with the bank or thrift institution on whose board they sit,

---

[4]"First Chicago: New Management to Bring Back the Past," *Business Week,* 4 August 1980, 68.
[5]Derek Bamber, "First Chicago: Under Sullivan, After Abboud," *Euromoney,* March 1981, 51.

they should agree never to let the institution suffer loss or embarrassment, regardless of what the letter of a loan agreement might permit. That should be the code of honor that binds together the members of this exclusive club.

The top officers of national banks are not prohibited from borrowing from their own banks, but they should be. How can an officer perform his or her fiduciary responsibilities and also be a borrower? I am not talking about middle-level or junior officers. I am talking about the top-echelon decision makers who sit on or meet with the board. They have to guide the board members in the establishment of the policies governing customer relations and borrowing requirements. Borrowing from their own institutions creates a conflict of interest. They should take their business to other banks that are independent and not in any way beholden to their own.

Some will say that the vast majority of local businesspeople are prudent, selfless leaders, well able to rise above petty, short-term considerations when pondering the future course of the local bank.

Well, we are all human and, in weaker moments, subject to temptation and emotion. I've had many directors tell me that being a director of a bank was nice because it allowed them to meet their counterparts around town and gave them a peek at everyone else's business. There is nothing wrong with that. "Networking" is good for the institution and good for the community. But being a director is also a job with responsibilities and accountabilities. You have to make tough decisions on loans coming up for approval. It's an information sharing experience where everyone is supposed to tell all, no holds barred, so that informed judgments can be made.

Directors like to think that their companies bring good business to the bank. In most cases, they do. But, here again, the directors are obligated to meet a higher standard of disclosure and must be totally forthcoming with both themselves and the institution. The toughest challenge occurs when things begin to go sour at a director's company. This is just about the time that the prudent banker is supposed to insert his glass eye and begin to protect the institution. It is easy to see how honest, well-meaning people can get into a situation where relations become strained.

One of my directors at First Chicago was Brooks McCormick, former chairman of International Harvester. When Harvester started running into trouble, I told him that, on the basis of our credit analysis, we were going to cut back on our loans to the company. Naturally, he thought that was terrible. He told me that Harvester had dealt with First Chicago from its beginnings, and that the McCormick family had been among the founders of the bank. He also pointed out that Roger Anderson, the chairman of Continental Bank, was on Harvester's board. Moreover, another of First Chicago's directors, Louis Menk, chairman of Burlington Northern, was also on Harvester's board.

I simply said, as politely and supportively as I knew how, "The credit of your company is, in my judgment, deteriorating." No one pressured me, directly or indirectly, to do anything differently. But such a situation is anything but comfortable for all involved.

A bank must attract good directors from among the movers and shakers in the business community and still be able to maintain an arms-length relationship. It isn't easy for the chief executive, let alone the staff, to deal effectively with these powerhouses when times are tough. In the words of Robert Barnett, a former chairman of the FDIC, "Directors should be constantly aware of the desirability of increasing the profitability of their institutions." Profitability is important to protect the individual depositor, a point so apparently obvious that it is never mentioned. Profitability, *per se,* is not the objective. Profitability is merely a means to build strength and expand the capabilities to service the community further. Board members lose sight of this aspect of their fiduciary responsibility. In fact, they don't like to question management policy too closely. Most of them are close friends of the chairman. And, boardroom debates can get unpleasant, even when cloaked in gentility.

At First Chicago in the mid 1970s, the once cohesive board of directors split into three factions. One small group identified with John Swearingen, the head of Standard Oil of Indiana, who had been saying repeatedly, in support of my position, that quality standards could not be maintained with overly rapid loan growth. A second group remained silent but uncomfortable. And the third group, primarily the Gale Freeman loyalists, remained firm behind the pronouncements of the chairman, upbeat and growth-oriented.

I suffered a great loss when John Swearingen decided to leave the board. He had previously been on the boards of two banking companies, Chase Manhattan Corp. and First Chicago Corp., and chose to resign the latter post when the regulatory authorities expressed reservations about such dual membership. Mr. Swearingen told Gale Freeman that the Chase was the older of his two relationships and, with the position of Standard Oil of Indiana throughout the world, he felt that he must maintain his membership in that organization. Mr. Freeman was not especially unhappy, as relations between the two men had never been close. Mr. Swearingen was succeeded as the in-house conservative by Bob Stuart of Quaker Oats and Bob Gwinn, then the chairman of Sunbeam. Both were good, sound directors and openly expressed their reservations about the course and direction of our rampant expansion. But to no extent did they carry John Swearingen's clout.

That was in mid-1973, and the Gale Freeman express was barreling down the track. The chairman was talking about First Chicago's stock going from $35 to $100 per share. The important thing was to obtain good quality assets, high-yielding assets, to become the premier wholesale bank in the country. Mr. Freeman said that there was no point incurring the expense of a large retail network to obtain the savings deposits of thousands of individuals. It was cheaper to buy wholesale money in large quantities. Dick Thomas, the vice chairman, was the great proponent of this theory that money would always be there for purchase. True, there might be a few occasions when the price for money would be higher than the yield on assets. But these occasions of negative spread historically had been few and far between. The board majority bought this philosophy because Mr. Freeman was eloquent and upbeat — always upbeat. He was comfortable and reassuring to be around.

Because of the widening differences in philosophy between Gale and me, management meetings became increasingly confrontational. He felt that the Fed Chairman, Arthur Burns, was an old fuddy duddy. With a smile on his face, Mr. Freeman chided me good-humoredly about being too conservative and, occasionally, an irritating nag not only to him but also to some of the other senior officers.

To his credit, he tolerated my opposition in the most senior councils of the organization. In return, I made certain that the opposition was loyal — that my most vigorous dissents were in private or in small management groups. I also made sure at the board level that we acted as one team pursuing a cohesive strategy. On the other hand, the positions of the different factions were obvious. It created tension. There is nothing wrong with constructive tension if it forces the board to deal with real policy issues. Throughout this period I never undermined Gale Freeman, even in the most private of conversations with any of the board members. Nor would I tolerate any campaign of insurgency within the organization.

The situation came to a head when our top executives were summoned to Washington to meet with Chairman Burns. Mr. Burns was concerned that too many of our loans were funded with money purchased in the open market. I didn't blame him for that, personally.

Picture the situation at First Chicago at the time. Dick Thomas, the bank's top commercial officer, was urging the major acquisition of a major consumer finance company on the East Coast. He had initiated these negotiations when he was running the holding company, and the discussions had proceeded quite far. He was also aggressively pushing the expansion of the leasing company and international wholesale lending. Others, like Chauncey

Schmidt, another vice chairman of First Chicago, previously the bank's top commercial officer, and now head of the holding company, were beginning to grow more cautious. But Mr. Schmidt was in an ambivalent position. As the primary executive of the bank holding company, he was not directly responsible for what happened in the bank. So he felt he had to yield to Gale.

Following the chiding from Chairman Burns, Mr. Freeman briefed the Executive Committee of the board, couching his message in terms of what was good for the country and for our shareholders. While he acknowledged that the Fed had ultimate responsibility for monetary policy, Mr. Freeman denied that the Fed had the power to dictate operating policies or rates of growth to private financial institutions. There was no such thing as too rapid a rate of growth, he said. If prosperity were to continue, business had to be financed.

The key, he said, was our loan quality. First Chicago's loan assets were good, and good loans could always be financed. At his most eloquent self, Mr. Freeman acknowledged that the internal classifications of the loan portfolio showed some deterioration. But they were still first-rate loans. Writeoffs were still minuscule in comparison to our earnings. Projections showed earnings rising much faster than writeoffs. Then he read a passage that seemed to state that almost every asset in the bank was eligible for rediscount, meaning it could be used as collateral for borrowings from the Fed on a dollar-for-dollar basis. He asserted without equivocation that it was the duty of the Fed to maintain the liquidity of the banking system, and also the liquidity of any member bank to the extent that it had assets suitable for rediscount.

The Executive Committee, and later the full board, listened soberly. There were only a few pained reservations expressed by directors such as Bob Stuart of Quaker Oats. Some directors nodded approvingly. At the luncheon that followed, individual board members went up to pat Gale on the back, congratulating him for his courage and statesmanship. Was this an expression of support for the CEO? Did it mean approval of the substance of his policies? Did it mean a vote of cohesiveness for the club? I don't know. I suppose each of these directors had his own reasons. But the effect on Gale was reassuring and supportive.

I couldn't help but admire Mr. Freeman's performance. He appeared determined, only giving in at the fringes enough to appear reasonable. His presentations were state of the art in terms of color graphics and slides. We were going to overtake Citicorp and Chase, Bank of America and Morgan—or that was the impression we got.

Meanwhile, in the real world outside the boardroom, funding grew ever more difficult, mostly because the increase in our loans required us to purchase ever increasing amounts of new money. Thankfully, the news media and Wall Street analysts treated us most favorably. Dick Thomas had them convinced that everything was in good shape.

Inside the bank, tensions were mounting. As Gale Freeman spoke more and more frequently of his impending retirement, the race for the chairmanship was in full swing. Chauncey Schmidt was unhappy at the holding-company level because it was not mainstream enough for him. Dick Thomas was jealous of Mr. Schmidt and was doing everything in his power to build up his own following, despite the fact that the team he was leading was built largely by, and loyal to, Chauncey. I had my own following, those generally regarded as conservatives or nay-sayers. The media had a field day profiling the candidates and assessing their chances.

As the annual meeting approached in April 1974, the economy was flattening and beginning to decline. What normally happens in such situations is that highly leveraged companies are the first to feel the pain. Their earnings decline, but their interest payments remain constant. The most leveraged and expansive industry at the time was real estate. As signs of trouble began appearing in real estate, our stock began to fall because of the bank's large exposure to real estate investment trusts. Mr. Freeman had boasted that we intended to be the largest real estate bank in the country. Now those words were being thrown back in our faces.

To their credit, some of the directors pressured the chairman into moderating the text for our annual report that year. He had been overly enthusiastic about First Chicago's stated goals and ambitions. It would have been an embarrassment if the original text had been published. The undercurrent of disquiet among the directors, triggered by the concern of the Federal Reserve, served us well. Everyone breathed a sigh of relief after that 1974 annual meeting. We felt more comfortable now that the bank was becoming more conservative. Mr. Freeman could feel it too. He had clearly switched over to my side in policy disputes. More and more it appeared that I was gaining the confidence and backing of the chairman.

The battle for the chairmanship was beginning to divide the board, and some directors started actively campaigning for their favorites. This left lasting scars. People have blamed Mr. Freeman for the "horse race." I don't. He did what he thought he had to do to prepare for his own succession. His motives were noble and unselfish. The problem was that the full board never dealt with the tensions that underlay the race for the chairmanship. Some board members continued to harbor visions of chasing and surpassing Continental and of maintaining the emphasis on wholesale commercial banking versus retail banking. This wasn't Gale's fault.

The moral of these lessons is that we have to be a lot tougher on bank boards. We have to demand a lot more of bank directors. Perhaps bank officers should not be permitted to serve on any boards of customers, something that I did myself with Field Enterprises and others. This is a hard and extreme position. I don't know the correct position or the proper intermediate guideline. If the banker joins the board of one customer, then other customers in the same industry—the Tribune Company in the Marshall Field instance—may be upset or at least feel discomfort. With all the problems in banking, the standards have to be reconfigured. Otherwise, we risk nationalization, just as Continental did, and that would be awful. It would stifle creativity and suffocate the economy.

Perhaps one answer may be to use advisory directors more generally. This would allow prominent members of the community to serve on bank and bank holding company boards without the responsibilities and accountabilities that must necessarily attach to a voting director. Advisory directors would provide confidence, generate business and serve as a communication link to the community at large. Meanwhile, the voting directors could meet more frequently, become better informed, and fulfill the surveillance function for which they are held accountable. They would, of course, be compensated commensurately.

We must infuse market discipline into the banking system, and we must liberate banking from the "bailout mentality" by making clear that poorly managed institutions will be allowed to go under. Accountability for failure and mismanagement will fall to the top officers and the boards of directors in whom we invest the public trust known as fiduciary responsibility. Not explicitly mentioned in the codes of conduct for bank directors is the need for them to adjust to the new economic realities of corporate restructuring. Directors will have to face them in running their own businesses as well as in the bank boardrooms.

EIGHT

Recapitalizing a Failing Bank

E ach of the regulatory agencies has a map showing the size and location of financial institutions receiving federal assistance since 1982. It is a sobering sight to see the clusters of little dots, east and west, north and south, but heavily concentrated in a spine in the midwest from Illinois to Texas. The troubles in the savings and loan industry are well publicized. The troubles in the banking industry are less well publicized. But the story is always the same, bad loans and investments resulting from too much growth, too fast.

It is interesting to note that the biggest problems have occurred in unit banking states, principally Illinois and Texas. New bank charters were easy to obtain in the early 1980s from both federal and state authorities. Organizers started new banks, ran them for short periods, and then sold them at a handsome profit to bank holding companies. Good management was not available to integrate and control these rapidly growing systems and institutions. Trouble followed, and we are now faced with a host of problem banks and savings and loans.

The challenge is to find an efficient and effective approach to aid these troubled institutions and restore them to good health with minimum disruption to the communities they serve. The challenge is not to be underestimated. There is a big job to be done because of the numbers of institutions to be serviced and because of the many billions of dollars of troubled assets they hold in portfolio.

The *Wall Street Journal* in a front page story headlined "Frightened Money," reports:

> So far this year, 122 banks have failed in the United States, double last year's pace, and 38 of them have been in Texas — a rate of one a week. Most have been small institutions whose collapse was handled routinely by bank regulators. But the steady drumbeat of failures is fraying the nerves of Texans, and they are quietly moving their funds from one institution to another or even out of state — despite the government's guarantee of deposits of $100,000 or less.

> While deposits at banks and S&Ls nationwide have been rising during the past several months, they have been falling in Texas, in what regulators call 'a gradual and persistent withdrawal' of money. Since the 1986 fourth quarter, Texas S&Ls report a $790.9 million net drop in deposits despite a slight gain in June. Texas bank deposits started shrinking early last year. The state's major banking firms say that as of March 31, their domestic deposit base had declined by more than $4.5 billion from year-earlier levels, including a $1 billion drop in the first three months of this year.[6]

The main line of defense is anchored by the two principal insurers, the Federal Deposit Insurance Corporation (FDIC) and the Federal Savings and Loan Insurance Corporation (FSLIC). These agencies were established in the 1930s to insure deposits in banks and share accounts in savings and loans and thereby to create and maintain public confidence in the system.

---

[6]Leonard M. Apcar, "Frightened Money," *Wall Street Journal*, 1 September 1987.

There is a big difference in the current capacities of the two agencies to accommodate the challenges they presently face. The FSLIC reserve insurance fund was nearly exhausted and, in August 1987, had to be replenished by a $10 billion infusion of funds voted by Congress and signed by the President. Hefty as that sum may be, however, it is by no means enough unless it is combined with funds from the private capital markets.

The FDIC, on the other hand, has over $18 billion in cash reserves. The challenge confronting its staff and directors is to maintain and build these cash reserves in the face of mounting numbers of problem banks, because the public measures confidence in the system by the level of available cash reserves.

It has been obvious for some time that the insurance funds, FDIC and FSLIC, would have to discover new financing techniques in rescue operations whereby the vast resources of the private capital markets could be tapped to combine with their own funds in order to maintain public confidence. The public must remain confident that the aggregate available resources are sufficient to do the job of rescuing ailing banks and thrifts and with ample margin to spare. To participate in this research, I started my own company, A. Robert Abboud and Company, in 1984 and then added Braeburn Capital with the specific purpose of investing in thrift institutions and community banks. The research in the area of troubled financial institutions led me to form an alliance with the investment banking firm of Donaldson, Lufkin and Jenrette and the law firm of Skadden, Arps, Slate, Meagher and Flom to compete for the right to recapitalize First City Bancorporation of Texas. First City was clearly in trouble. The FDIC would have to provide assistance. The Southwest, in general, and Texas, in particular, offered attractive turn around potential and First City was large enough, the second largest rescue after Continental Illinois Corporation, to become a prototype private investor recapitalization for smaller banks and thrifts. Since First City was a bank holding company comprised of insured member banks, our bid would have to be submitted to the FDIC.

Following a lengthy process involving intense negotiation, the Abboud group was informed that it was the winning bidder to recapitalize First City with FDIC assistance on September 12, 1987. The Board of Directors of First City Bancorporation approved, and I was named a consultant to First City to oversee the implementation of the recapitalization to finalize the assistance package. During this implementation phase, I learned about the difficulties and complexities inherent in any rescue operation. I also gained new appreciation of the valuable services routinely performed by both the FDIC and the FSLIC. The mission assigned to these two agencies is indispensable to the maintenance of public confidence in our depository institutions.

Eventually, it may make sense to merge the FDIC and the FSLIC. However, this will require the savings and loan industry to restore itself to good health and to make the additional contributions to the fund to restore its surplus. Because of this potential levy for additional contributions to replenish the FSLIC surplus, savings and loan shares will continue to sell at a lower multiple of book value than bank shares.

The threat of a possible charge on each and every savings and loan to refloat the cash ravaged FSLIC is similar to the cloud that overhangs the values of the shares of the big banks that have large exposures to developing country debt. Everyone knows that the developing countries cannot pay their outstanding foreign loans in full. The big banks have suffered one round of charge-offs already. One or more rounds is sure to follow, and the stock market values of the common equities of the big banks reflect this possibility. Needless to say, the major charge-offs of bad loans deplete capital. To replenish the capital account, the big banks will have to sell more common equity, and the result will be dilution in the book and market values enjoyed by present shareholders. The same impact will fall on the present shareholders of savings and loan institutions. A capital assessment to aid the insurance fund will cost money and depress stock market values of savings and loan shares.

Who is to blame for this depressing state of affairs? Obviously, managements and boards of directors are to blame. In conducting the business of their own institutions, they produced losses and created the need to issue new capital, thereby causing existing shareholders to suffer dilution in the values of their holdings. Others ran their own institutions properly but did not exert leadership or influence to thwart or dampen the excesses practiced by the errant members within the industry. The result, at least for the savings and loan industry, is depletion of the insurance fund, the injection of resources from the U.S. Treasury, and the prospect of a special assessment on the survivors.

The consequence is that both banking and thrift insurers face major challenges to preserve public confidence and still help the troubled institutions in their industries. One avenue open to the insurers is to close the failing institutions. Sometimes, conditions have deteriorated to the point where closure is the only viable alternative. The mechanism employed by the insurance agency is called an "insured deposit transfer." This means, in the case of banks, that the deposits up to $100,000 per account name are sold to a healthy institution and the owners of those accounts (the original depositors) are assured that their money is safe and that they can use the money right away. These depositors, with $100,000 or less in their accounts, are protected and need have no concern about the safety of their money. The system works and is one of the main reasons why the October 1987 stock market collapse cannot be compared directly with 1929, when this system did not exist.

Depositors with more than $100,000 in any one account or combination of accounts under the same name are not protected for amounts over $100,000 in an insured deposit transfer. To the extent they have deposit balances over $100,000, they get receivership certificates for the excess over $100,000. For such amounts they are unsecured general creditors, ranking equally with all other unsecured general creditors. Other general creditors might include suppliers, lenders, note holders, beneficiaries of guarantees or letters of credit, and holders of bankers acceptances.

111

A second alternative means of rescuing a failing bank is called a purchase and assumption transaction. Under this alternative, the FDIC offers potential bidders the opportunity to purchase certain of the assets of a failed bank and to assume the liabilities of the bank, including, of course, the prized deposits.

Valuing the deposits in preparation for submitting a bid is often difficult and highly judgmental. Estimates must be made regarding the volatility of such deposits, the costs of maintaining them, the prospects of the economy in the market area being served, the competitive pressures that will be brought to bear by other banks and thrifts in the area to lure the deposits away, and the prospects of being accepted by the customers and maintaining relationships. The decision-making process to develop the proper bid is subjective at best, and the FDIC does a good job of getting bidders to compete with each other and of maintaining total confidentiality so that no one bidder knows what the other is offering.

The result, of course, is protection of bank customers and depositors, minimum disruption to the communities served, and less total cost to the FDIC. The purchase and assumption mechanism has been used with sufficient frequency to be well understood and procedurally predictable.

A third, and newer, alternative of rescuing a failing bank is the total asset takeover. In this alternative, the FDIC offers all of the assets as well as all of the liabilities of the failed bank to the successful bidder. Unlike a normal bidding process whereby the bidding party offers to pay a certain sum of money to acquire an asset, the total asset takeover is a process whereby the bidding party specifies the amount of money it seeks from the FDIC to cover the estimated losses in the asset portfolio.

The successful bidder takes the money, recapitalizes the bank according to predetermined ratios established by the various regulatory authorities with jurisdiction, and is on his or her own thereafter for success or failure. This total asset takeover is the most pure of the free market alternatives and is to be commended for placing both the risk and the reward where it properly belongs, i.e. on the bidder or investor. Obviously, with accountability for risk or reward also comes the obligation for stewardship or management.

The very newest alternative is the bridge bank legislation. This newly enacted law empowers the FDIC to take over a failing bank, appoint management, achieve stability and hopefully renewed values, and then put the bank up for sale. The procedure is much too new to rate on the basis of experience. However, the record of government appointed management has been inconsistent at best. The fact is that investors with capital at risk manage banks, thrifts, and other companies better than hired managers with little or no private capital at risk. It is difficult to explain but that's the way of the world, and we are foolish not to recognize this basic law of human nature. No one protects assets better than the owner.

Such a statement would suggest that I do not believe in trustees or fiduciaries or government officials charged with the responsibility of protecting the public trust. Not true! I am a great supporter and admirer of public officials and other true fiduciaries. I firmly believe in bank trustees for private property and government officials for public property. These individuals are among the most dedicated I have met in my business career.

Continental Illinois was, of course, the largest failing bank situation of all time. The FDIC moved in, provided capital, assumed majority control, appointed management, and operated the bank in a manner which many now believe to be the first prototype of the bridge bank concept. It frankly hasn't worked. It was a bold and valiant effort, but something new was needed. The Continental Illinois bailout did not include a private investor group with their own private capital at risk and a firm long-term business plan to be implemented beginning on day one of the rescue. Consequently, the bank's identity was for a time uncertain, its progress was slowed, and three years later, it still labors under the handicap of adverse public perception, because of its majority ownership and control by the FDIC.

The next stage evolution after Continental was the Bowery and, then, Bank Texas. The Bowery is now a major success story and the criticism is that the entrepreneurs who bid for the bank, and put up their own capital at risk, made too much money—about $100 million in profits on a $100 million investment over two years, if the transaction is finally consummated in its present form. Forgotten is the reality that this was the least expensive alternative for the FDIC, that the customers and communities dependent upon the Bowery have been well served, and that the employees and the insurance fund have been protected. Yes, the transaction resulted in a handsome profit for the investors. Wonderful! Would we have been happy if the transaction resulted in a loss and returned the bank to the protection of the FDIC? Would we have been happy if the Bowery failed and the customers and communities dependent upon its services were denied those services? Would we be happy if the jobs provided by a vigorous and healthy Bowery were lost because the institution was losing money and had to be contracted? Ridiculous! Our free market system is predicated on risk taking, with reward and applause for the successful and loss and accountability for the unsuccessful.

After the Bowery came the next step in the evolution of bank rescues, Bank Texas. Unlike the Bowery, this did not involve a select group of private investors putting up their own money but a syndicator, Hallwood, committing to bring in investors through a private placement. The concept proved successful. Hallwood was the approved bidder, and the new management team introduced by Hallwood is now managing the bank. The losses are shrinking and the final report card is yet to be written.

The latest phase of evolution is First City Bancorporation of Texas. Building on the Bank Texas model, the First City plan not only contemplates a private placement but also a follow-up registration into the publicly traded markets. It not only contemplates a recovery or "collecting bank" to house the troubled assets but also a noncash infusion by the FDIC together with a rescue plan on a massive scale. The amount of the FDIC guarantee is nearly one billion dollars. The amount of additional investment from the private markets is over $500 million. Consider these numbers in context. When I joined The First National Bank of Chicago in 1958, it had only $1.5 billion in total loans and discounts and, at the time, was the fifth largest banking company in the United States.

The structure of the First City rescue plan is, on the one hand, new but, on the other hand, rooted in precedent. Each part of the purchase has been done before. The innovation is simply the packaging and the scale.

If there is credit to be accorded, it goes wholly and without reservation to the staff of the FDIC with help from staffs of the Comptroller of the Currency, the Federal Reserve Bank, the Texas State Banking Commission, and the other governmental agencies that had to play a role, such as the Internal Revenue Service, the Securities and Exchange Commission, and the various Congressional committees charged with regulatory oversight. The effort was a combined endeavor, but the laboring oar was the staff of the FDIC led by their very able and dedicated Chairman, William Seidman.

Bill Seidman assembled a remarkably talented team. He set the standards and established the values. The goals were clearly enunciated. These goals are to protect the system and to preserve the capital in the insurance fund at all costs.

Why is protection of the capital in the insurance fund so important? Because it translates directly into public confidence. The insurance fund presently has cash equivalent assets of $18 billion. As long as this fund is perceived to be stable and increasing, the public maintains confidence in the banking system. When and if the fund should decline, public confidence in the banking system would decline commensurately. This is what happened to the savings and loan industry when the Federal Savings and Loan Insurance fund began to decline and then was exhausted. To restore confidence, Congress had to vote a $10 billion infusion from the U.S. Treasury.

The First City recapitalization is the latest evolution in protecting the integrity of the insurance fund. By accessing the private capital markets directly, it supplements the insurance fund by many billions of dollars. In fact, based on price, the potential of supplemental capital is enormous. If the concept is successful, it becomes a prototype to use for ailing thrifts as well as banks. Theoretically, public confidence in depository institutions should no longer be in question because of direct access to the private capital markets for forced recapitalizations.

The essential ingredient, of course, in any such system is a dedicated staff of government employees, incapable of corruption and influence, and dedicated to maintaining the integrity and values of the system. I would never forgive myself if I did not digress at this point to record my own observations as to how the staffs of the FDIC and its companion agencies worked in a real live situation such as First City.

In 30 years of business I have never seen a harder working and more dedicated group of people. I would call them at home or office all hours of the day or night, seven days a week, with never a complaint from them or their families. You couldn't buy any one so much as a cup of coffee. Their salaries are government scale. Their sole objective is to get the cheapest possible deal to protect the insurance fund and yet save failing institutions and the banking system as a whole. They are literally economic patriots.

Why do I emphasize the role and character of these dedicated regulators? I do so because they are pivotal in the dynamics of building and preserving public confidence in the banking and depository system as a whole.

The reason that the stock market collapse of October 1987 has not tipped the economy into a downward spiral toward recession or depression as in 1929 is because the public at large did not lose confidence in the strength or viability of banks or thrifts. The public remained convinced that the regulators, with the regulatory tools at their disposal, could work viable solutions to restore and protect troubled institutions. If that confidence should ever be broken, the runs on depository institutions would begin and economic collapse would surely follow, worse than 1929 and pervasively around the world because of trade and investment linkage.

Public confidence is at the soul of economic prosperity. It is the heart of the economy. If it is strong, prosperity reigns. If it is weak, economic trouble follows. Creating and preserving that confidence is the seminal role of any leader and any federal administration. Central to the endeavor is a strong and healthy banking system. The paramedics, emergency room personnel, trauma ward attendants and critical care specialists in this system are the regulators and the staffs of the insurance funds.

This is why the Continental Illinois, Bank Texas and First City transactions are so important. They are not just individual banks. They are the highly visible examples by which the public measures the capacity of the banking system to cope with the challenges at hand. Frustration or failure to complete the rescue in these highly sensitive economic times would cause unpredictable consequences. The ripple effect throughout the economy would have the potential to be bad and pervasive. It is not a good gamble.

Isn't this obvious, you might ask. Why do you belabor the point? I do so because the rescues are far more difficult and the tools available to regulators to do the job are far less adequate than might readily be suspected. Much needs to be done to simplify and strengthen the powers for intervention in troubled situations. The authority of regulators to accommodate corporate laws designed not for this purpose but to protect shareholders and creditors in nondepository institutions should be reviewed and appropriately strengthened. A bank or savings and loan holding company is not just another company to be governed by the same laws and regulations that apply to other ordinary commercial concerns. A bank or a thrift houses community savings and is the central mechanism for spurring or retarding overall economic activity. Its viability directly affects public confidence.

The First City story gave me insights into the weaknesses and inadequacies of the system in which the regulators and staffs of the insurance funds must work to achieve a large scale rescue. The details of that transaction belong in another book. For purposes of this book, I'll simply make the following observations.

The bank and savings and loan holding company system requires a thorough revamping. The original theory—that risk activities can be contained in a holding company structure and financial failure of those activities will not weaken or damage the depository institution or institutions within the structure—simply has not worked out in practice. Moreover, the double leveraging capabilities built into the system, permitting bank holding companies to borrow in order to put more capital into the depository institution of which they are the parents has proven in some cases to have been at the root of the problem bank situation.

The separation of holding company boards and managements from the subsidiary banks' boards and managements requires superior communication and leadership. Sometimes tension arises between the holding company board and management and the lead bank board and management. This tension often allows each group to blame the other in case of trouble. Accountability and responsibility are blurred.

Creditors and shareholders of the holding company are led by the investment bankers who sell the securities to believe that they are in the same position as the creditors and shareholders of the subsidiary banks. In fact, the creditors and shareholders are subordinated to the creditors and shareholders of the subsidiary banks. It is a classic double leveraged system, but it has not been marketed or explicitly explained as such. The treatment accorded the Continental Illinois holding company creditors and preferred holders further confused the difference in ranking between bank and holding company securities. The FDIC clearly made a mistake in that rescue package.

In certain holding companies, some of the member banks are state-chartered and some are national banks chartered by the Office of the Comptroller of the Currency. In addition, the Federal Reserve supervises the holding company structure. The triple jurisdiction adds infinite complexity to the rescue operation.

The requirement that holding company shareholders must approve forced recapitalization packages under the terms of individual state corporation statutes that were never designed for such situations makes rescue packages very risky to consummate. For example, in the First City situation, Texas State law specifies that the common shareholders and each class of four classes of preferred stock approve the transaction by a two-thirds majority of the total number of shares issued and outstanding. This means that any shareholder who doesn't vote casts a *de facto* "no" vote. Small classes of preferred stock controlled in one case by one individual can single-handedly block the whole transaction. Creditors or lessors who refuse to accede to the concessions demanded by the FDIC can also block the whole transaction. And when such transactions are blocked, the consequences and hardships are severe.

The consequences are that the recapitalization package fails, the insurance fund has to deplete its reserves because it has to pay more money to do a bailout, and public confidence in the ability of the system to cope with problems is eroded. At a time such as the present, when the financial markets are highly sensitive, the impact on the economy as a whole could be devastating.

The hardships occur because the alternative to a forced recapitalization is insured deposit transfer, purchase and assumption, total asset transfer, or bridge bank. In other words, the alternative to an FDIC negotiated forced recapitalization is a bailout. This costs the insurance fund more money and depletes the reserves.

More than the costs in money and public confidence, the disruptions to customers, depositors, and the communities served by the member banks are incalculable. Individual banks within the system must be closed, charters must be pulled and reissued by the appropriate authority—state or federal, employees lose their jobs, borrowers lose their lines of credit and commitments, creditors soon discover that their leases and contracts with the member banks can be terminated, and communities lose the services hitherto provided by the bank. It is a disruptive process because the regulators do not presently have the legal authority for a "cram down," forced recapitalization solution on holding company creditors and shareholders. The regulators can only operate by getting the required cooperation from such creditors and share-holders or resorting to the banking equivalent of nuclear deter-rent, the individual takeovers or closings. New legal authority is needed for the regulators to mandate a cram down. A cram down is the ability to impose a solution without a vote by those required to make concessions. Some procedure will have to be devised to insure fairness.

At present, the system is definitely unfair to bank customers, the communities served, and the insurance fund. Holding com-pany creditors and shareholders can thwart the recapitalization of a failed bank or thrift by withholding their cooperation or by voting "no," or by not voting at all since failure to vote prevents the necessary affirmative vote needed for approval. These are the same shareholders and creditors who permitted management to remain in place and permitted the institution to fail.

The tactic sometimes used by holding company creditors and shareholders is to frustrate the recapitalization and then to use the judicial process to carve out the healthy banks in the system to be sold for their benefit. This leaves the losses in the bad banks within the system for the insurance fund to absorb. The tactic is to make the insurance fund take all the losses while the credi-tors and shareholders retain for their benefit the good assets. This is despite the fact that, in the good times, the holding company is operated as one integral system, funded as one integral sys-tem, and presented to the capital markets as one integral sys-tem. Present legislation permits holding companies to present themselves as an integral unit in the good times and to become severable when there are losses to be absorbed. Clearly, there is an inequity. It is a situation where personal interest is in conflict with the public interest and when the blocking action is taken by a shareholder — director, it could even be viewed as an out-rage. More than that the potential of major hardship to the pub-lic is intolerable. Worse yet, the potential hazard to the system and the economy is unacceptable.

So far, we have been lucky. The regulators have done the job despite the inadequacy of the tools at their disposal. This is a tribute to Chairman Bill Seidman of the FDIC and his staff. The newly installed Chairman of the FHLBB, Danny Wall, is just beginning to build a comparable level of public confidence through accomplishment. Mr. Wall's decisive move to close Vernon Federal Savings and Loan in Dallas on November 19, 1987 was the largest ever thrift bailout and the second largest federal depository bailout after Continental Illinois Corp. Under the terms of the Vernon Federal restructuring, $1.3 billion would be injected to refloat the troubled institution, with $1.1 billion of this amount in notes and $200 million in cash. But with the problems still to be solved in both the banking and thrift industries, we are at great risk. A failure to complete an important recapitalization could precipitate a confidence crisis that could be difficult to manage or contain. This is needless risk because it can easily be corrected through legislation.

NINE

Old Values, New Realities

The old adage that time and tide wait for no man has a special significance in the world of finance. Businesspeople and bankers who resist these forces do so at their peril.

Today, the financial markets are crying, nay demanding, that managements restructure their asset portfolios to increase earnings and raise the market value of their publicly traded stock. If they do not, they must accept the consequence of being swept away by the tide of change.

In one instance with which I am intimately familiar, T. Boone Pickens made a pass at acquiring Cities Service. He wanted the big reserves at Hugoton (a large gas field in Kansas that spills over into Oklahoma). Cities thwarted him by making a deal with Gulf Oil. Instead of proceeding apace with asset redeployment, both Cities and Gulf took refuge in theologic adherence to tradition and size. For whatever reason, the Gulf-Cities merger fell apart. Occidental Petroleum moved in, paid four billion dollars to acquire Cities, sold off or redeemed more than three billion dollars of cash from Cities' own assets, and retained the domestic exploration and production business plus important foreign concessions. These earned $500 million a year pre-tax and generated approximately $800 million a year in cash for a net out-of-pocket cost of less than one billion dollars. Neither Cities Service nor Gulf took the avenues of restructuring open to them, and both became engulfed by the onrushing tide.

What are the driving forces that have given rise to the need for asset restructure? Some of the more obvious forces of the 1980s are as follows:

1. *Inflation.* By 1980, the rate of inflation peaked and then began a steady, sustained decline to what became, in total, a quantum drop. Managements and corporations that based their strategies on continued inflation at double-digit rates discovered the fatal flaw in their assumptions. The assets they accumulated in implementing the original strategy did not produce as planned because inflation subsided.

2. *Real Rates of Interest.* With the drop in inflation, the financial community found that, by slowing the rate of drop in nominal interest rates, a negative real rate of interest could be converted to a positive real rate of interest. The real interest rate is the difference between the nominal, or published rate, and inflation. With inflation falling, the spread between the published rate of interest and the inflation rate helps banks increase their earnings. They need to cover loan losses. By dropping their nominal rates more slowly than the inflation decline, banks create abnormally high real rates of interest. In the early 1980s, these high real rates of interest pushed down the rate of inflation even further, strengthened the dollar, and put downward pressure on real estate prices, particularly in the energy belt. A major casualty of the high real rates of interest was the savings and loan industry. With property values not increasing and in some cases declining, the turnover of mortgage portfolios declined, slowing the roll-out of old loans at low rates.

3. *The Dollar.* With real interest rates above normal, the dollar became an attractive commodity in foreign exchange markets. Everyone wanted the safety of the U.S. market and the attractive investment opportunity it presented, particularly in the securities area. As the dollar kept increasing in value relative to foreign currencies, there was additional profit to be made in holding dollar-denominated assets. Money poured into the United States seeking investment opportunities, but investors were discriminating. They wanted the protection of high-quality financial instruments or hard assets. Thus, money was in plentiful supply to fuel the so called "junk bond" market. As prices were bid up for assets being accumulated by corporate conglomerates, market activity accelerated.

4. *Energy Prices.* With the decline in inflation and a stronger dollar, energy prices tumbled. Earnings and cash flows of energy companies tumbled commensurately. Drilling companies and oil company suppliers, in generally capital intensive businesses, lost volume, cut prices to keep their equipment working, and reported big losses. Conversely, the heavy energy users, whose shares had dropped in value during the period of high energy prices, suddenly found their fortunes reversing. Their earnings began to increase along with the value of their shares.

5. *Agriculture.* The farmer, having accumulated acreage and expensive machinery to satisfy the hungry commodity markets of the late 1970s, suddenly found the markets in oversupply. Commodity prices for grain fell precipitously. Farmers became unable to service bank loans, which spelled trouble for the banks in the farm belt. The once expensive land that collateralized the farmers' bank loans plunged in price. A result of the farm problem was a sharp cutback in fertilizer usage and new equipment. Moreover, barely used equipment, now in excess supply, was dumped back into the

market. Prices plunged on equipment, fertilizer and other farm-related supplies.

6. *Banks and Thrifts*. The onslaught of deregulation compounded the management problems facing the leaders of financial institutions. Along with the vast inflow of liquidity from abroad, competitors invaded the financial services market, a progression that started in the 1970s with the advent of money market funds. Moreover, new powers were conferred on the banks and the thrifts, whose managements were not always prepared to take them on. Banks and thrifts that tried to do too much too quickly ran into trouble, and some were allowed to fail. When the banks and thrifts reached out to private, nonbank entrepreneurs or service companies to handle their excess liquidity or their bond portfolios, they suffered more losses when a few of those entrepreneurs, corrupted by the limitless flow of easy money coming their way, suddenly failed. Moreover, with deregulation and competition, the prices of services dropped. The institutions could no longer afford to be all things to all people, and so they began to specialize. Once choices were made, costs had to come down and productivity had to go up on a product-by-product and customer-by-customer basis. This process is still in its infancy, and institutions that lag will find themselves prime candidates for takeover by others.

7. *Developing Country Debt*. Loans to less developed countries continue to overhang the international financial system. There is little likelihood that this debt can be repaid anytime soon out of trade surpluses or foreign exchange inflows. Some sort of asset swaps will have to be devised on a case-by-case basis, which, for the lending institutions, may present new business opportunities. On the other hand, they may in the short run cause these loans to be viewed as nonperforming assets, severely reducing bank profits.

The result of all these forces is more perceived risk, and more risk in fact. Risk implies opportunity for those who recognize change and seek to harness its potential, and failure for those who refuse to understand it and to adjust accordingly.

The interplay of these new economic forces is complex, but the reasons for them are basic. The stock market values some companies at less than their liquidation value. Hence, they are bargains to be bought, broken up, and sold for a handsome profit. In other cases, companies are purchased by their own managements through leveraged buyouts, using the companies' own credit to finance the purchase. The company purchased in the leveraged buyout is then managed differently, primarily for cash instead of book earnings. Low-yielding assets are sold for cash, and unnecessary overhead is cut. The result is a much leaner, healthier company. The cash flow is improved materially. Loans are paid off and the managements, together with their investors, make a lot of money.

Why, then, don't companies do this automatically in the ordinary course of business? There are probably as many answers as there are companies. However, at many fine, well-established, companies there is a conflict between deeply ingrained traditional values and short-term opportunities that present themselves.

How many times have you heard these new adages of corporate life: "We are building for the long term. America wasn't built by people without vision who had no faith in the future. We are not going to turn over our company to those quick-buck asset players. We are builders, willing to sacrifice earnings in the short term to build for the future."

Maybe these are the appropriate philosophies for a privately held company, but the realities of the marketplace for a publicly held company indicate that shareholders are profit-conscious. They vote to sell their stock to the highest bidder, whoever that bidder might be, leaving it to the new owner to redeploy assets and earn the returns commensurate with the purchase price.

The traditional values were the ones ingrained in all of us when I went to business school. These values ordained that short-term credit was provided by banks and should only be used for seasonal needs; that longer-term loans were also provided by banks and were to be used for, and liquidated by, specific projects; that total long-term public debt should be no more than 25 percent of total capitalization; that the return on shareholder equity was more than adequate at 13 to 14 percent and that, of this return, no more than 30 percent was to be paid out in dividends, the rest to be plowed back into the company for future growth. This was the time-honored formula for mature or established companies. So-called growth companies earned less and paid out smaller percentages of earnings in the form of dividends.

Traditional values were the formulae for success in the 1950s and the 1960s, when interest rates were low. Bond yields were low. Long-term money at low fixed rates was plentiful. Double-digit inflation was beyond the realm of imagination. America was the dominant commercial and industrial force in the world, and global investment opportunities abounded.

Also during the 1950s and 1960s, Europe, (West Germany, in particular) and Japan were rebuilding their war-torn economies. In the process of being rebuilt, these economies introduced a radical new concept, i.e., leverage. Investors in these economies were afraid to take the risk of purchasing equities. They preferred to invest in high-yield debt instruments, with the perceived comfort that there was some equity cushion below them. With leverage (debt exceeded equity by two to three times) equity investors demanded a much higher rate of return to compensate for the overlay of debt. By U.S. standards, it was an inverted pyramid and very dangerous. But capital-short Japan and Europe had little choice but to invert the pyramid and rely heavily on debt. The banks and financial institutions in those countries borrowed from abroad, paid premium rates to attract money into their seemingly over-leveraged institutions, and then passed the money along to their over-leveraged industrial managers. These managers ran their enterprises primarily for cash so they could service their heavy debt loads. To survive, they placed maximum emphasis on efficiency, productivity, and technological excellence so as to earn the high returns for the very risky equity at the bottom of their inverted pyramids. The rest was history. We called their post-World War II recoveries a miracle.

Today, it appears that the roles are reversing. It is the United States that is in the process of refurbishing and revitalizing its economy. The conditions of the 1950s and 1960s no longer pertain. Interest rates are high, bond yields are high, double-digit inflation is a renewed possibility, and the United States is no longer the dominant commercial and industrial force around the world.

U.S. industry is undergoing a metamorphosis. It is rebuilding. It is slimming down, getting the fat out, managing for cash, placing a priority on efficiency and productivity, and searching desperately all over the world for technological frontiers.

The evolution of this metamorphosis drives today's financial markets. Investors find it difficult to rate managements. They don't know which ones are on their side and which ones are not. They are turned off by the so-called professional manager or administrator, believing, rightly or wrongly, that a new breed is necessary to lead commerce and industry through the current transformation. Thus, investors are demanding high-yield bonds or preferred stock at contractual rates to ensure an expected return, with some measure of protection provided by equity. The market for high yields at contractual rates will continue to prosper. Simultaneously, equity holders are demanding much higher rates of return and dividends as their risk has increased.

Managements and other investors are attracted to leveraged buyouts by the higher rate of return for straight equities. Because of the inverted pyramid — proportionately smaller amounts of equity and much larger amounts of debt — managements and private investors can now attempt to purchase even the very largest companies. The objective is to take control of these companies and redeploy the assets, selling off low-earning assets and increasing the rate of return on the other assets. Maximizing cash flows permits them to service the debt. Book earnings are irrelevant in leveraged buyouts and companies that are taken private, because cash flow becomes the key. Anything and everything that generates more cash becomes paramount, including drastic reductions in overhead. One might argue that such policies benefit the present at the expense of the future. On the other hand, such policies are long overdue in many businesses.

Managements' best course of action is to redeploy assets voluntarily in accordance with carefully prepared, long-term strategic goals. This requires the development of well-reasoned strategies to meet profitability goals and minimum acceptable rates of return. It also requires the discipline to sell or liquidate activities or assets that do not fit in with desired "hurdle rates" or the long-term strategies. Almost every management will claim that this process not only is underway in its own business but also has in fact been underway for a long time. I think most senior managements sincerely believe that is the case, but it just isn't so. The stock market is very discerning. Whenever a company is selling at less than its book or its liquidation value, it is a clear signal that asset redeployment is called for.

There is nothing magical or mystical about asset redeployment. It is merely a matter of working first from the top down and then from the bottom up.

The top-down exercise is to establish acceptable performance standards for returns on assets, balance-sheet ratios, cash flow requirements, and ultimately after-tax rates of return on equity. It is also to establish the credo of the business, the rank order of priorities, and the degrees of acceptable risk. More often than not, a catalogue of standards is neglected. Policies are needed to set codes of conduct, controls, checks and balances, and procedures for periodically monitoring progress toward predetermined goals. Most important of all is the establishment of human resource development, training, and measurement programs, and a compensation system that only rewards performance in furtherance of stockholder interests.

The bottom-up exercise is for line managers, the ones entrusted with corporate development resources, to draw up business plans and programs that meet the standards agreed upon in the top-down planning process. These business plans must include monitoring and measurement systems that permit day-to-day managers to tell the difference between value-added business and value-subtracted business. Moreover, the bottom-up business plans should not exceed the financial or resource constraints that are determined in the top-down approach and allocated to specific business units.

Once an effective asset redeployment program is instituted, the results can be impressive. The businesses that refuse to review their deeply ingrained, traditional beliefs, those that fight the new realities, will become the prime targets for takeovers. Moreover, the public at large will often support the attacking investor if it is generally perceived that the asset values in the target company are not being utilized to their optimum.

Asset redeployment was a pressing need at Cities Service when first Boone Pickens, then Gulf, and later Occidental Petroleum went after them. Once acquired by Oxy, a top-down process defined the core businesses of Cities, established priorities, and then determined the needed cash flows and rates of return to extinguish the heavy debt load incurred in making the acquisition.

A list of companies or business units to be sold or liquidated was prepared. Business units of both Oxy and Cities Service were on the list. Specific assignments were made with expected cash yields to be obtained, and weekly review meetings were scheduled to track the progress. Simultaneously, performance standards were set for the companies and business units to be retained. Reinvestment capital was no longer plentiful and everyone had to learn to do better with fewer resources. Consensus was achieved and the results exceeded expectations.

This type of review process is imperative for companies that wish to stay at the leading edge of their industries and command premium prices for their securities in the public markets. As the environment changes, so must asset redeployment. Perhaps it will not occur as dramatically as the first time around, but always it will go forward in discrete steps, both from the top down and the bottom up.

Even the most successful businesses can profitably use an asset redeployment audit for senior line managers and top management to review. Even when no changes are required, software measurement and monitoring tools can assist the execution and implementation of programs already in place. Businesses confronting deregulation or the onslaught of new competitors must undergo this review process, and generally it is useful to call in outside professionals. They can help to question assumptions and introduce new perspectives. They can play the role of devil's advocate, and, if necessary, challenge and rechallenge the standards of the marketplace and the resistance of those who adhere blindly to traditional values.

TEN

Black Knight, White Knight

Since the mid-1970s, nothing has had a greater influence on the corporate and financial worlds than the struggle between the corporate "raiders" and the entrenched "establishment"—the "black knights" versus the rescuing "white knights."

That black knight-white knight imagery is strangely ambiguous. Back in the Middle Ages, a knight who kept his armor polished and therefore "white" was obviously wealthy enough to have a squire to do it for him. Anyone in unshined, "black" armor very likely had no squire to tend to his armor. He was probably some penniless adventurer, back from the Crusades, trying to become a robber baron—quite literally.

Soon the distinction broke down. Black enameled armor became fashionable with the wealthy, notably the famed "Black Prince," son of Edward III of England, who wore magnificent black armor with considerable distinction at Crecy and Poitiers during the Hundred Years War. No one could accuse the Black Prince of being a penniless adventurer, not even the French.

Update the expression to the 20th century and that "black knight" is a would-be corporate raider who buys a large block of stock in a potential takeover target. Until T. Boone Pickens' ill-fated bid for Unocal, the black knight had generally run very little risk. As long as he looked rapacious enough, chances are he would have been bought out at a profit either by "greenmail" from the takeover candidate's management (as a medieval robber baron might have been paid off by a traveling nobleman) or by a competing bid from another establishment company called a "white knight."

If black knights are supposed to be gold-digging troublemakers, where do they get the capital to play the game — the horse and armor needed to enter the joust, if you will? Initially it comes from banks. Without the banks and, as the scale increases, other institutional investors, the "raider" often cannot raise enough money to buy a block of stock in the takeover target. And without the banks, managements cannot obtain the money to propose "leveraged buyouts," the take-over technique popularized by Kohlberg, Kravis and Roberts (KKR) in the mid-1970s. (Incidentally, First Chicago, through its talented loan officer, Robert Judson, was the first major bank to back KKR as they pioneered leveraged buyouts.) The objective of the management-sponsored "leveraged buyout" is no different from the buyout by a white or black knight. It is to realize inherent values by managing for cash instead of managing for book earnings, all of which raises the question of why management did not assume this responsibility in the first place. In any event, buyouts by black, white, or grey knights (as I'll label the management) usually requires heavy bank financing.

This poses difficult questions for bankers. Should they loan money to black knights who may use it to raid the bank's own corporate clients? Should they welcome the opportunity to support white knights whose sole purpose may be to frustrate shareholders' right to seek a higher price for their stock in the marketplace? Alternatively, in the management leveraged buyout, isn't there a conflict of interest if the management is trying to capture latent values for itself instead of achieving these values for all the shareholders? And are these legitimate issues for bankers to ponder and judge?

Bankers have no special qualifications to weigh these very serious policy dilemmas. Takeover loans can be very lucrative, short-term investments. Shareholders of the takeover candidate, many of whom may also be depositors of the bank, can profit handsomely. Certainly the pension funds, which own most of the common stock in the country, have been delighted to sell out to the top bidder — black knight or white. Where should the bank's loyalties lie?

There are several schools of thought on this. Ever since there was a stock market, shrewd investors have been picking up bargains when the intrinsic value of companies they bought exceeded the market value of the companies' shares. Warren Buffett is a living legend on Wall Street for doing just that. The only difference between Warren Buffett — acting through his corporate vehicle in Omaha, Berkshire Hathaway — and your average black knight, one might argue, is that the black knight threatens takeover (and management departure) whereas Buffett has conveyed the image of being merely a passive investor. The true black knight is just a little more ostentatious.

This argument works only up to a point. For whether they be white knights, "grey" managements in leveraged buyouts, Warren Buffetts, or black knights, all must either "turn the acquired companies around" to justify their investments, or disassemble the companies and sell off the pieces at premium prices so that the sum of the parts equals more than the whole. This is a lesson that most white knights still have to learn.

There is yet another phenomenon at work. Nobody seems to mind if a black knight acquires small, unfamiliar companies at bargain prices — companies that are not household names, and, therefore, supposedly lack a broad-based constituency to express dismay and a sense of loss. But the public and politicians seem to mind if you mess with the Establishment companies whose managements belong to the right clubs. Among those clubs might be the local bank's board of directors.

That's when the banker starts to hear about how nasty the black knights are and how faithless he, the banker, is to loan that black knight money. "The bank owes a fiduciary responsibility to its customers," they say. . . as if the bank were a silent partner of management, functioning in the same kind of staff capacity as a law firm. The reality is that a bank has many customers. Many may be the client corporation's shareholders. "The bank's loyalty should be to the existing management of a customer company," argue the Establishment board members. "After all, it is the management that chooses the bank, not the shareholders."

True enough, but to me the question remains: Who owns the customer company? The classic answer is that the stockholders do. That remains true, legally. But times have changed. In some corporations, stockholders are indeed the true owners, particularly if they are owner-managers. However, more than 50 percent of the outstanding common stock in American corporations is owned by institutions, not individuals. Institutions tend to be interested in the cold and unerring yardstick of stock market performance. Also, nonstockholders whose lives are touched by an organization have increasingly asserted more of an "ownership" interest. And they make an interesting case.

Take, for example, a railroad. The bondholders may be protected by the value of the rolling stock, but they also have what approaches an equity interest in the road's welfare. So do the regulators. Charged with protecting the public welfare, regulators often have more to say about running the railroad than its own directors do. So, in a larger and more political sense, do the communities served by the railroad because the company's welfare affects the industries served by the railroad, and these industries provide jobs? And how about the employees and their unions?

One could make the same observations about any large utility or corporation that is granted the right to operate in a limited-access business. Such businesses must accept the reality that the stockholders are not their only owners.

In open-access industries, the important questions that determine true ownership are: How big is the company? And how capital intensive is the business?

There's little doubt that in a small company the shareholders are the true owners. Control resides in a board of directors appointed by, and responsive to, those shareholders. But the large corporation is totally different. There may be hundreds of thousands of investors who, in any practical sense, have no active say in management. Moreover, the board of directors may be incapable of running or directing the corporation. The corporation may be too big, too diverse, too technically complicated to be run by a board with 15 to 25 members. This is not to say that the board is not composed of very bright, sometimes brilliant, successful professional managers from other fields. It is to say that, no matter how brilliant, upright, or wealthy, one cannot stay on top of a complex corporate enterprise in once-a-month meetings. Some boards do not even meet that often. Nor are directors generally paid to spend the time and effort to understand the nuances and complexities of a large corporation, particularly a large financial institution. They claim that their primary responsibility, if not their only responsibility, is to sit in judgment of management.

In banks, directors generally understand very little about liability management or the monetary system. Because they are lending their names to the financial institution on whose board they sit, they like to see it praised. Most consider it an honor to be asked to serve, a kind of status symbol.

When the board of directors gets that elitist feeling, as mine at First Chicago did, it generally loses its sense of balance or historic perspective and can point the corporation in a disastrous direction. Some on my board thought I had gone off the deep end when I pointed out to them in the late 1970s that the Continental Illinois bank would face more problems than any bank could imagine and that we were not about to follow. Some of my directors would then go to the Chicago Club and listen to their peers on the Continental Board brag how fast that bank was growing, how much the earnings were increasing, and how the poor

First was losing ground. The media echoed the message. Continental acquired the reputation of being a leader and others sought to follow. Greenwich Research Associates emphasized to its consulting clients what they had to do to keep pace with the Continental. Few took the time to understand why the First, the Continental's principal competitor, took the exact opposite tack.

Let's be honest. Directors are there symbolically, to inspire confidence for the public and to attract business. The board is a club, self-nominating and self-perpetuating. Individual members are at the mercy of the management and the security analysts. And, if analysts label their management out of "sync" with the industry, God help the management. What criteria do the analysts generally use? They use the obvious, of course: short-term reported book earnings and peer group ratings.

Institutions, particularly lending institutions, are likely to move together like a herd. That is why we seem to roll from crisis to crisis. Whether it be investments in REITs, energy loans, foreign loans, or farm loans, because everyone is doing it, there is no individual to blame if something goes wrong. I have witnessed the same phenomenon in the savings and loan industry, where the irrepressible herd instinct was encouraged and fortified by the regulators, industry trade associations, and accountants and lawyers. Few dare to buck the trend. Most retreat to the security of the herd.

As chief executive of First Chicago, I chose to "lean against the wind." In the 1974 to 1977 period there were real questions whether we could keep the bank afloat. I resolved not to go through that again. I had become familiar with the history of First Chicago and its more than 100-year cycle of competition with the Continental. Time after time, one bank would do well and surpass the other, only to get in trouble and fall behind. During the early 1970s, we experienced the heady exhilaration of analyst acclaim. We did not surpass Continental in size, but we were the leadership bank until we received our comeuppance in mid-1974. Then Continental took off with style and panache. I knew what would happen because it had happened before: Continental would stumble; and, if we kept our balance sheet strong, our capital strong and our growth moderate, the First would emerge as the leader once again. The strategy required restraint, tight control, and patience. But, the pressures against that strategy were overwhelming—from directors no less.

Congressman Jim Leach of Iowa summed it up best at the conclusion of the Congressional hearings on the Continental. He said on page 125 of the September 18, 19, and October 4, 1984 *Congressional Record*, and I quote:

> ...let me just comment for those of us that follow Chicago banking, from the Midwest, there was kind of a feeling a few years back that the bad guy of Chicago banking was Robert Abboud of First Chicago.
>
> As I have listened to this testimony, it appears to me he is taking on almost heroic dimensions as the tough guy who says, "We don't want to follow the procedures of our main competitor." I stress this because, as I review the examination reports, as put together by our staff, there are a lot of comments about peer bank pressures and peer bank analogies...

I thank Congressman Leach for those kind words, and I don't disguise my pleasure in hearing them, because it was certainly not the way it was described at the time.

The directors of large financial institutions are, at best, part-time players with very little in-depth knowledge of the risks inherent in banking. Very few are selected to represent specific constituencies, even though, strangely enough, the boards of the local Federal Reserve Banks are so selected.

Management, like the board, is self-perpetuating. The chief executive officer will groom one, two, or three handpicked candidates to succeed him. The board goes through the motions of selecting a new chief executive. Once one of them is installed, he or she does everything possible to create a cohesive group of loyal followers who will maintain the self-perpetuating establishment.

This is not to say that new blood cannot gain access to the inner circle through sheer ability. That happens more often than might be expected. But the new entrant must have not only the ability but also the willingness to pay rather intangible dues of loyalty, allegiance, and open support for the established common causes.

My predecessor at First Chicago, Gale Freeman, used to say that stockholders own the corporation and the only responsibility of management and the board was to make money for the stockholders. He said this with considerably more vehemence during his early years as CEO than in his later years, after the REIT bubble burst and we went through three funding crises between May and December 1974. He ultimately realized that depository institutions are different than other private businesses whose shares are traded in public markets. Unlike other businesses, depository institutions cannot be managed just for cash, earnings and higher dividends. Depository institutions must be managed first and foremost for safety and liquidity because they are answerable to constituencies other than their shareholders and holding company creditors.

As is true of a railroad or utility, stockholders are not the only owners of a large financial institution. Bank depositors have in the aggregate substantially more invested in the enterprise than the shareholders and, therefore, have some rights of ownership.

Also, the Federal Government, to the extent that it assumes regulatory responsibility for the continued viability of a financial institution, is a form of owner. So, also, is the insurance fund that guarantees its deposits. Employees often feel that they too have a vested right of ownership in a bank, particularly since their pension funds often have large stockholdings. The borrowers also have vested interests in the institution because lines of credit and other services provided by that institution are crucial to their financial planning. So a financial institution is unique in terms of the diversity of its ownership. It must exhibit loyalty to all these constituencies as well as to the general public and the financial system at large, of which it is an integral cog.

But some corporate managements, whose corporations are customers of the bank, tend to feel they are owed special loyalty. Indeed, they demand it. During my years at the helm of First Chicago, I felt I had to set down some sort of policy to assert the bank's role in financing corporate acquisitions. What I did cost us some business because it meant that First Chicago was no longer the darling of acquiring companies as it once had been. No more would we be the lead bank in putting together takeover loan syndicates.

I decided that we would honor all credit lines that had been granted to customers and for which the customer had paid a fee. If a contest developed between two customers, where one sought to take over the other in a hostile takeover, the bank would not increase its commitments to the would-be acquirer, although it might increase its commitments to the target company. While that might seem inconsistent, it seemed to me that we had a duty to maintain our obligations to those who had paid fees to maintain those lines and to support customers who were under attack with additional credit in their "hour of need."

To be honest, that policy suited no one. Would-be black knights regarded us as an unreliable partner. The Establishment companies felt that we had not gone far enough in cutting off credit to the black knights. I felt it was wiser to have an unequivocal, announced policy than to be opportunistic and consider each case on its merits. There is no question that we could have made substantially more money by aggressively funding "black knights." I chose not to do that. However, many banks, certainly our principal competitor, did just that and profited handsomely. I still believe First Chicago's policy was best for the time because it was clear that we stood for predictability. On the other hand, I also accept the market's verdict on those who practiced "constructive ambiguity" and deftly played both sides. In retrospect, they did better for their shareholders during that period.

This issue is by no means resolved. In August 1987, Gillette severed its relationship with Citibank because Citibank was helping to finance Revlon in its takeover bid for Gillette. Citibank's creditor position with Gillette was allocated to other line banks. It is reported that Citibank reviewed its policies and decided to remain with its position of deciding each case on its own facts — in other words, to be opportunistic.

Today, the takeover stakes are even higher, the combatants more experienced, and the suits and countersuits sufficiently original to warrant inclusion in Grimm's Fairy Tales. Arguments have been advanced that the anti-racketeering statutes should be invoked to thwart would-be acquirers. Federal and state legislators have jumped into the fray with laws designed to curb greenmail and various other perceived abuses. Absurd legislation has been passed by individual states in what has clearly come to be viewed as a challenge to free markets. The argument is that a state doesn't want to lose business and wishes to protect its own. On the other hand, one state's loss is generally another state's gain.

The use of criminal statutes is also misused. Carl Icahn humorously relayed an anecdote about the time his wife asked him why he was being publicly attacked under the so called RICO (Racketeer Influenced Corrupt Organizations) Act, the anti-racketeering statute. He said he told his wife, "Oh, that's just another name for arbitrageur." The point is that the rules of the game need to be defined. I personally think we have gone overboard in the name calling, regardless of the merits in any particular takeover situation. I also think that a few arbitrageurs, typified by Ivan Boesky, have abused the code of market ethics, bringing mistrust and political criticism on this important scavenger function.

I am often asked, "Do you approve of these pirates who cruise the corporate waters and steal other people's companies?" I respond by asking, "Whose company is it in the first place?" By definition, the companies are publicly traded. That certainly suggests ecumenical ownership with free access for anyone willing to pay the price to acquire shares. How can you steal something that is publicly offered for sale and is paid for with coin of the realm in an established market?

Moreover, it is not a question of approval or disapproval. The black knights are sometimes called sharks. The shark is a fearsome predator, a magnificently evolved fighting and eating machine. But the shark also performs a cleanup function without which the oceans would be a worse place or, alternatively, something else would evolve to take the shark's place. The same with the black knight. A function that needs to be performed is being performed because managements are not satisfying their shareholders and are not realizing values in the stock market equal to the price that the black knights are willing to pay.

The white knights also perform a needed function. Just like the black knights, many of the "good guys" are opportunists seeking to profit from the weak or embattled. Some perceive an opportunity to grow more quickly or acquire skills and markets that could not be developed with internal resources. Again, as with the black knights, the primary motivation of the white knight is to buy value cheap. It is not altruism. Yet, the public applauds white knights and decries black knights.

Isn't management really the culprit in all of this? Isn't it management's job to perform in a way that the process need never be started? I think shareholders are demanding precisely that by their actions in supporting takeovers and voting against the myriad defensive measures being proposed by self-perpetuating managements.

As for the politicians, regulators, and the courts, they should perform only the functions strictly mandated by their offices and otherwise let the market operate naturally. The jurists, of course, have no choice but to act if a suit is filed. Their operative guideline, however, should be strict construction of the law. The regulators, such as the SEC and similar state regulatory bodies, should do the same. The politicians should stay out of the fray altogether to the extent possible. Everyone is better off with the least interference.

The banker cannot stay detached. In a takeover battle he or she must decide whether to lend support or to withhold support and whether the stock held in discretionary fiduciary accounts is to be tendered or not.

A bank's chief executive must take the lead in making the toughest decisions for the most unpopular reasons. There is not time to wait for a general consensus to develop. The CEO is running a highly leveraged institution whose assets exceed capital by 10 to 20 times. That means he or she has to be prompt and make correct judgments. A chief executive officer cannot be sensitive only to public relations and politics. He or she must be a shrewd, skilled practitioner with a gut feel for danger and a clear sense of the overriding priority, which is to run a safe institution.

I would suggest that if you are a trustee and a fiduciary and a good profit is available in good currency, then take it.

If you are a community bank and a local industry is being threatened with shrinkage or removal, then fight it with all the resources at your disposal.

If you are a money center bank and you can help aggressive managements to grow through acquisitions, then back them.

If you are well acquainted with managements who need support to finance a leveraged buyout in order to restructure a company, then back them.

If multiple constituencies are involved and there are conflicts, honor any moral or actual commitments, regardless of the profit motive. If there are no commitments, then listen carefully and do whatever makes the most money for your institution, assuming that such action does not hurt and hopefully helps the communities you serve.

If you are backing an arbitrageur, then, for everyone's sake, get all the collateral you can with adequate margin to spare and marketable title to the proceeds.

ELEVEN

International Banking

To those who may be contemplating a career in banking, international or foreign banking sounds romantic. It is romantic. I went to First Chicago directly from business school because Gale Freeman, who recruited me, promised I could concentrate in that area.

What is international banking? In a general sense, it consists of all the business a bank normally transacts, but with customers outside one's own country. Banks have gone global to meet the needs of their customers for foreign currencies, to facilitate payments, and to meet the demand for credit.

An international bank's first basic function is to buy and sell foreign money, an activity known as foreign exchange. As every traveler to another country knows, U.S. dollars must be exchanged for the currency of that country. This exchange is generally performed by banks, at the airport, in the city, or sometimes through clerks at hotels, or in some countries by special foreign exchange dealers who set up shop on the streets or in other public places.

But whoever initiates a foreign exchange transaction, it always ends up being entered on the books of a bank. The bank buys the dollars and pays for those dollars in local currency. When travelers leave the country, they convert the foreign currency that they have not spent back into dollars. The bank buys the local currency and pays for the purchase in dollars.

This is a lively business for banks because they buy dollars at one price and sell them at a higher price. They do the same with all other currencies. The difference between the "buy" rate and the "sell" rate is called the *spread*. Banks often compete by offering narrower spreads than other banks. Hotels usually have wider spreads than banks, since they act as middlemen between customers and the bank. The currency trader on the street usually has a spread inbetween that of the hotel and the bank.

Multiply this "retail" trade in foreign currencies by the much larger requirements of big, and not so big, multinational corporations, and it becomes a huge, profitable, virtually riskless business for which banks compete vigorously. All the trade that moves from one country to another involves banks, which exchange the currency of the purchaser into the currency of the seller, just as they do for the tourist or traveler. Again, the banks make money because they buy at the low rate and sell at the higher rate, and thus their profit margin is the spread.

To compete effectively for the business of large commercial customers—for example, companies included among the Forbes 500, such as General Motors, General Electric, and IBM—the banks must quote very attractive rates. In other words, their spreads are very, very narrow. So, they assign specialists to do nothing but trade currencies. The large banks sometimes have specialists who trade only one or two currencies. Thus they become expert in those currencies and can quote the best rates possible. To provide the most comprehensive foreign exchange service, the banks trade all day long, seven days a week, 365 days a year through their strategically placed foreign branches. Because of the time changes on the different continents, and because the different countries and religions celebrate holidays on different dates, there is always a market open somewhere in the world. When the workday ends in one city, the currency specialist can pass along his or her "position" to the specialist in that currency at the next branch, and the trading goes on uninterrupted around the clock and around the world.

By allowing the currency trader to take a "position" and pass it along to the specialist in another, open market, a bank hopes to make more money and to quote better rates to its customers. For example, a bank trader who believes that the Japanese yen is about to increase in value relative to the dollar, will spend dollars to buy a "long position" in Japanese yen. He or she will then keep the excess yen in inventory to sell to customers at bargain rates when the market price for yen increases. The trader still makes a profit because the "position" was bought when the price was low. The bank then has an advantage over competitors whose traders were less astute.

Conversely, if the trader believes the price of Japanese yen will go down relative to the dollar, then he or she reverses the process and sells Japanese yen, taking a "short position" at the present high price. The trader hopes to fill in the open short position when the market price for yen drops. Once again, he or she can quote advantageous rates to customers because the trader has anticipated the market and positioned the bank properly.

This process of converting currencies so that buyers and sellers can move goods freely amounts to billions and billions of dollars. You might, therefore, conclude that the banks must make a lot of money. Some do. . . but some don't. They lose by guessing wrong and taking the wrong positions at the wrong time, and they end up having to eat the loss. Some banks have been known to lose a great deal of money in this business because, it is, after all, a form of gambling. It is the responsibility of bank management and directors to set limits on the positions traders are permitted to take and then to police those limits to make sure they are not exceeded.

This process of establishing and enforcing limits for currency positions is not an easy task. For each currency, there are "short" and "long" positions. There are overnight and forward positions, where traders contract to buy and sell at future times. There are "gap" positions to balance the immediate, or "spot," transactions and "future" transactions. And there are positions limited by capital restraints and foreign exchange regulations in the countries where the branches are located in the chain of trading around the globe.

Alongside the billions of dollars in foreign exchange trading that permits goods and services to flow freely across national boundaries are billions of dollars in other trades known as "hedges." A hedge shields a company from the risk of an unexpected swing in a currency's value.

IBM, for example, might have a sizable investment in West Germany, which is denominated in deutsche marks (DM), the German currency. But, IBM is an American corporation, publishing its consolidated balance sheet in U.S. dollars. If the value of the deutsche mark goes down relative to the dollar and IBM has done nothing to hedge this downward movement, then IBM would have to record a loss on its income statement in accordance with applicable accounting rules. The IBM Treasurer's Department, which is among the finest in the world, knows this and watches the changing value of the DM just as closely as do the banks. If the IBM Treasurer's Department thinks the DM is about to drop in value relative to the dollar, it will sell the DM "forward" before the rate drops. When the rate bottoms, the IBM Treasurer's Department will buy the DM back at the new, lower price to close out the future sale contract. The profit made by IBM in selling and then buying back the DM offsets the accounting loss IBM must record in valuing its deutsche mark investment in Germany in dollars at the close of the accounting period. Every businessperson or investor doing business in another country must hedge the same as IBM or risk a severe loss. Thus, thousands and thousands of hedging transactions take place each week with the banks, and bank managements must set limits for currency positions to accommodate their customers' hedging requirements, just as they must set limits for currency positions to accommodate their customers' trade requirements.

Another strategy is required when IBM believes that the deutsche mark is likely to go up relative to the dollar. Then IBM might elect to carry an "open position" in whole or in part. That is, it may choose to do nothing. When the valuation occurs at the end of the accounting period, IBM would be able to record a profit equal to the amount by which the DM has risen in value since the last valuation. This is big and serious business. Again, it is a form of gambling.

As multinational corporations and the trade they generate grew, leaving billions and billions of dollars at risk all the time, the banks discovered that they did not have sufficient capacity to accommodate the swings in the rates. This became all the more apparent with the advent of "floating" exchange rates. The system of floating rates was adopted in 1971 and contrasted with the system that had existed since the Bretton Woods agreement in 1944. The Bretton Woods agreement "fixed" the value of the free world currencies relative to the U.S. dollar within a relatively narrow trading range and then fixed the value of the U.S. dollar in terms of ounces of gold. At the start, gold was valued at 35 dollars per ounce. With the passage of time, however, balance-of-payments deficits buffeted the world economy, particularly in the late 1960s and early 1970s during the Vietnam War, and these fixed currency and gold values could no longer be maintained. There were some attempted adjustments, called devaluations when the currency in question was adjusted down relative to the dollar, or revaluations when the currency went up relative to the dollar. Modest adjustments had also been made along the way in the price of gold.

By 1971, the pressures driving the currency values apart and a run on the U.S. gold supply caused the Bretton Woods system to collapse. In the new free market of floating exchange rates, the U.S. dollar and other currencies would float freely as supply and demand dictated. In some regions, such as Europe, currencies were officially valued relative to each other. This was the so-called "European Snake," which cushioned the fluctuations of any currency in the group. The theory was that supply and demand would set the relative rates of all currencies globally.

In practice, some nations, such as Japan, to use a prime example, did not let their currencies float freely. If they thought their currency was appreciating too rapidly versus the dollar, their central bank would buy dollars. This would support the value of the dollar, preventing the foreign currency from appreciating further. Conversely, if the foreign country saw its currency dropping too far, it would sell dollars and buy its own currency to keep the value within desired parameters. With this process, called *intervention,* the theoretically freely floating system quickly degenerated into "managed float" or the "dirty float," depending on how pejorative you choose to be.

The net result was a system of wide and sudden swings in currency rates.

To protect their customers from these gyrations while staying within the foreign exchange limits permitted by their capital, the banks needed help. And from that necessity was born the International Monetary Market (IMM), a division of the Chicago Mercantile Exchange. The IMM was the brainchild of Leo Melamed and Everette Harris, and I was privileged to be numbered among its founding directors. Its purpose was to spread the risk of open currency positions among willing investors. It obviously is gambling, but gambling in the good sense. It is the same type of informed gamble that any investor takes in buying or selling shares of stock. And the advent of the International Monetary Market, which was soon copied in New York and in other financial centers around the world, permitted the market to accommodate the open positions that had to be hedged in the system of floating exchange rates.

As important as currency transactions may be for international banks, they are not their bread and butter. The staple business of international banking is the processing of documents, import letters of credit, export letters of credit, collections, and bankers acceptances. This is high-volume technical work that requires experience and precision. The fees are small and the work is labor intensive. Thus, volume is important to justify mechanization and, most of all, to generate "float," the credit balances or deposits in customers' accounts.

What are letters of credit? They are guarantees of payment that come in basically three types: import, export and travelers letters of credit. The travelers variety has now been largely replaced by credit cards. Before credit cards, if someone were traveling in a foreign country and needed to buy something or to pay for services, he or she could take a letter of credit to a local bank. The bank would advance the money, ask the traveler to sign a draft (equivalent to a receipt stating that he or she received the money under the terms specified by the letter of credit) and immediately charge the account of the bank that issued the letter of credit. This was a great convenience. It eliminated the need to carry large sums of cash or travelers checks. The credit card with pre-negotiated limits has made the travelers letter of credit, once widely used and highly profitable to banks, a relic of the past.

The import and export letters of credit are something else again. They continue to be useful in accommodating the flow of foreign trade.

The import letter of credit permits a resident of one country to order goods or services from abroad. The letter of credit assures, in writing, that the goods or services will be exactly as specified and will be shipped or performed in the agreed-upon time period. If there is any deviation from these terms, then the bank authorizing the payment makes good on the loss. The buyer is protected.

The procedures in this business are of long standing and are well recognized in international law. Court decisions have been rendered on almost every conceivable set of circumstances, and arbitration is readily available to expedite the settlement of disputes.

Export letters of credit are the reverse of import letters of credit. For example, an exporter will receive an order for goods or services from a buyer in another country. However, the exporter does not want to order the materials or hire the people or incur costs unless it is certain he or she will be paid in good funds with his or her own currency on the specified date of delivery. The exporter asks the purchaser to open an export letter of credit through a bank, naming the exporter or his or her company as the beneficiary of that letter of credit.

The two parties negotiate the terms of sale with the understanding that these terms will be incorporated in the letter of credit. When the exporter ships or delivers, he or she signs a draft to that effect, presents the draft to the bank that confirmed the letter of credit (that is the domestic bank that received the letter of credit from the buyer's bank in the buyer's country). The exporter also presents any other documents called for by the letter of credit, and is paid the amount owed.

There is still another type of documentary business involving imports and exports. This business involves *collections*. Collections are drafts (checks) drawn on someone in another country who owes you money because you have shipped the person goods or provided him or her with services. The collection is routed through a bank simply because that is the easiest way to deliver the bill, collect the money, and get the sums converted into the desired currency. The bank charges a small fee for performing this service and makes certain that all the documents specified are delivered in the precise form requested.

As in so many aspects of banking, the successful conduct of documentary business—letters of credit, drafts, collections, travelers checks, and so forth—is more an art than a science. The challenge is to generate volume, handle this volume efficiently and with minimal error, and, most of all, to generate deposits and other business from the importers, exporters, and their banks at both ends of the transactions.

The best at this business is probably Citicorp, with its extensive international branch system. The overseas branches are able to generate documentary business in the countries where they are located and to handle the transactions sent them from other branches or head offices. It is a network approach to generate volume.

Banks that have no overseas branches or only a few can create the same kind of network through *correspondent banking.* They establish interbank credit lines and come to an understanding of how the documentary business will flow between the banks in both directions.

Whether using networks of branches or correspondents or, as is most often the case, both branches and correspondents, it is essential to have an expert trade department to assist customers in their development of foreign trade. Most customers need and want this help. They can use advice on potential markets, customer introductions, and skilled assistance in opening letters of credit, drafting collections, or handling documents with the corollary foreign exchange contracts to protect themselves until payment is actually received.

One benefit of the letter-of-credit business is the opportunity to generate *bankers acceptances.* Bankers acceptances are the drafts drawn on a buyer by a seller under terms of a letter of credit. When this draft is "accepted," or stamped across its face by the bank, the bank becomes directly liable to make the payment. Thus, the bankers acceptance is truly "three-name paper," backed by the buyer, the seller, and the bank. As such, it trades and circulates in the financial marketplace on almost the same basis as Treasury bills. Bankers acceptances may run in duration from 30 days to 180 days, depending on the the letters of credit under which they were drawn. What makes them so special is that they are eligible for rediscount with the Federal Reserve bank.

The bankers acceptance business is the real prize in international banking. It is productive because it facilitates the movement of goods. And it is far less risky than the big syndicated country credits in which many multinational banks became bogged down during the 1980s. The acceptance is a reliable bank-to-bank transaction, with goods or commodities often constituting the collateral.

It is especially romantic and personally satisfying because the business generally flourishes in the developing world, where transactions are seldom done on open account (unsecured credit) and where the intermediation of banks provides payment protection through letters of credit and/or guarantees.

International banking is played out amid a host of economic and political forces that, at times, find the banker as a witness to history and a participant in it.

I remember in my own early career, around 1960, traveling to such places as the old market in Aleppo, Syria, with the castle of Saladin, of crusader fame, scanning the horizons in all directions. There was a little bank there called Banque Albert Homsy. It was in the old city, where the narrow, winding stone streets date back to 1,000 A.D. I would stay in the old-style hotel, whose lobby looked like Sydney Greenstreet should be sitting in a chair underneath a ceiling fan. One night, while I was having dinner with Mr. Homsy at his home, a political revolution took place and toppled the government. After dinner, he accompanied me to the hotel, and as we entered the car, his driver said, "Now, Mr. Homsy, with this revolution I will be like you." To which Mr. Homsy replied, "No, my son, now I will be like you."

In Iraq, I sat out a couple of revolutions in the Hotel Baghdad, with the objective of establishing a correspondent relationship with Rafidain Bank so we could accommodate exports of agricultural and road building equipment from the U.S. Midwest.

I traveled to the bazaars of Jeddah, Saudi Arabia, which in 1960 had not yet experienced the wealth that flowed from the oil boom in the 1970s. Again, I was interested in commercial lines that would promote exports from the U.S. of automotive equipment and foodstuffs.

Kuwait was a short trip from Saudi Arabia. It, too, had not yet experienced the flow of petrodollars, but construction was already beginning. Hotels were being refurbished to accommodate the influx of foreigners, and there was need to import construction materials and plumbing supplies.

Belgrade, Yugoslavia, was a stopping-off point on the way back home because the Pan Am plane stopped there and it cost very little extra to make bank calls. Yugoslavia required development in almost every sector, and the banks required lines of credit to finance the importation of U.S. goods.

Our long-range targets were big countries with substantial wealth in the ground or institutions or countries known for their entrepreneurial flair. One was Sudan because it had substantial mineral and agricultural wealth in the ground and the potential to be the breadbasket for the entire region. I remember my first visit and how impressed I was with the happy, proud people. These were the people who broke the famed British Square, and all the history surrounding General Gordon took on reality.[7] I remember standing at the point where the White Nile meets the Blue Nile, forming a line straight as a razor's edge, and I marveled at the bountiful flow of fresh water on its way to the Mediterranean through Egypt.

Amman, Jordan was another stopping point because it was the headquarters of the Arab Bank, the largest privately owned indigenous regional bank. I received a banking education under the tutorship of Abdul Hameed Shoman, the brilliant entrepreneur who founded the bank in 1929. Mr. Shoman subsequently visited me at The First National Bank of Chicago. We were still in the old building in 1963 when I took him to visit with our then chairman, Homer Livingston. Mr. Shoman proceeded to lecture Homer on how he should be ashamed to have the bank headquartered in such an old, dirty building. I thought I had lost my job right then and there. Little did I know that Homer was already planning the magnificent edifice that is now First Chicago's headquarters.

---

[7]General Gordon was the commander of the English occupation forces in Khartoum, the capital of Sudan, during the late 1800s. He was killed when the citadel was stormed and the English forces defeated. Such a victory by the Sudanese was hitherto considered impossible.

I commenced relations with the banks in Egypt, spurred by the Commodity Credit Corporation. It was profitable and risk-less business because it was guaranteed by the U.S. Government. The Banque du Caire in Cairo was the cotton growers' bank and it needed lines of credit to import fertilizer and pesticides from the United States. Antoine Zananiri, whom I later hired for First Chicago, ran the foreign department. And, in the late 1960s, I arranged with Mohammed Abu Shadi, then chairman of the National Bank of Egypt, a loan to finance the purchase of Boeing 707s for Egypt Air. To my knowledge, this was the first bank commercial loan that was collateralized by gold.

I also traveled through the Mandelbaum Gate and motored down the roadway, past the spent tanks and armored vehicles, to Tel Aviv to visit Dr. Foerder, then chairman of Bank Leumi. There I met my good friend, Ernest Japhet, then chairman of Union Bank and later chairman of Bank Leumi, and his deputy, Eli Lerner. Together we worked out a loan to finance the importation of diamonds from South Africa to be polished in Israel and then exported. As this was a continuing business, the loan set up a field warehouse, whereby the diamonds would be segregated in the Union Bank vaults for account of First Chicago.

Later I made business development trips to Portugal, Spain, South America, Mexico, El Salvador, Guatemala, Honduras, Costa Rica, and Panama. I also traveled to Colombia, Venezuela, Brazil, Argentina, and throughout the Caribbean, seeking out and consummating trade related business. These were, at the time, developing countries requiring credit to finance their imports and to manufacture, assemble, or grow their exports. It was good business and generally self-liquidating.

In the early 1960s, Portugal was beginning to develop its northern regions with major hydroelectric projects along the Douro River. This was also the wine country, centered commercially in Oporto. First Chicago made the loan to help finance construction of the hydro project, collateralized with a commercial bank guarantee and, in the process, picked up the letter-of-credit business for the early importation into the United States of Mateus wine.

Costa Rica was attempting to develop light industry in the early 1960s. One project sponsored by the International Finance Corporation, an affiliate of the World Bank, was a paint and detergent business called Kativo Chemical Industries. First Chicago took a small equity position, extended credit to finance Kativo's import requirement for materials, and I agreed to serve on the board of directors. I'll never forget the day that Walter Kissling, Kativo's chief executive, called me to report that the local volcano had erupted and the flowing mud and lava had carried away all the 50-gallon drums of materials that constituted Kativo's inventory. I asked Walter if he had volcano insurance. He said, "Why would we have volcano insurance? The mountain hasn't erupted since 1600." This was a tender moment for a junior international banking department officer. What to do? I extended an additional loan to Kativo to replenish the inventory. Walter Kissling, genius that he is, offered five Colones apiece (about one dollar) for the return of any unopened 50-gallon drum and thereby recovered a surprising number. Moreover, he decided that the falling ash from the volcano could be utilized as raw material for a line of detergents. In the end, the company recovered, became profitable, and was subsequently sold to a U.S. company at a gain to the shareholders.

There was also a big credit for PASA, the big chemical complex in Argentina, which is still going strong today. It was a project financing led by Dillon Read and involved a joint venture between the International Finance Corporation and U.S. Corporations. First Chicago was one of the bank participants and I was the loan officer. First Chicago's objective was to help its domestic customers become established in overseas markets. The bank's expectation was that it would share in the processing of documents covering the movement of goods between the U.S. parent and the overseas subsidiary.

This was the motivation for First Chicago's rapid overseas expansion in the late 1960s when I became head of the International Banking Department. I was convinced from my experiences in opening and heading the branches in Frankfurt, Germany, and Beirut, Lebanon, that strategically located branches could be key instruments in promoting the flow of trade and then in profiting from financing that trade. Auxiliary branches in places such as Zurich, Switzerland, important financial centers, would assist this effort while providing services to the Trust and Bond departments.

The greatest thrill was the opening to the People's Republic of China, a project begun in 1972 and brought to fruition in 1978 when First Chicago became the first U.S. bank to have a correspondent relationship with the Bank of China.

We had an excellent cadre of top international officers. Bill McDonough, as head of International Banking, was in overall charge. Neil Hartigan, my special emissary, was in charge of China for the trip and did an outstanding job. Ahmet Arsan was in charge of Asia, and many other officers who were the senior executives in their own territories participated with distinction. Our board decided to meet in China. The Far East tour was successful and capped an initiative that was six years in the making, and the subject of controversy both within and outside of the bank because of the criticism it generated among some Taiwanese and Taiwanese supporters. But, at long last, our efforts paid off and First Chicago was in a commanding position to lead in the emerging China trade. Because of this position, the bank was accorded new respect in Japan, Korea, and Singapore. It was a great triumph.

Later, First Chicago, The Bank of China, and the Industrial Bank of Japan formed a joint venture to promote a continuing flow of trade and investment. China is home to one-fourth of the world's population. Its success in rebuilding its economy, feeding its people, and promoting commerce and industry is one of the modern-day marvels. I felt it important that the United States, and not just Japan and Europe, be a major player in this endeavor and maneuvered First Chicago into a respected position with the Chinese. Subsequently, I had the privilege as President of Occidental Petroleum to maintain this involvement. Even today I am seeking ways to stimulate trade and investment between our two countries so that our economic relations can achieve their latent potential.

The thrust of all of these transactions—the objective of our entire international approach—was commercial banking, not investment banking. The bank constantly sought to open avenues of commerce that would bring business to the bank and potential export and import opportunities to our domestic customers. The international business of a bank can be described as trade-related financing, correspondent relationships, and personal friendships with colleagues of different nationalities working to stimulate the profitable movement of food or goods or services.

Sadly, in the middle-to-late 1970s and early 1980s, this emphasis on basics began to wane and the new priority became the "mega-dollar" country loan, a sovereign risk, unsecured loan floating at some interest rate spread over the London interbank offering rate. There were fees to be collected up front. There was no ongoing operational work in the back office as with documentary credits. The dollars per transaction were huge, and syndicated $100 million credits became bite size. The MBA crop flooding the bank personnel rosters loved it because the years of experience needed to transact the documentary credit business seemingly were not needed. The result was a total aberration in the scope and nature of international banking. This was the beginning of the developing-country debt problem discussed in the next chapter. It was folly from the start, but it seemed so easy to put out big money fast with healthy fees and good spreads that the practice accelerated exponentially. The excuse was that the excess liquidity generated by petrodollars (the dollar balances flowing to the Middle East following the rapid escalation in the price of oil) had to be recycled.

It was carried out in the name of "merchant banking." But, it wasn't merchant banking in the classic sense. True merchant banking is one activity that causes me no problem as a banker. First Chicago built a successful merchant banking operation in London. Merchant banking involves arranging financing for a

specific project, for the assembly of goods preparatory to ship-
ment, for the construction of a factory where a market is assured,
for the seeds and fertilizer to grow a cash crop, or for a hotel or
business facility where a feasibility study indicates that the income will pay out the loan.

In the late 1970s and early 1980s, banks crossed the line from
merchant banking into full-scale, high-risk investment banking.
They made loans to foreign development banks, central banks,
or national treasuries simply to make up the shortfall in the particular nation's dollar reserves. Banks made money syndicating
the loans—selling pieces of them to other banks—without iden-
tifying any commercial project or benefit. The argument was that
the countries had to pay out so much for high-priced oil and high-
priced interest on existing debts that they couldn't make ends meet
from the proceeds of their exports. As a result, they did not have
the resources to pay for other essential imports and still properly
service their debt. In other words, their expenses exceeded their
income and they needed a loan. And the reason given for the
shortfall was the strain that higher oil prices placed on their national budgets.

This hardly explains the eagerness to lend to oil-exporting developing countries like Mexico, Venezuela, and Nigeria. But there
the explanation was equally creative: These countries were at long
last building their economies and taking a giant leap into the 20th
century by commencing long-overdue capital projects. The enormous wealth of their oil reserves in the ground, it was said, gave
them the means to finance such projects.

Meanwhile, the oil-exporting nations of the Middle East, such
as Saudi Arabia, Kuwait, and the United Arab Emirates, to name
a few, were accumulating huge excess balances in their dollar
reserves as the money from high-priced oil poured into their treasuries. These excess balances were placed on deposit with banks
in Europe, principally London. The world economy was booming, so the interest rates were high and huge dollar balances earned
a good rate of return. Because the world economy was so robust,
demand for oil was more than ample to maintain high rates of

production at ever increasing prices, reaching at one time as much as $40 per barrel.

The banks that paid interest on these deposits had to do something with the money. Because the deposits were largely in the Eurodollar market, there were no reserve requirements to slow down the velocity. Without reserve requirements, the multiplier was theoretically infinite, limited only by an individual bank's capital constraints. The regulators were exercising leniency in this regard and turning their heads in other directions. So anyone and everyone who needed liquidity to finance new loans and investments could get access to deposits by simply paying one-sixteenth or one-thirty-second percentage point more in the interest rate. It was a virtual money machine fueled by the difference in value between the price of old oil ($10 or less per barrel) and the price of new oil (up to $40 per barrel). Because the free world's consumption of oil was approximately 18 million barrels per day, new and added liquidity had to be invested to the tune of about $500 million per day, or about $150 billion per year.

If the oil-exporting countries were receiving it, someone had to pay it. Who paid for it? Naturally, the oil-importing countries, including the United States. The United States could do it, of course, because we just printed the money to make up the shortfall. The developing countries, however, which did not own a machine to print dollars, had to borrow the money in the international financial markets and would pay anything it required to get the money. The banks, awash with cash taken from their oil-exporting clients, were glad to oblige because they made a profit on the spread. This was the greatest chain letter, pyramid club, or Ponzi scheme ever invented. And the game went on until the price of oil collapsed, first down to $10 and, now, with some artificial props, back up to about $18 per barrel.

The banks called this process *recycling*. Perhaps so. But the point is that it is not international commercial banking and it is not merchant banking.

At best, it is investment banking. But the usual rule in investment banking is that investment bankers are solely middlemen and do not hold the paper themselves. The check and balance in the system is that the ultimate purchaser of the paper will analyze the true worth of the paper before buying. But, in the country-debt situation, the banks were both investment bankers and the ultimate holders of the paper. The check and balance in the system was lost.

In truth, the task at hand was not investment banking but *central banking,* the concern of the International Monetary Fund or the World Bank or the Bank for International Settlements. It was a job for the monetary authorities of the world's governments, not private commercial bankers. But the monetary authorities adopted a hands-off policy on the theory that the free market would take care of itself, as if the free market could ever operate adequately when a monopoly or a cartel artificially inflates the price of an essential commodity in great demand, such as oil. When the central bankers did not take charge, commercial bankers were more than happy to jump into the breach. The profit was seemingly big, easy, and readily available. It was a temptation too big to resist.

TWELVE

The International Debt Crisis

International bankers' enthusiasm to lend did much to create the overhang of developing-country debt, one of the most critical and pressing economic problems of the 1980s. It had profound effects on borrowers and lenders alike, and indeed on the entire world monetary system.

In the banking community, the developing-country debt almost exclusively affected big banks. They made the bulk of these loans, in amounts disproportionate to their capital or reserve accounts. Figure 12.1 shows the vulnerability of the biggest U.S. banking companies as of June 30, 1986, as compiled by Donaldson, Lufkin and Jenrette. Note that the capital figures used in the calculations include perpetual but redeemable preferred stock. This is misleading because redeemable preferred (even if nominally perpetual) can be called in extenuating circumstances. Even perpetual preferred stock should be excluded because it offers no extra protection to the common shareholder. Managements issue it because it is easier to sell than common equity and it is protected, but it is a time bomb waiting to explode as far as the common

163

FIGURE 12.1:
EXPOSURE TO SIX TROUBLED DEVELOPING COUNTRIES
Eleven Selected U.S. Banking Companies
($ Millions)

Company	Mexico	Brazil	Vene-zuela	Argen-tina	Philip-pines	Chile	Six Country Total	As % of 1: Total Loans	As % of 1: Shldrs' Equity(a)	Total Exposure to the Six: As Multiple of: Loss Reserve	As Multiple of: Pretax Earns.(b)
BankAmerica	$2,512	$2,697	$1,377	$475	$350	$300	$7,711	9.4%	193.5%	3.5X	NM
Citicorp	2,700	4,700c	1,200	1,400	1,700	600	12,300	10.2	143.9	8.3	7.1X
Chase Manhattan	1,630	2,770	1,230	980	400	700	7,710	12.2	190.2	8.1	8.8
Manufacturers Hanover	1,960	2,309	1.057	1,472	500E	786	8,084	14.5	221.8	8.5	15.2
J.P. Morgan	1,147	1,914	475E	861	300E	300E	4,997			5.9	3.7
Chemical	1,475	1,425	700	400	375	400	4,775	12.2	160.9	7.9	8.6
Bankers Trust	1,275	875	425	275E	200E	300E	3,350		123.9	7.4	5.5
First Chicago	911	782	230	265	200	272	2,660	10.9	119.5	5.6	7.7
First Interstate	700	493	27	97	143	96	1,556	4.7	59.2	3.2	3.8
Security Pacific	512	570	60	190	135	170	1,637	4.4	63.5	2.8	2.8
Wells Fargo	597	589	248	140	60	100	1,734	4.8	78.1	2.5	5.1
Total/Average:											
8 Money Centers	$13,610	$17,472	$6,694	$6,128	$4,025	$3,658	$51,587	11.9%	157.2%	6.9%	7.1%
13 Regionals	2,912	2,178	509	535	383	542	7,059	2.4	29.3	1.4	2.8

Note: Shown are "cross border risks," i.e., loans denominated in dollars. Exposures in most cases are from published company reports, or "ballpark" numbers based on conversations with bank managements. Data are as of June 30, 1986.
E#DLJ estimate, i.e., guestimates with little or no assistance from management.
(a) Includes common and preferred (b) Actual first-half 1986 earnings annualized.
(c) In addition to its cross-border exposure shown above, Citicorp has approximately $1.6 billion of domestic banking business in Brazil carried on in cruzeiros.

Source: "Bank Stock Quarterly," Donaldson, Lufkin and Jenrette Securities Corporation, 11 February 1987.

equity holders are concerned. In some bank holding companies, it is not a small sum when the capital is adjusted downward for goodwill or possible losses in the asset portfolio. For example, First Chicago's capital base includes subordinated floating rate notes, equity commitment notes, equity contract notes and preferred stock while other bank holding companies may have purer capital and less leverage in the equity base. Thus, for the common shareholder, the ratio of risk loans to effective capital varies qualitatively from bank to bank.

If the above table were expanded to incorporate the top 35 banks, almost all of the developing-country debt would be included. This is an important point. The players in this drama are all big and sophisticated and able to fend for themselves. If they invested to excess, then it is up to them to bail themselves out. It is not a responsibility of the U.S. taxpayer to come to their rescue.

The trouble is that the big banks don't have sufficient reserves to deal with the writedowns that might be required. Additions to those reserves at long last are now being made, thanks to the leadership provided by Citicorp in May 1987. A table published in the *Wall Street Journal* lists the reserve levels of the major money center banks and the additional reserves required to absorb a 25 percent writedown of Latin American debt and still cover all remaining nonperforming loans (Figure 12.2).

FIGURE 12.2:
FOLLOWING CITICORP'S LEAD
($ Billions)

	PRESENT LOAN-LOSS RESERVE	RESERVE INCREASE REQUIRED TO COVER 25% OF LATIN LOANS AND 100% OF OTHER NONPERFORMING LOANS
Citicorp	$4.90	$0.00
BankAmerica Corp.	2.17	3.01
Chase Manhattan Corp.	2.72	1.00
J.P. Morgan & Co.	0.95	0.74
Chemical New York Corp.	1.05	2.33
Manufacturers Hanover Corp.	1.02	2.76
Security Pacific Corp.	0.76	0.88
Bankers Trust New York Corp.	0.59	0.96
First Interstate Bancorp.	0.54	0.84
Wells Fargo & Co.	0.73	0.53

With the exception of Citicorp, present levels of loan-loss reserves were inadequate to meet the new 25 percent standard without substantial additions. In setting that standard, it cost the Citicorp shareholders at least one year's earnings and a 20 percent drop in shareholders' equity.

Nor was there assurance that the 25 percent Citicorp standard was enough. Conditions could conceivably worsen and a 25 percent discount on Latin American credits would be too little, particularly if all lenders chose to reduce their exposure all at once. Other nonperforming loans could also increase if loan administration at an institution happened to be lax. This is why financial institutions should make sufficient disclosure regarding the quality of their asset portfolios. Then the marketplace can make meaningful judgments as to the adequacy of the reserves and the institution's safety.

To date, regulators have not required financial institutions to mark their assets to market, reflecting their current values; and public accountants have not disclosed the extent to which the balance sheet, as published, may be above market values. Regulators and accountants have not seen fit to use a market test.

Why shouldn't they? Isn't this their job and their duty to the public at large? In effect, they are cooperating in the myth that the emperor has a fine suit of clothes when everyone can plainly see that he has no clothes. There is a solution. That solution is to provide adequate disclosure so the public can make its own evaluation.

The harsh fact is that debtor nations cannot afford to repay their loans, even if the loans are sharply discounted, unless economic conditions make it possible for them to experience growth. International Monetary Fund austerity policies, which we insist on shoving down the throats of these debtor nations, choke off this growth. Bankers in the lender countries cannot afford to write off more debt than is presently proposed by the Citicorp standard. The monetary system cannot afford the chaos that would result from full-fledged repudiations by debtor nations.

This leaves us in a dangerous standoff, with the world's monetary system and economic well-being hanging in the balance.

The time has come to be honest with ourselves and with the rights of others, particularly the emerging generations in the developing world and in our own nation. Developing-country debt is too big to pay back in full under the original terms. It is so big and so pervasive in its implications that it has become capable of crippling the management of the entire monetary system. It is like alcoholism in a family. At first no one wants to admit it exists. Then the relationships within the family degenerate and the family unit fails to function properly. Finally the sickness is acknowledged, professional help is sought, and a cure is put into place.

Developing-country debt is a BIG problem, and it is not going to go away because we pretend it doesn't exist or pretend we can keep it suspended indefinitely until the economies of the debtor countries grow large enough to sustain the load.

This situation reminds me of the driver of a five-ton truck carrying 10 tons of canaries. The driver constantly reaches out the window to beat vigorously on the side of the truck. Asked why he does this, he replies, "I have 10 tons of canaries in a five-ton truck and I have to keep half of them in the air at all times."

This is exactly what the monetary authorities are attempting to do with the developing-country debt. They have to keep far more than half the developing-country debt in the air all the time. All of us share in paying the price to do this.

The U.S. consumer is paying through an unprecedentedly high real rate of interest. Banks maintain a wide spread between the rate they charge borrowers and the inflation rate to make enough money to compensate for the bad loans. Obviously, the bad loans will have to be written down at some point, as Citicorp, Norwest Bank, Chase, and then others recognized in their May 1987 increases to reserves. The loan-loss reserve is created by a charge against earnings. Thus, earnings must be pumped up to support such a charge and still leave sufficient earnings to retain public confidence in the soundness of the bank. To pump up earnings in expectation of a charge, banks will inflate the real rate of interest.

Recently, the real rate of interest has been ranging between four percent and five percent. Historically, it had been three percent or less. Even the real rate of interest adjusted for inflationary expectations has been double the normal until recently. The current inflation in the real rate of interest is a powerful depressant on the economy. It also raises the nagging question about the true cost of money to selected groups of customers. For example, banks historically set a prime rate, which they charged to the most creditworthy customers. All other customers paid a percentage above this rate.

With the growth of commercial paper as an alternative mode of corporate finance, the prime rate soon gave way to short dated "money market rates." In the early 1970s, concerned that confusion in terminology could precipitate litigation, I forged an agreement within First Chicago to publish, instead of a prime rate, a corporate base rate that could be defined precisely for our bank. Today the confusion on prime rate persists, and, in fact, has led to litigation.

The smokestack industries also suffer from the high real rate of interest because they borrow a lot and because their customers are interest sensitive. In the end, the consumer is the one who really pays. The credit card customer not only pays an annual fee to carry the card, but also interest rates as high as 19.8 percent despite significant drops in inflation and interest rates across a broad front. Credit card prices rose for good reasons in the 1979–81 period, when First Chicago and other banks had to pay 20 percent for deposits and other money. The assumption at the time was that the rate of credit card interest would float downward when the cost of money dropped. Because of the bad loans, the rate of interest has not dropped.

There are still other costs. The regulators are inhibited in the exercise of interest-rate policies. Perish the thought that we should any time soon have to tighten the money supply. That would raise interest rates and increase the debt service burden for the borrowing countries. The same fear inhibits regulators from giving free reign to growth policies in the debtor nations. And they are inhibited in the effective management of bank balance sheets in the creditor countries.

There are examples throughout history of what happens when nations are saddled with debt burdens they cannot afford to meet.

Germany after World War I is a case in point. The consequences are always unhappy. Governments fall, revolutions occur, and the debts are repudiated.

Foreign lending by banks is a risky business requiring experience, focused skills, and historical perspective. In an article entitled, "Bank Criteria for Foreign Loans," published by *Bankers Monthly* in November 15, 1964, I outlined the necessary cautions and procedures in some detail. They are as relevant for today's circumstances as they were in 1964.

Two excerpts from that article are worth quoting. The first deals with the profitability of foreign lending:

> Contrary to popular opinion, earnings on good foreign loans made in U.S. dollars are not much higher than earnings on domestic credits. Certainly, there are exceptions, but when the additional costs of supervision and surveillance are considered, along with the possible unavailability of compensating balances, the rate of return is roughly comparable to or only slightly better than that normally prevailing in the United States. With this small differential, therefore, the risk of loss must be commensurate with generally accepted standards, and analysis and surveillance must be just as comprehensive. All of the normal criteria, such as knowledge of the borrower, understanding the purpose of the transaction, and access to information, are just as important. And the availability of a seasoned, skilled staff is critical.

The second excerpt deals with the areas of caution in making foreign loans:

The following economic conditions appear to breed the seeds of financial trouble:

- Conditions where there is an insatiable and unrealistic appetite for foreign goods without a realistic means to produce a comparable volume of domestic goods for export—or at least to make up the deficits by invisible or incoming capital investment;

- Where there is an overall external debt that is growing faster than the economy and faster than the nation's ability to service it;

- Where, because of inflation or fear of inflation, there is a reduction in bank deposits that results in tight money conditions and prohibitive interest rates, thereby choking industrial expansion;

- Where there is an undisciplined and uncontrolled economy leading to financial speculation, graft, and a general flight of capital.[8]

The excerpts suggest that we, as an industry, knew way back in 1964 that foreign lending was risky and required close care and attention to fundamental tests of creditworthiness. There were clear "dos and don'ts" developed from experience, and it was an area commanding special attention and surveillance.

So, how and why did we plunge into the present mess? The popular excuse is that the commercial banks had to recycle the liquidity imbalances that followed the oil embargo of 1974. Then followed the oil-price hikes of 1978 and 1979 with more transfers of wealth to oil-exporting countries, when banks again had to move this money back into the mainstream. This, of course, was just a public relations pitch, a rationalization to mask the real objective, which was to make money. The banks were driven by greed to make what seemed to be easy profits. The commercial banks found customers, i.e., the oil-exporting nations, begging them to take their excess funds on deposit, and the banks obliged. They also found a ready market for loans in the developing world. They could convince these borrowers to pay premium rates of interest on the loans. It was too juicy a target for the bankers to pass up, and they didn't. With the needs of their people staring them in the face, the leaders of the developing world

---

[8]A. Robert Abboud, "Bank Criteria for Foreign Loans," *Bankers Monthly*, 15 November 1964, 26,32.

saw the ready availability of credit as an opportunity to be seized, and it was.

The regulators also played a role by not requiring minimum capital or reserve levels to support the large Eurodollar loans. The opportunity to take Eurodollar deposits and on – lend them became a very lucrative business for banks. Without reserve requirements, there was no limit to the multiplier and the growth was virtually without limit. With money plentifully available and the regulators permissive, banks made risky loans without proper safeguards or supervision, and those loans went bad. Now there is a big problem, and it is time we acknowledged the truth and started the cure.

To some extent, the cure has already started. Bank examiners are tougher. Capital is now required for off-balance-sheet lending and contingent liabilities. It is a start, but only a start. As always, true solutions can only be found and imposed within the banks, by managements dedicated to safety, backed by actively involved directors.

In the mid 1970s, I instituted the allocation of our capital accounts to First Chicago's various business units as a way to measure both capital sufficiency and true profitability. The riskier the business, the more capital required, and the capital charge to the business unit was computed in measuring its profitability. For example, government bond trading required less capital and could support higher leverage than factoring or venture capital. All business units were assessed relative to perceived risk experience and industry norms. I also required an internal capital charge on our Eurodollar lending and a special reserve for cross-border risk, i.e., lending dollars to other nations for employment internally in their own currency. I also instituted a policy to monitor how much First Chicago was owed by each sovereign foreign borrower compared with how much we had on deposit via Eurocurrency deposits from that same obligor. The difference was not to exceed the bank's legal lending limit. In addition, we set up an International Advisory Committee of the board to monitor regional developments and to review country cash flows in order to assess that country's ability to service its debt. All these measures were unpopular because they imposed constraints. Some of our senior officers complained that they made First Chicago noncompetitive, gave it a bad name among borrowers, and stunted our growth. Dick Thomas, the president of First Chicago, told me that I couldn't fly in the face of the market and that smarter bankers than Abboud weren't imposing these constraints.

Having come up through the international banking operations, I perceived the risks. It was not popular but I was determined to lean against the wind, much to the consternation of some of my directors. I frankly was amazed at their failure to comprehend the risks involved. I was confronted with the old refrain: First Chicago was losing ground by not growing as rapidly as others, notably our principal competitor, Continental Illinois. This loss of position was said to be adversely affecting our institutional pride and, therefore, morale throughout the organization. Needless to say, after my departure, the constraints I imposed were removed and First Chicago's loans, including loans to developing countries, soared. Many of them subsequently turned into problems.

Mexico's debt is a good example. Mexico is reported to owe foreign creditors $98 billion. First Chicago's share of that debt was reported by Donaldson, Lufkin and Jenrette to be in excess of $911 million as of June 30, 1986, a figure that shocked me when I read it. What in the world is First Chicago doing with $911 million in outstandings, equal to about half its common stock equity, in one developing country? In January 1980, the figure was $356 million. Nor is First Chicago alone. Some other banks are relatively more exposed than First Chicago. Yet, why is the fact that others did it an excuse for any institution?

Congressional testimony about the near collapse of Continental Bank revealed time and again how peer pressure was given as the excuse for dumb decisions. Peer pressure is nonsense. The reason is ambition and greed. Some know what they are doing when they take such risks but, unfortunately, most who follow these leaders do so at great peril.

It is the responsibility of the boards of directors to monitor exposure and risk and to keep their institutions safe. I have no sympathy with the ruling of a Chicago judge in the Continental case that, because the directors only received a retainer of $15,000 per year plus meeting fees, they could not be expected to know what was going on. If true, then let's have fewer voting directors, pay them more, and make sure that they do know what is going on. How else are we going to protect our privately managed institutions from overconcentration of risk?

The only alternative is to charge the government with this responsibility. This, of course, would signal the end of the private banking system and its advantageous flexibilities. But, if there is to be freedom and flexibility, there must also be accountability. In the case of developing-country debt, the banks got themselves in voluntarily, although, in fairness, with government encouragement. Let them use resourcefulness and pay the price to get out. Moreover, that price must not be at the sacrifice of future trade, economic growth, or foreign policy.

Brazil recently announced that it cannot service its external debt in accordance with the original terms. Keeping that debt in force without discount was exacting a terrible price on Brazil and other countries like Brazil (with attendant foreign policy implications on monetary authorities around the world and on the U.S. economy directly).

The first step in facing such facts is to disclose the enormity of the problem.

At present, banks are not required to reveal how much developing-country debt they have written down by providing specific reserves against these debts, if any. They are required to list the amount of nonperforming loans, but there is no way of knowing whether developing-country debt, public or private, is included in whole or in part. Examiners are forbidden to reveal how they are classifying this debt in their periodic examinations. Yet, in First Chicago's case, we saw an exposure in Mexico alone equivalent to half its common stock equity, and depositors, investors, borrowing customers, and the financial markets do not know how much is reserved. The same can be said about loans to Brazil, which, for First Chicago, amounted to an additional $800 million, up from $364 million in March 1980. For free-market discipline to work, we must have proper and timely disclosure. Without disclosure, the government, and hence the taxpayer, is left to underwrite the risk. Then it is only a matter of time before commercial banking is nationalized. As much as I would resist nationalization, there is no way anyone will prevent it if those entrusted with governance of our financial institutions aren't willing to accept accountability and absorb their own losses, even if they have to sell substantial amounts of new capital to pay for their own mistakes. And there is no way the public should tolerate a continuing subsidy through maintenance of an abnormally high spread in the real rate of interest.

According to Donaldson, Lufkin and Jenrette, the 30 largest borrowers among less developed and Eastern European countries as of June 30, 1986 had borrowed an aggregate $108 billion from U.S. banks. This is a big number, and the first order of business is for each institution to tell the marketplace how it assesses the risk and what it proposes to do to accommodate the situation, if anything. Some institutions may take the position, "We are reserved to this amount. We believe our borrowers will recover and will pay, and we don't propose to do anything further." Wonderful! The marketplace will vote by placing or withholding its business. Others may say, "We have reserved or sold all." Some may say, "We have such and such a program working with the borrowers to effect recovery over a specified time period." Also wonderful! Every shoemaker to his own last.

One commonly accepted position is that the Treasury and the Federal Reserve should provide the leadership and the formula for exit. However, the Treasury and the Federal Reserve didn't make these loans. Private bankers made them. Let those same bankers collect them. This is the only way to save and preserve the private banking system.

I don't blame the bankers with the biggest problems for wanting to maintain confidentiality and follow the pack or wait for an industrywide approach to a solution. I was similarly tempted in 1975 and 1976 with the REIT and troubled real estate loans that First Chicago had at that time. There is nothing more uncomfortable than the glare of attention during such a period. I firmly believe that a decision I made in 1976 to disclose was the correct one for the shareholders and staff of First Chicago. Otherwise, we would probably have ended up like Continental, with funding problems we couldn't handle when the market discovered the true situation. The gamble worked. First Chicago muscled its way out of its problems.

I can understand the temptation to seek confidentiality when confronted with a difficult situation. However, it doesn't work. A program of self-help must be put in place to correct the situation. I knew no one was going to help our bank. So, First Chicago took its medicine over a five-year period and survived. Shortly after I assumed the chairmanship, First Chicago revealed the extent of its REIT loans, its nonperforming loans, the amount of interest reversals, and the step up in provisions for reserves. It wasn't comfortable but, because First Chicago had a workout plan in place, the bank survived.

This does not mean that banks must reveal details of individual customer relationships. Here the privilege of privacy must be preserved without compromise. It has only to do with broad aggregates in the balance sheet and the answer to the most basic of all questions in a free market: Are the assets as represented in the published reports truly worth what they are reported to be? There is nothing wrong with disclosure as to whether the capital as published is true and hard. There is nothing wrong with disclosure as to whether the earnings as published are real and not overstated because of a failure to recognize latent losses.

This may sound like "apple pie and motherhood." How can anyone be against it, you ask? Let me count the ways. Consider, for example, what the Federal Home Loan Bank did with so called "regulatory capital." This procedure was adopted to "cushion" the results of savings and loans, institutions authorized to collect and hold our primary savings. Regulatory capital's premise was to take losses and negative net worth and capitalize them as assets on the left-hand side of the balance sheet. It obscured the reality that the institution in question was short of capital. It was a device adopted not by some charlatan out to dupe the public, but by the principal enforcement and regulatory arm of the U.S. Government with responsibility for surveillance of our primary savings system.

How about the practice of accounting for developing-country loans by institutions, their independent auditors, and their directors, all with the sanction of the regulators? Everyone knows there are country loans that are not worth face value. Why did it take until Citicorp's $3 billion addition to loan-loss reserves to face up to reality and to take the necessary charges to earnings? Let's examine the rationalizations, one by one:

- "Nations don't go broke."

  True! *Nations* don't go broke but governments sure do. That explains why Russian Czarist bonds representing sovereign obligations are good only to paper our closets. Even Walter Wriston, the retired chairman of Citicorp and one of the best bankers the United States has produced, who is the acknowledged author of the doctrine that "Nations don't go broke," praised Citicorp's recent action to increase reserves against developing-country debt. He said he "probably" would have followed the same course and that "nothing more nor less than the world has changed" (Laurie Cohen, "Bet Pays Off for Citicorp, Ups the Ante for Debtors," *Chicago Tribune*, 24 May 1987). Or, as Citicorp's current Chairman, John Reed, said on March 13, 1987, "It's a crummy world out there" ("Citicorp Sharply Lifts Loss Reserves, Putting its Rivals on the Spot," *Wall Street Journal*, 20 May 1987). On May 19, 1987, Mr. Reed elaborated, "These problems will be with us until the 1990s. We don't see anything in the global economy to get out of these problems soon" (Eric N. Berg, "Citicorp Accepts a Big Loss Linked to Foreign Loans," *New York Times,* 20 May 1987).

- "Banks perform an indispensable function by recycling liquidity from areas of surplus to areas of need, and this intermediation function is essential to the preservation of our financial system."

  If what the banks did was merely recycling in the intermediation process, then why can't they get their money back? They can't get it back because they made bad loans, because much of the money was wasted, because some of the money went into long-term development projects that won't begin to pay out for decades, because the principal credit criteria used by the banks was the presence of a guaranty by a central bank, development bank, or local commercial bank without any real information as to how good such a guaranty might be. This isn't recycling. This is converting large pools of liquid resources into long-term structural illiquidity.

- "Don't be precipitous in dealing with the problem because such action could cause a panic with untold consequences to the entire financial system."

  This assumes that no one recognizes the problem and that everyone will remain fooled. The markets are not that gullible. Failure to acknowledge and to take action is what will cause a panic. The stock market automatically discounts the securities of institutions that do not face up to the problem and whose balance sheets are therefore bloated.

- "We are making progress, the worst is over, things are getting better."

  If so, why does the aggregate debt keep going up and not come down? Why is the financial burden on debtor countries, with rare exceptions, becoming more oppressive rather than less? How come even friendly democracies are saying they will, at some point, have to break with us on this issue?

- "No one institution can deal with this problem by itself because of its magnitude."

If so, institutions should form consortia to deal with it collectively. There is merit in speaking with a group voice. However, the leadership should not be a Government voice. Certainly, the Government must be consulted and convinced to cooperate, but the private sector made the investment and it is up to the private sector to find a solution. One suggestion might be a common workout fund owned by all the banks that wish to trade their developing-country debt for shares of stock. Banks transferring the loans would guarantee their liquidity and pay any interest on deposits or borrowings taken to fund them. The new fund would take the loans at discounts negotiated on a case-by-case basis. The fund could sell senior equity to provide a broader capital footing. Purchasers of this new capital would then have the opportunity to share in the capital gains when and if the loans were collected, or converted to hard assets in the debtor countries, or bartered for goods to be resold. The advantages to participating banks would be manifold. Management of these assets would be consolidated on a scale that would permit the retention of top-quality entrepreneurial talent. Depositors and stockholders of the institutions that originally made the loans and transferred them would be relieved. The chances of recovery would be enhanced in an organization specifically set up to seek such recovery. Fresh capital could be brought in without diluting the capital structures of the participating institutions.

The bottom line is that the preponderance of outstandings represented by developing-country debt must be converted to equities in local currency in the debtor nations. It also must be done in a way that does not fuel inflation. This is standard workout procedure with any commercial credit. As John Reed, chairman of Citicorp, observed in the *Wall Street Journal,*

> An equity investment is a better asset today in Brazil than
> a loan to a central bank—when that loan is 20 years, subject

to renegotiation at the will of the borrower, at what would appear to be at an ever declining rate. Our stockholders are better served if instead of having that loan, they have the same exposure in the form of a productive investment.[9]

There is a widespread but unjustified skepticism that this cannot be done when dealing with foreign governments. It is in the interest of all parties to stimulate growth in the debtor nations, to reinvigorate world trade, and to finance mineral and agricultural programs that stimulate production for export. This appears to be in line with a new U.S. Government policy which is backing away from the austerity-driven formulae of the IMF and promoting growth-oriented strategies in the developing countries. Part of this is the new focus on managing exchange rates and the dollar stabilization activities, through intervention both up and down, all steps in the right direction—finally!

Secretary of the Treasury, James Baker, in January 1986 made a plea to a London meeting of finance ministers for coordinated interest-rate reductions to spur worldwide economic growth. That plea was accepted and implemented in March 1986 in what was heralded as a most unusual action, wherein several major nations would together coordinate monetary policy. Some said it couldn't be done. Finally, on February 22, 1987, the group of seven leading industrialized countries (minus Italy, which chose to abstain) announced an agreement to stabilize exchange rates and foster growth-oriented policies in Europe and Japan to stimulate consumption of foreign goods.

The operative word is *growth*. What is needed is an arsenal of growth-oriented policies—in trade, in investment, in capital markets, in services—to produce real honest-to-goodness growth across a broad economic front.

This is where government involvement can be helpful, creating the mechanisms to facilitate commercial transactions across

---

[9]"Citicorp's Reed Outlines Path on Third World Loans," *Wall Street Journal*, 28 May 1987.

borders; to make negotiations possible between debtor and creditor countries. Government-to-government cooperation can be harnessed to frame the rules to make trades, swaps and commercial exchanges possible. It is a proper role for government to define the marketplace and police the rules so that buyers, sellers, investors, borrowers, and creditors can properly assess the commercial risks and then take their chances.

Businesspeople are trained to assess their markets and then to risk capital for profit on the basis of these assessments. The businessperson is not properly trained to assess the combination of military and political risks, nor does he or she have the means to protect against these risks. Therefore, businesspeople are intensely concerned with world peace, the rule of law, and the availability of impartial legal mechanisms for the settlement of disputes with nationals of other countries and with foreign governments. Businesspeople become terribly concerned about the Cuban example of repudiating debts. They view with alarm the intervention of a nation such as Cuba in Africa and the Caribbean because of its previous disregard of universally accepted law. Their alarm has nothing to do with political orientation. Almost all nations, both East and West, respect international law and the rights of creditors. Cuba has simply chosen to live outside the law accepted by everyone else, and it may now be regretting its isolation.

Having acknowledged the enormity of the problem of developing-country debt, the first step toward a solution might be to approach it on a regional basis, for example, Latin America.

The next step is to create a model as close as possible to something already done in the past. The more familiar and comfortable the procedure, the better.

The third step is to ensure that nonnegotiable sensitivities are respected, such as national sovereignty, jurisdiction, ownership, and equality of bargaining power. Respect, equality and mutual benefit are the watchwords.

To test the theory, let's try to formulate such a market mechanism, just for practice, focusing on the Americas.

Suppose governments in the hemisphere that choose to participate agree to establish a new regional international authority. Let's call it the Americas Reconstruction Bank (ARB), because the underlying concept is similar to the Reconstruction Finance Corporation of the 1930s. Figure 12.3 illustrates the general role the authority would play.

The basic idea would be to stretch out repayments by collateralizing specific producing assets within the debtor nation, allowing developing countries to get out from under the debt load. At the same time, debtor nations would not have to accumulate specific currencies to service the crushing level of current debt, nor would creditor countries have to withhold further loans or investments. If such debt relief could be accomplished, the constraints on new trade and investment would be relieved or even eliminated. The objective, of course, is to recreate the climate for growth, growth being the only true solution. Growth of world trade and investment is the healing process. For the seeds of growth to germinate, we must cleanse the soil from the hyperacidity of the debt burden. We cleanse the soil by creating a marketplace, with rules agreed to by all, to encourage workout negotiations between lenders and borrowers. In our example, that workout forum is called the Americas Reconstruction Bank (ARB).

The organizational details are almost incidental. As in the present Inter American Development Bank, governors would be appointed to the ARB from every member nation, each of which would also be asked to make a contribution to capital. Like the present World Bank, the ARB would have a professional executive staff.

The chief executive and the staff would report to the board of governors and would administer policies established by the governors.

The ARB would be authorized to issue special *Repayment Depository Receipts* (RDRs), something like the special drawing rights issued by the IMF. These RDRs would be used to repay debt to foreign financial institutions. Debtor nations would pledge specific

FIGURE 12.3:
THE AMERICA'S RECONSTRUCTION BANK PLAN

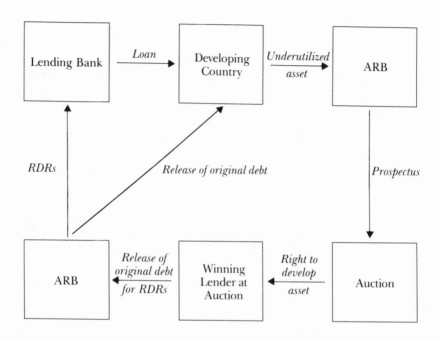

assets as collateral, say a closed mine not currently in operation. The ARB would obtain commercial jurisdiction over the collateral within the debtor country, subject to agreement with the host country. The ARB would be able to authorize the inflow of foreign investment for its development and for the export of its product for foreign exchange. An agreement with the debtor nation would give the collateralized property public utilities and other services on terms no less favorable than those for domestic enterprises. Obviously, there would be a time limit on both the note and the pledge of collateral.

The purpose would be to surround the collateral in a kind of "enterprise zone," where it has every opportunity to succeed unencumbered.

The ARB would then prepare a prospectus describing the collateral. The collateral would invariably be an idle or underutilized asset, such as a mineral resource, an oil field, or a factory capable of producing a product for export. That's what makes the program attractive to debtor countries. Lenders would be forced to bid for the chance to develop the asset for commercial purposes, thereby supplying the debtor nation with new capital, new management, and possibly new markets.

The lender, who is awarded the property described in a prospectus, would assume all the obligations that the prospectus assigned to the collateral. In return, the lender would receive RDRs, obligations of the ARB, which would be regarded as full payment of the debtor country's obligation. The RDRs would be collateralized by and repaid through the stream of income from the pledged asset. If the pledged asset did not perform to expectations, then the RDR would depreciate in value and the institution holding it would have to write it down. If the asset's performance exceeded expectations, then the RDR would appreciate in value and the institution holding it would realize a capital gain.

The program would not work unless monetary authorities and regulators in the nations having jurisdictions over the creditor banks' agreed to permit RDRs to be exchanged for developing country debt. Then the bank lenders could book RDRs on the balance sheet at some negotiated rate of writeoffs or reserve additions. Such writeoffs or reserve additions would have the effect of discounting the obligations of the debtor nations.

Aside from the necessary recognition of RDRs by regulators, critical to this proposal's success, is a political sensitivity in the presentation of this concept internationally. It should not appear "imperialistic" to debtor-nation electorates, which would render it unacceptable at the outset.

The value of this program is that a developing country would get out from under its preexisting debt load. Economic activity within the country would be stimulated by the new investment flowing in to restructure idle factories or other resources. There would be no taint for political leaders because the developing country would be dealing with an international institution (the ARB) of which it is a shareholder and on whose board of governors its representative sits. Its participation would be purely voluntary. The country would not be selling out the national patrimony, but merely putting up as collateral for a finite period of time a presently defunct or idle asset. It would be much like a foreign direct investment to develop mineral or hydrocarbon assets or agricultural or timber land. The only difference is the presence of an agreed upon mediator and market maker, the Americas Reconstruction Bank, which would provide an RDR.

Under this umbrella, the lending institutions would have an opportunity to work out their loans. By developing the resources they have agreed to reinvigorate, they can govern the rate of return and repayment sufficiency of the RDR they hold in their portfolio. Admittedly, this role will require additional investment. On the other hand, any experienced lender understands that workouts generally do require additional investment.

Lender countries will also have to put up some more money. But it is not sending good money after bad. It is sending good money to recover a bad loan. That is just good banking!

The ultimate solution might be along these lines or totally different, but some solution is required and it needs consensus. The use of a multinational development agency such as the proposed Americas Reconstruction Bank is not a new concept.

Back in the early 1930s, President Roosevelt sanctioned the Foreign Bondholders Protective Council, Inc. to negotiate private bondholders' unpaid claims on foreign governments. The founding directors were Cordell Hull, Secretary of State; W.H. Wooden, Secretary of the Treasury; and Charles H. March, Chairman of the Federal Trade Commission. Also deeply involved and subsequently a director and president of the organization was Harvey H. Bundy, Assistant Secretary of State under President Hoover, who had been one of the original proponents of the concept during the latter months of the Hoover Administration. Mr. Bundy had traveled to England to study the mechanism of that country's established bondholders council, founded in 1868.

The U.S. Foreign Bondholders Protective Council was set up in New York City in 1933. Its preamble stated that the negotiation of outstanding claims was properly a matter for the private sector, but that government should facilitate the process and create the mechanism whereby such negotiation could effectively occur.

Although a private, nonprofit, public service organization, the council received support from government officials at all levels. William O. Douglas, then chairman of the Securities and Exchange Commission and later a justice of the U.S. Supreme Court, wrote a book on bondholder rights, entitled *Democracy and Finance*, with particular emphasis on railroad bondholders. He favorably discussed the activities of the Foreign Bondholders Protective Council at some length.

After World War II, James Grafton Rogers, former assistant secretary of state, became head of the council and Kenneth M. Spang became its vice president. Mr. Spang became its president in 1953, served the council until 1958, and was its longest tenured full-time officer. Subsequently, he became an officer of Citicorp.

John McCloy, head of the World Bank after World War II, formerly chairman of Chase Manhattan Bank and military governor and high commissioner for Germany, was also actively involved in the council's activities as was another World Bank President, George Woods.

Despite close working relations with the banks, who were principal creditors, the council was independent of the banks and not paid by them. In fact, Mr. Douglas stressed the fact that the council should not be paid by the banks in order to avoid any perceived conflict of interest and to preserve the council's role as a disinterested and fair intermediator.

Mr. McCloy and Eugene Black of the World Bank were key players in the council's post-war success. The World Bank needed to sell its own bonds to United States financial institutions, the proceeds of such sales to fund the bank's loans. However, savings and loan associations balked at purchasing bonds of an institution which planned to lend to countries who were in default on their own bond obligations. To sell its bonds, the World Bank adopted a policy not to make loans to any country that had not worked out a settlement acceptable to the Foreign Bondholders Protective Council regarding its outstanding bond indebtedness.

Thus, to obtain loans from the World Bank, foreign nations had to negotiate and reach agreement with the private, public service organization, the Foreign Bondholders Protective Council, Inc.

Each negotiation, country by country, was a saga unto itself. The point is that negotiations on outstanding foreign country debts often take years to settle satisfactorily. History teaches us this lesson over and over again. Moreover, some catalyst is required, an "adequate and disinterested," public service organization.

Also required is a new source of money, such as the World Bank provided in the late 1940s, 1950s, and 1960s, to create an incentive for borrowers to settle in order to qualify for new credit. That is why I suggest the formation of an Americas Reconstruction Bank or perhaps a separate division of the World Bank. Mr. Barber Conable, the current president of the World Bank, is giving high priority to the problem of third-world country debt.

It takes time, and we should not expect miracles. There will undoubtedly be disappointments. Thus, the need for the banks to provide large-scale additional reserves is an expensive but essential process that has only just begun. That is why some composite international financial structure is needed to preserve a measure of obligation and commitment. Without such a structure, there is a very real danger that new credit will dry up and world trade flows will decline dangerously. We are at a critical, critical juncture, and don't let anyone tell you otherwise!

THIRTEEN

Retail Banking

International banking may carry the glamour, but the key to any bank or thrift's underlying strength is its retail deposit-gathering network. These deposits include NOW accounts (negotiable orders of withdrawal or retail checking accounts that pay interest), savings accounts, money market accounts, individual retirement account (IRA) balances, small-denomination certificates of deposit, credit balances for money orders, the float (the purchase price not yet paid out) from sales of travelers checks, escrow accounts, tax accounts, and other deposits arising from mortgage and real estate transactions, private banking deposits from high-net-worth individuals, Christmas clubs, savings clubs, travel club accounts, direct payroll and dividend accounts, discount brokerage and investment accounts, and a host of other accounts limited only by the imagination of the aggressive, creative retail banker.

Retail banking is the true test of any depository institution's usefulness to the community and the measure to which it has earned the confidence and support of the community it serves.

The first thing I do when I study the balance sheet of a depository institution is to look at the book of savings and related accounts and the trend of growth of those accounts. I do the same when I review the liability structure of a branch or a subsidiary or even an overseas branch in a foreign country. Too many institutions expect their foreign operations to survive and prosper by simply purchasing money in the interbank money markets. This is a tragic mistake because the branch will never develop stable roots in the local economy with such a program. If a branch is worth opening, it is worth supporting with sufficient product to attract stable, long-term retail deposits.

The operative word is *product,* a service or an investment opportunity designed to attract customers. It is the art of merchandising, the same as one would practice in any fine department store. A good retail banker has buyers, general suppliers, private-label suppliers, merchandise managers, sales personnel, controllers to set and monitor margins, advertising and promotion personnel, customer-service representatives—every dimension of a primary retail establishment. In my opinion, this is the part of banking that is the most fun and the most personally rewarding. It is also the basic underpinning of the business, particularly when conditions are turbulent or uncertain.

To be marketed successfully, the retail banking merchandise must be displayed in attractive, pleasant surroundings. Any retailer knows that you cannot successfully merchandise designer clothes and fine jewelry in dark, dingy, unpleasant surroundings. Nor can such items be merchandised where customers must wait in lines, or where they are served by untrained sales personnel conveying the impression that the customers' business is unappreciated or somehow unworthy. Sound, sight, and smell in a comfortable, contemporary, inviting atmosphere are all important. So also is a tie to the local community served by the facility or branch. A good bank that truly wants your business will invest in these amenities. First Chicago did. Homer Livingston approved it. Gale Freeman executed it and gave it grace and style, and I eagerly continued in that tradition.

The most important product in that setting is insurance on deposits. Guarantees are provided by the FDIC to banks and the FSLIC to savings and loans, in both cases up to $100,000 per name account. Material should always be prominently displayed describing the insurance and its terms and conditions.

There is a difference between FDIC and FSLIC insurance, although both are U.S. Government corporations. The FDIC promises to pay within 90 days of any default. The FSLIC, on the other hand, insures the share accounts in a savings and loan, which are technically not deposits but rather equity investments. In the event of a savings and loan's default, the FSLIC promises to pay when the institution is ultimately liquidated or sold and there is determined to be a shortfall. This could take years. Since such a delay would be unacceptable in the marketplace, the practice of the FSLIC has been to pay as quickly as possible.

The differences in insurance coverage offered by the two agencies will have to be eliminated. In fact, the two agencies should be merged. It makes no sense to have two government agencies offering the same service in overlapping jurisdictions.

The three pillars of retail banking are operations, marketing, and product development. Each is challenging and great fun, but the one I find the most exciting is new-product development.

The object is to keep pace with the economy, changes in the tax laws, inflation and ways to offset it, the desire to invest and to make savings grow, the bank's need to provide more convenience at lower cost, and the need to simplify and to make banking a pleasure instead of a bother. Simple things, such as preparation of an easily prepared statement, understandable wording on forms and applications, and timely mailings of such items as the 1099 interest income-tax form are essential.

It is always dangerous for a senior officer, much less a chairman, to interfere in the product development side of the retail bank. I knew this, but I couldn't resist the temptation.

I remember the days when gold and silver prices were soaring. I would stand by the head of the escalator looking down on the retail floor where we sold gold and silver coins and where we also housed the safe deposit boxes. A steady stream of customers would go to the gold and silver windows, buy coins or bullion, and then march directly to their safe deposit boxes to store the items purchased. I thought it was a waste of time. Why don't we offer gold passbooks and silver passbooks whereby the customer could buy ounces of bullion recorded in a passbook and redeemable in kind on demand? The service would be inexpensive compared with the cost and inconvenience of storage, and every bit as safe.

This is now big business for banks and thrifts that offer the service. The May 5, 1987 *Wall Street Journal* said small retail investors "can buy gold and gold-related investments at more than 2,000 U.S. banks and brokerage firms. Industry analysts estimate that these purchases represent about 35 percent of U.S. gold-related sales, up from about 10 percent in 1980. Gold certificate programs, in which investors purchase gold stored and insured by banks, have been especially popular. Balances in Citibank's program, for instance, have surged 135 percent in the past three years, says John Norris, Citibank's director of precious-metals trading."[10] And now, the investment bankers are offering warrants to buy gold in the future at predetermined prices.

In electronic banking, First Chicago pioneered automated teller machines with the Cash Station system in Chicago, and the bank-by-phone system. I was fascinated by the possibilities of customers using the touch-tone telephone to access accounts, pay bills, and conduct a host of routine services without having to wait in line during banking hours.

The credit card was another masterful invention, brought to First Chicago by Gale Freeman with Bob Wilmouth. The operation was losing money when I became chairman, but the hard work had been done and the big credit losses associated with start-up had been written off. Within a short period, the program became profitable and grew in all directions. It is, after all, a volume

---

[10]Michael Siconolfi, "Gold Finally Becomes a Respectable Holding for Investors in U.S.," *Wall Street Journal*, 5 May 1987.

business. New services were added for cardholders. Additional card systems were purchased. We built a processing center in Elgin, Illinois. And, most of all, we applied new electronic technologies to process card transactions and to prevent counterfeiting. You have no idea how many attempts are made to defraud the system. Buyers' cards are counterfeited. Blank, unissued cards are stolen and sold. Genuine cards are stolen, sold, and used with forged signatures. Sometimes crime rings work out arrangements with disreputable merchants to falsify sales slips using legitimate names of cardholders. Defending against these and other dangers are a cadre of talented enforcement investigators and up-to-date computer technology and electronics. The most important link in the security chain is the merchant. Most of the fraud can be tempered if the merchant asks for identification, calls into the central computer files for card and amount validation, and remains generally alert to anything that may seem unusual or extraordinary.

Soon, card usage spread to overseas markets. This compounded the security problems. However, the service was essential because people wished to travel and to use their cards in place of travelers letters of credit or travelers checks. The international travel market was dominated by American Express. Thus, VISA and Master-Card, which are associations of thousands of banks, had to incur major expenses in advertising and special promotions to enter the market. They did successfully, and today VISA and Master-Card are known and used around the world. Without satellite communications and big modern computers with interconnecting modems, this would not have been possible.

In the late 1970s, VISA introduced the VISA travelers check and solicited member banks, of which First Chicago was one, to join. It was a difficult decision because American Express was so dominant. First Chicago had been an issuer of its own travelers checks in the 1950s and 1960s and, after absorbing what for the time appeared to be a large loss to pay off some counterfeit notes in Canada, decided to sell out. We deliberated long and hard when VISA came along. Jim Cassin and Bob Richley, both distin-

191

guished bankers who ran our retail banking operations, recommended we go ahead. Tony Tuke, then chairman of Barclays Bank in London, telephoned me to ask our decision, as they, too, were considering converting their own travelers check program to VISA. I told Tony that we had decided to proceed. Barclays also decided to go ahead. Unfortunately, I left shortly after the program at First Chicago started and the new management disbanded the program. I believe that was an unfortunate decision—all the more so because I had visions at some point of introducing a travelers check that pays interest.

My policy was never to let a retail customer leave without a choice for a substitute service. Retail depositors make the institution, and it is important to accommodate them. With this in mind I became consumed with the idea of a travelers check that carried interest from date of purchase. It would be like a mobile, interest-bearing NOW account that would serve the convenience of the small saver. The processing could be handled electronically. There would be no individual accounts to maintain. The customer could buy the certificates in $100 denominations, earn interest until the day cashed (the merchant would check the date of issuance and add the monthly credit amount from date of purchase) and still be economical to service. We researched this long and hard. There are legal and operational problems. Most of all, the big issuers of travelers checks do not want the practice to start. But someday we will see it, not just to accommodate travelers, but also to service small savers in poorer communities where banking and thrift institutions do not choose to maintain branches.

Serving the small saver profitably is an art. If balances fall too low, many institutions give up and say "close the accounts, we don't want them." This is shortsighted, particularly for the large international banks that seek to build overseas branch systems. An overseas branch cannot live exclusively on purchased money in the interbank market. Strategies must be devised to provide a local service to attract local currency deposits. If products are created to serve the small saver, it is only a small step forward to add a prestige product for the large saver or the high-net-worth trust company client.

I was always impressed by the fact that First Chicago prospered and maintained a reputation for strength and safety in the late 1940s and 1950s because of its large retail savings base, the largest of its kind anywhere in the world for a unit bank. (A unit bank is one that cannot open branches. Illinois, until recently, did not allow branch banking domestically.) But, this did not come about by accident. In the 1930s, in the teeth of the depression, Edward Eagle Brown, then president and chief executive officer of First Chicago, offered to pay interest on savings accounts at a time when other banks were paying nothing on savings. They merely agreed to keep your savings safe, an important consideration at the time. First Chicago stood out from all the rest by offering to pay savers one-half percent, compared with a three-quarter percent prime rate. As a result, the savings deposits were used to buy U.S. Government bonds. After the war, they provided the resources to finance First Chicago's leadership position in the term loan business to corporate customers. There was no such thing at that time as a broadly based interbank money market where banks could augment their resources with purchased money. So, savings accounts were the base to support two-, three-, four-, and five-year term loans to business customers seeking to convert their businesses from wartime production to civilian production. This was the pay-off for First Chicago. Despite its unit bank status in Illinois, it grew to become the nation's fifth largest bank by the mid-1950s.

The thrifts, too, provided a needed service to the small saver in the 1930s and 1940s. The thrifts used the resources to finance home ownership and, in the process, earned a tremendous reservoir of political goodwill that preserved their advantageous tax status until the recent deregulation.

The point is that it is good business for financial institutions to serve the broad-based mass market. Walter Wriston and Citicorp understood this concept both in the United States and abroad. I believe this explains why he named John Reed, a retail banker, to succeed him as Citicorp chairman in 1984. At First Chicago, retail banking was a top priority for me. The savings base that Ned Brown attracted in the 1930s and 1940s was aging, and the balance of power had shifted to corporate lending. I sought to readjust the balance in the hope of establishing a new "yuppie" savings base for the decades to follow.

Thus, First Chicago jumped into the forefront of the campaign to eliminate the ban on branch banking. Although the effort was well underway under Gale Freeman, I took on the leadership role for our bank personally.

I tested the limits on opening off-site facilities, first on Wabash Avenue and then on North Michigan Avenue at the corner of Chicago Avenue. This was an historic site move into a territory that bankers in the region had vowed would never be opened to the big "Loop" banks. The Continental Bank opened two blocks west in a more remote developing area. But I vowed we would challenge the opposition and, under the leadership of Jim Cassin, First Chicago succeeded.

I also initiated a system of 12 "facilities offices" in and around Chicago that conformed to the Comptroller of the Currency's rulings on loan production offices. The Illinois bankers who opposed branch banking immediately filed suit challenging the legality of these offices. It was a bold move with modest chance of success, but it was necessary to implement the overall First Chicago retail strategy. *Business Week* wrote about the confrontation as follows:

> Accordingly, First Chicago and Continental Illinois last year began quietly installing remote electronic bank terminals in such locations as office buildings. After a federal court ruled that the terminals were performing some illegal branch-banking functions, Abboud this past April brazenly opened 10 "community offices"—so-called to avoid the word *branches*—around Chicago. Costing about $1 million, the offices not only were equipped with electronic machines but also were staffed with people soliciting loan applications.

In one stroke, Abboud gained scores of enemies, as many admirers, and several hundred fascinated onlookers. He may also have come within a deposition of being found in contempt in a suit against the offices.[11]

The article went on to note that I was politically and personally close to Mayor Richard J. Daley, who had come around to agreeing to our proposal to permit "community offices" by way of a city ordinance. We had also established close relations with the city's finance department, in keeping with the community responsibility of a bank of our stature.

Looking back, these machinations seem modest, since the banks and thrifts are now branching all over. However, at the time it was formidable because the strategy of the thrifts and the independent community banks was to keep the loop banks contained within the downtown business district.

First Chicago even had a problem opening a banking site in the Xerox Building, which it financed, and at the building called First National Three, which it built. Both are located across the street from First Chicago's head offices. After considerable legal effort, First Chicago obtained permission only because it owned the land on both sides of the street and the terms of the deed stipulated that ownership of the fee joined in the middle of the street. (For that matter, the joining of the fee on Madison Street was the only reason permission was obtained to build the enclosed walkway above the street level between First National One and First National Three, but this is another story.) Permission was denied, however, to offer retail banking services in First National Two, across Clark Street from the head office, because the deed of ownership did not abut or join at the middle of the street.

And the battle did not end there. The initiative to extend automatic tellers out into the community was another major struggle.

First Chicago needed a delivery system to supply the innovative product line it was developing. The product was good, the

---

[11]"Abboud: Mr. Tough Guy of U.S. Banking," *Business Week,* 28 June 1976, 91.

advertising and marketing were good, but the delivery system was virtually dependent on the U.S. Mail, the quality of which was deteriorating rapidly. Something had to be done. One answer was to open new offices like the facilities just discussed. But the number and geographic reach of these facilities were severely limited. Another answer was the bank-by-telephone system, already mentioned, but this service was new and had a long way to grow. A third answer was the off-site, conveniently located automated teller machine.

First Chicago began experimentation on the development of such machines with a company called Docutel. In fact, First Capital, First Chicago's successful venture capital subsidiary, invested in the company. This relationship went sour and ended in a lawsuit. I was not privy to those arrangements and do not know the circumstances.

But the thrust was established. We needed hardware. To that point we had relied on IBM and the service had been excellent. I always thought IBM would come forward with an automated teller machine, but it was not within their product line when we needed one. Somewhere, somehow, we found satisfactory hardware and the initiative shifted to building a network.

The obstacle again was the Illinois law on branch banking. Opponents of branch banking took the position that automated teller machines were the equivalent of branch banks and, therefore, restricted in their placement away from the head office. A compromise had to be struck and it was, under the leadership of Messrs. Cassin and Richley. The compromise stated that one or two networks could be tolerated as long as they were viewed as public utilities and anyone could join. The basic ingredient was the central switch that allowed the customer of any member bank or savings and loan to route the transaction back to the home institution. The first to sign onto the system, which we called *Cash Station,* was the Northern Trust, and then a savings and loan. At last, an off-premises delivery system had been born.

The restrictive branch banking laws in Illinois have since been all but dismantled. Looking back on the pain and drama, it seems like so much effort for so little gain. But those early efforts, occurring before the deregulation wave enveloped banking and other industries, instilled a cultural attitude that was to serve the organization well through future battles. The new attitude was a recognition that service and product had to be delivered to a broadly based, mass market everywhere First Chicago operated, both in the United States and abroad. For promoting such thinking, I was branded a "populist." I frankly took this as a compliment, convinced as I am that banking can thrive only if it serves all the people, the mass market.

Within the corporate culture, there was great resistance to this policy because the "fast track" people were thought to come from commercial lending, not retail banking. Large financial institutions have more of this sibling rivalry than the public might suspect. Institutions go through phases when first one discipline is in ascendancy and then another. At First Chicago, corporate commercial banking had been dominant since the mid-1950s. In the 1970s it was overtaken by international banking. I wanted to bring equivalent prestige to retail banking. But to do this, we needed people, time, and product.

The credit card was a great beginning, but as interest rates rose in the latter 1970s, profit margins began to be squeezed. The *coup de grâce* occurred in the fall of 1979 when the chairman of the Federal Reserve, Paul Volcker, decided to adopt the monetarist philosophy propounded by Milton Friedman and the "Chicago school" of economic theory. From that point on, the Federal Reserve was going to manage the money supply by taking reserves out of the banking system and letting interest rates go where they would. This was a radical departure from the old method of keeping interest rates within predetermined brackets.

Interest rates promptly escalated from about 12 percent per annum to over 20 percent and brought interest-sensitive markets like real estate and fixed-income securities to their knees. The impact on credit cards was devastating. Usury laws in the various states limited the amount of interest to be charged and, in almost all cases, this rate of interest was below the cost of funds that banks had to pay to get the money. The spread had disappeared. The only card systems making money were those like American Express that charged an annual fee. VISA and Master-Card banks charged no fee, relying solely on the merchant discount (the amount the card-accepting merchant must pay to get the service), which did not compensate for the disintegration of the interest-rate spread. Cardholders who did not borrow, who paid their balances in full when they received their bills, got a free ride for the services provided. And the borrowing customers got a good deal because their costs of borrowing were limited by the various state usury ceilings. Clearly, it was an unworkable situation and something had to be done.

There was pressure within the bank and within the industry to curtail the use of credit cards and to limit borrowings. First Chicago, at the time, had about 1.8 million VISA cards outstanding and about one-half were borrowing accounts, as opposed to free-ride convenience accounts. Our policy was to expand product and service, not to curtail it. The obvious solution was to increase the price in order to restore profitability. We could not increase the interest rate charged to borrowers because we were already at the Illinois usury ceiling of 18 percent. We could not increase the merchant discount fee appreciably because of competition. Because cardholders who did not borrow were basically receiving a free service, I asked our people to explore the feasibility of an annual membership fee along the lines of the American Express card.

The recommendation came back to levy a $20 per year annual fee that would automatically be charged to the account at the anniversary date for each cardholder. Bob Richley presented the recommendation to our Credit Policy Committee. The fee would yield $36 million in added revenue, a direct benefit to the bottom line.

However, there was strong opposition to the recommendation among my senior colleagues. They argued that a price increase would cause us to lose a substantial number of cardholders. We could lose our leadership position in the Chicago market. Bob

Richley and I believed that the annual fee provided considerable flexibility to remain competitive. The interest rate charged to borrowing customers could be lowered to float with the prevailing level of interest rates at any given time. This was of critical importance to preserve market share and leadership in our area. If we wanted political support and flexibility under applicable usury laws as rates went up, we had to be similarly responsive and accommodating as they came down. The annual card fee was the answer, leaving the interest rate to float with market conditions. Bob Richley stuck with his fee recommendation and I approved it.

When we communicated the decision to our board's Executive Committee, my senior colleagues again voiced their opposition. The outside directors supported the chairman's recommendations and the annual fee went into effect.

Other banks quickly began to follow suit. I heaved a sigh of relief. To his great credit, Bob Richley never evidenced the slightest concern that we were going out on a limb. He assured the outside board members that we would not lose more than 100,000 cardholders. The Continental Bank, our primary competitor with MasterCard, tried to be cute and announced a $15 annual fee. Their tactical jab did not work. Our number of cardholders did not go down a bit and we were now in a position to continue to expand the product line with profitability restored and everyone comfortable with our aggressive posture to seek additional market share.

I never realized how much this fee continued to bother some of my most senior colleagues. On April 10, 1987, on the day of First Chicago's annual meeting, President Richard Thomas announced that the $20 annual fee would be dropped for customers who charge $2,400 or more on their VISA card during the course of a year. This was in response to consumers' allegations of gouging and demands to lower the 19.8 percent annual rate of interest in view of lower interest rates generally. Chairman Barry Sullivan also stated that cardholders are most sensitive to the annual fee, while over half of them don't know the interest rate.

I can't argue about his research. But I do know that the interest rate is more important in building a retail product among the moderate-income public than waiving the fee in return for aggregate purchases of $2,400 or more. This rebate induces the wealthy to use VISA more instead of other cards they may possess. Nothing is wrong with this strategy. It just doesn't address the main concern raised by the interest-rate controversy.

The moderate-income person who may have $1,000 of loans outstanding on his or her VISA card is more concerned with the $198 in annual interest cost than with the $20 annual fee. The poorer the person and the fewer new purchases he or she can afford to charge on a card, the more likely the person is to pay both the high interest cost and the fee. And under the new tax code, the interest is no longer deductible, which makes it that much more expensive.

This rebate strategy drives away the lower-income customer while providing benefits to the upscale customer. It is the same strategy that dictated fee schedules on small savings accounts to drive them out of the bank. This is not broad-based retail strategy. It is purely and simply focused on the people who don't need to borrow. It is 180 degrees away from my strategy, which was to offer a quality product at a fair price to every sector of the mass retail market.

Under my stewardship the retail banking objective was to expand both services and the product line. No longer did we view retail banking as a simple savings-gathering department, which is the mistake that many banks and savings and loans make. A successful retail operation must be much, much more. It must keep pace with the changing environment and continually introduce new products compatible with the times. Home mortgages and personal instalment loans are basic to the lending function, but the product line must also conform to the spirit of the legislation that grants banks and thrifts their charters to serve the public interest.

First Chicago was head and shoulders above its immediate competition in this regard. It became a prime depot for the purchase and sale of precious coins and rare metals. It also introduced the retail bankers acceptance, which for more than 100 years had been accessible exclusively in the professional investor market. The interest rates paid on bankers acceptances were substantially above the rates paid on savings, which were limited by the Federal Government under Regulation Q. And a bankers acceptance carried the full faith and credit of the issuing bank, although FDIC insurance probably didn't apply.

Because of the Regulation Q limits on savings account interest, customers began in the 1970s to withdraw their deposits, which earned 7.5 percent annually or less, and invest the money in newly popular money market funds paying 12 percent annually. These money market funds, which were managed by innovative brokerage houses, would in turn buy a First Chicago certificate of deposit in a $100,000 denomination paying 14 percent per annum. The system made no sense and penalized the savers who could not or were reluctant to move their savings accounts.

At a meeting in the board room of the Federal Reserve System in Washington with Chairman of the Board Paul Volcker and the heads of the major banks in the United States, I raised the competitive dilemma we faced with the money market funds. I asked the chairman if the Federal Reserve could either subject the money market funds to the restrictions of Regulation Q or, in the alternative, give the banks and thrifts relief from the limitations of Regulation Q. The request was noted but nothing was done, and the disintermediation—the flow of money out of the banking system to higher-yielding investments—continued at an accelerating pace.

First Chicago, as the largest savings depository in the Midwest, was bearing the brunt of this disintermediation. Something had to be done in response, and that something was new product. We had to circumvent Regulation Q and find lawful ways to pay our savings customers more.

We invented a certificate called First Rate Investments (FRIs) which provided savers with the 90- to 180-day portion of a pool of bankers acceptances. After a short period, the Federal Reserve

Board halted issuance, stating that the certificates resulted in the "creation of a deposit subject to interest-rate limitations." The "big guy" who could afford to buy the entire bankers acceptance could get the high rate, but not the "little guy." Bob Richley, then senior vice president, summed up our attitude with a quote in the June 19, 1980 *Chicago Sun Times:* "Unfortunately, the consumer is the real loser here. We disagree, particularly in view of the Congressional mandate to deregulate interest rates to encourage a more competitive, consumer-oriented environment."

To carry out these innovative and challenging strategies, First Chicago became the incubator of a new breed of talented, creative bankers with unlimited vision. The roster included Dave Brooks, who later became vice chairman of Crocker Bank and is now a senior executive with Citicorp; Pete Hart, who now heads retail operations for First Interstate; Homer Holland, who now heads Crescent Savings; John Rau, now president of Exchange National Corporation; James Cassin, now president of First Empire in New York; Bob Richley, president and chief executive officer of the First National Bank of San Diego; and Ray Einsel, whom I hired from Bankers Trust to head our Credit Card Operations and who is now with Great Western Bank in Arizona. Our retailing success and the depth and quality of our personnel made First Chicago a prime target for management recruiters. This was great for our people and actually served as an incentive to the talented younger people in the Retail Department, who were flattered by the recognition.

An additional challenge was to impart this aggressive retailing posture to our overseas branches. We had a modest start in Germany, where I opened a subsidiary in 1966, and we had a major presence in Beirut, Lebanon, where I opened a subsidiary in 1967. The plan was to move the retailing capability to other branches around the world by introducing products adapted to each local market. This was not an easy task because the indigenous banks in those retail markets were very well established. Moreover, the global thrust was considered impractical by some in our own organization who were wedded to the notion that corporate banking and big-ticket country credits were the only feasible ways to build international business and earn profits. I was not convinced. As in the United States, any branch must put down roots in the community it serves. It must become a visible and useful member of the community. It must offer a continual stream of new products in local currency. The local deposit base will gradually grow as a direct consequence. For example, the subsidiary in Lebanon had branches in the major communities and offered a wide array of retail services including money transfers, remittances, foreign exchange, safekeeping, and a variety of other products. It has since been sold. Some of First Chicago's best all-around bankers served in that branch, including Leo Garman, now retired; Dr. Ziad Idilby, now managing director of Holland Park Investments; Harry Tempest, who became a senior officer at Bank of California; Bob Yohanan, now president of Lakeshore National Bank in Chicago; and Abdul Jallad, now managing director of a London based company. The Beirut unit and other First Chicago offices in foreign cities, even those offices located off of street level in high-rise buildings, became lucrative generators of retail deposits.

I do not agree with Mark Twain, who said, "Put all your eggs in one basket and then watch that basket." In the banking business, the secret is to provide a continuing stream of baskets for people to put their eggs in. And the secret in international banking is not only to provide multiple baskets but also to demonstrate staying power through good times and bad. George Moore, who was the chief executive of Citicorp before Walter Wriston, told me of times when his bank was under pressure to close foreign branches or limit new openings because of economic conditions. He said that he successfully warded off those pressures because, if the major strategic thrust of the bank was to be multinational, then it must exhibit staying power to weather the bad times in order to participate in the good times. Without such commitment, don't get into the business. It will be nothing but an expensive ego trip.

I am sorry to say that First Chicago appears to have lost the zest for an aggressive retail thrust domestically and around the world. Small accounts have been closed in Chicago with, to my knowledge, no alternative service provided. Small local currency accounts abroad are also being closed, all in the name of cost savings or efficiency. I was a victim of that policy because I maintained a small deutsche mark savings account in our Frankfurt branch (about $200 in U.S. equivalent). It was account number one, opened on the day I opened the branch, and I kept it mainly for sentimental reasons. There was no activity in the account. It just sat there earning interest. Instead of receiving a note on each anniversary date expressing appreciation for my business—and perhaps more festive notices of the fifth, 10th, and later anniversaries coupled with a request to increase balances, use other services, or refer other business to the bank—I was told the account did not meet the new balance requirements. This happened to a former chairman and the first general manager of the branch. I guess the bank became too big and too structured to consider such things, which is precisely my point. This is a great example of how not to market retail products.

A better policy would be to encourage all such deposits in every branch and subsidiary (London, Dublin, Paris, Brussels, Rome, Milan, Athens, Abu Dhabi, Seoul, Hong Kong, Singapore, Tokyo, Panama, Brazil, to name a few). Market the retail product within the local communities and introduce new and better products on a continuing basis. Once accepted, never, never kick a customer out the door without cause. If necessary, offer and market a substitute product. Upgrade the customer. Ask the customer to refer other business. But never tell an existing customer, "You are too small (or, your business is unprofitable), I cannot serve you."

This open and aggressive spirit guided First Chicago when we set out to build the international network, and did we ever succeed! Dick Thomas was drafted briefly from the domestic side by Gale Freeman to open the London branch and then headed the international department while I was opening the branches in Frankfurt and Beirut. He returned to domestic corporate banking after that stint. It was really Chauncey Schmidt who got the London branch off the ground and made it profitable. Typical of our attitude was our pioneering entry into the People's Republic of China. The operative command was get in, establish a beachhead, and build from there for centuries to come. Build the trade-related wholesale and build the retail, serve our customers setting up shop in those regions, and refer customers from one location to other installations served by the system.

A major initiative such as overseas expansion cannot be turned on and off every few years. Nor can the global marketing of retail product be turned on and off every few years. To be effective and to reap rewards for the shareholders, these strategies must be implemented with consistency over decades, ideally with a minimum of personnel changes. To do otherwise is to waste manpower and money and to lose other, alternative opportunities. Foreign banks opening branches and subsidiaries in the United States understood this. Hesitant, start-and-stop approaches are inimical to a major retail thrust.

Retail marketing, like product development, is both a science and an art. The science is to understand and traverse the myriad laws and regulations that govern the sale and distribution of financial instruments, particularly when dealing in multiple foreign jurisdictions. The art is capturing the attention of the right population to buy the product, recognizing an advantage in your brand. Brand differentiation, a concept more commonly associated with mass-market consumer goods, is essential with financial services or instruments that most people regard as all alike. Brand recognition should be identical with product differentiation in the target population's mind, even if the differentiation is an appearance of quality, superior service, safety, or ease of inquiry for explanations and detail.

We did not always succeed at communicating a brand identity. When First Chicago introduced IRAs in the Chicago market, the bank sponsored a half-hour classical music program on an FM radio station to reach the desired, upscale target market.

First Chicago's community development Vice President, Norman Ross, served as host. No one in the Chicago market was more beloved, admired and believed than Norman Ross, but the volume of IRA business generated wasn't all that great. It is hard to say what went wrong, but as best we could determine, we were too much of a soft sell, not crisply defining the solid benefits to be obtained, and not differentiating our brand from others offering the same service. Even in the high-net-worth market, it doesn't pay to be too genteel.

At Christmas time, First Chicago would market Christmas club accounts. As a promotion, we offered to sell watches, radios, television sets, toasters, jewelry, stuffed animals, and even travel tours at discount prices. First Chicago always excelled in this merchandising. One year Harris Bank offered a stuffed lion called Hubert and hired Gary Coleman to play the part of a youngster with eyes aglow, delighted to receive his lion. The television spots were devastating, and the Harris beat our socks off. Gary Coleman later went on to star in the television show, *Different Strokes*. Harris discovered a winner who could move a product.

We also did poorly in marketing services to high-net-worth customers. A major investment was made in refurbishing offices in First National Two to allow individual large depositors and senior corporate executives to gain immediate access to an account officer and to transact business quickly and conveniently. The Harris and the Northern Trust still beat us in consumers' perception and in new sales generated. We had a better product than the Harris' "personal banker," and a product as good or better than the Northern Trust, given our worldwide scope. But we failed to make an impact in the delivery of our message whether via direct mail, the printed media, or the electronic media.

On the plus side, we did well with marketing credit cards. The strategy was to grow the outstandings steadily but within controlled limits to keep credit quality from deteriorating and losses from escalating. This is the secret in all of banking: steady, programmatic, and moderate growth. The flashy, "go-go" alternative invites trouble.

Compare my strategy with that adopted by First Chicago after my departure. I had made the card system profitable even at a time of double-digit inflation and interest rates. Barry Sullivan's strategy was the same in general principle but different in that he jumped on the accelerator to increase outstandings. In an interview with a Smith Barney analyst, R.B. Albertson, on May 16, 1987, Mr. Sullivan said that First Chicago's credit card outstandings had grown from zero in 1966 to $800 million in 1982. They doubled that year with the acquisition of Bankers Trust Company's card operation, then doubled again to more than three billion dollars following direct-mail solicitation in 1983–84. Meanwhile, credit card losses, known as charge-offs, grew to 3.50 percent of outstanding loans in 1986 and will probably be closer to four percent in 1987.

I agree totally with Mr. Sullivan's desire to pursue the credit card business. My differences with him are solely with regard to speed and pricing. Heavy solicitation results in deterioration of credit quality. This means that prices must be kept high so that the borrowers who repay their loans cover the losses of those who don't pay. This creates pressure to build even greater volumes to keep the ratios in line, and meanwhile vulnerabilities continue to mount. Like everything in banking, good judgment is always a balancing act between quality and volume.

Under my stewardship, the bank promoted credit cards, but I also encouraged the expansion of the broad base of our retail savings product. We did well marketing most standard products, and we did particularly well with some new products such as the rare coins and precious metals. The general image campaign of "We are Chicago's Bank" was a clear winner both in the United States and abroad and is being repeated currently. Being Chicago's bank means finding product globally, packaging it in bite sizes for the retail market, and selling it. Solid, product-specific marketing is all the more important when the policy is to take wholesale products generally reserved for corporations, the rich, and the institutions, and break these products down into small-denomination units for marketing to the public.

I have already discussed the pioneering effort with retail bankers acceptances. We also studied foreign exchange contracts, all the products offered on the Chicago Board of Trade and the Mercantile Exchange, mortgage loan pools, instalment loan pools, and bond pools.

The objective of this product development research was to pull together a pool of assets, mortgages or instalment loans, and to sell undivided interests in a common pool in denominations as low as $1,000. The purpose was to provide upscale products to small retail customers at attractive rates from a source they trusted. This could also make home equity loans, real estate mortgage loans, and instalment loans self-liquidating at a time when deposits were both expensive and hard to obtain. A successful product in this area would not only have met a crying market need but also would have redressed the imbalance in our mix of fixed-rate assets and variable-rate liabilities during a period of rapidly escalating interest rates. My motives were to create new products for our retail customers. If it worked, we would clone the process for use in our overseas branches.

The difficulty was not conceptual but legal. The Law Department opined that certificates representing an undivided interest in the asset pool would have to be registered as securities. This meant that we, as a bank, would be prohibited from selling the certificates under the securities laws. Mechanics to work out these problems were being formulated when I left. Today, of course, they are attractive investment instruments.

The same was true with the bond portfolio. I was particularly interested in pooling the municipal bond portfolio and marketing it in small denominations at retail. If it worked, we would do the same thing with foreign currency denominated government bonds generated by our overseas branches.

I initiated the concept in 1975. New York was in the midst of a major credit crisis, and its bonds could not be refinanced. The Public Building Commission in Chicago was about to issue bonds and the underwriters were the Continental in the lead, the First, the Harris, and the Northern Trust. The prospectus was written, the bonds were placed, and the pricing meeting was to take place on the afternoon when news was received that the market had rejected a New York bond issue. John Perkins, president of Continental Illinois, called Mayor Daley's office and told the mayor's administrative assistant, Tom Donovan, that the sale would have to be called off because of market conditions. I was furious when I learned the news. Calling off the bond issue would have placed Chicago in the same questionable credit category as New York, while a successful issue would measurably differentiate Chicago from New York.

I checked with our Law Department to see if First Chicago could underwrite the whole issue if that should prove necessary. The general counsel said yes. I then called Tom Donovan, explained the dilemma in which Chicago found itself, and asked to speak to the mayor. Mayor Daley was out of town, but Tom thought he could reach him.

A short time later, the mayor called back. I explained the dilemma and strongly recommended that the issue go ahead as planned. His Honor was ecstatic. He asked, "Do you really think we can pull if off?" I told him I thought we could. He said, "I'm coming right back, let's meet in my office later this afternoon." I called John Perkins, explained the dilemma to him, and again urged that we go ahead. Now *he* was furious. He said the committee had met, had agreed to call off the issue, and it was dangerous to proceed. I told John that our bank was convinced it was best for the city to go forward and, if the Continental chose to drop out, we would pick up their share. John said, "You can't do that!" I told him that I could and would. He then said, "You leave us no other choice, we'll go ahead."

After that, it was easy. The Northern Trust and the Harris fully understood the problem and agreed to join in the issue. It went forward and was favorably received by the market. Mayor Daley was bubbling over with pride. Chicago was differentiated in the credit markets and held up as a shining example of "The City That Works." It was at this time that I wondered why, on future occasions, we couldn't purchase such bond issues in wholesale amounts, package the bonds in a pool, and sell small-denomination certificates of varying maturities to the citizens of Chicago. The professional bond markets be damned! The citizens of Chicago had faith in their city, and selling $25 million or $50 million of small-denomination bonds with shortened maturities over the course of a few days didn't seem like such a big deal. Or so I thought at the time.

As hard as we tried to find a legal mechanism to do this, we never succeeded. I still believe that there is a solution that will permit the bank to buy long-term municipal bonds (seven to 10 years) and sell short-maturity certificates (one to two years) to its customers. It would be good for everyone, including the municipalities.

I was prepared to do something along these lines when I made the offer to buy City of Chicago bonds at the time of Mayor Daley's death. Following the announcement of the mayor's death, the quoted price for Chicago bonds plunged. First Chicago promised to buy all the bonds offered at the price which existed on the day before the mayor's death. The price stabilized and no bonds were offered. If a large volume of the bonds had been presented pursuant to our offer, I was going to package them as "Daley bonds" to the small retail buyers, irrespective of the prohibitions imposed by prevailing legal opinions.

As an aside, there was also a technical problem with City of Chicago checks, signed by Mayor Daley. The city treasurer was uncertain whether the checks were good and whether the banks would honor them when presented for payment after the mayor's death. First Chicago pledged it would stand behind the checks, and thereafter there was no problem.

Today, there are interest-rate swaps and hedges for any and every type of financial security. The challenge for the retail banker is to put these services into small packages for sale at the retail level. If a homeowner takes out a home equity loan at a rate floating over prime, there is no reason why he or she shouldn't be able to hedge that rate of interest at some reasonable cost. The automobile instalment loan has been pretty well preempted by the captive auto finance companies. This should pose a challenge to the banks and thrifts to find a competitive product.

Retail banking is fascinating because it is not deposit gathering in the primitive sense. It is product development, marketing, and merchandising on a global scale—in short, mass merchandising. It requires commitment of talent and money. It also requires scale to afford the electronic support systems so essential to make loan and deposit administration safe and convenient.

The need for scale poses a real challenge for the smaller banks and thrifts who wish to remain independent. How can any one of them afford the talent base to produce product, to finance advertising and marketing programs competitive with the giants, and to pay for the elaborate and expensive operating systems?

The truth is they cannot unless they federate together. Generally, they have good delivery systems within their communities and good rapport with customers. What they lack is product development capability and operating systems to keep administrative procedures in proper order. A group of independents could join together to fill that gap. Or, independents can pay fees to become franchisees of larger institutions. Or, independents can band together and buy a larger institution. Clearly, they will have to do something. But, no matter what they do, the total number of banks and thrifts will progressively decline. Consolidations and buy-outs will take their toll. To some degree, we must control this evolution and not let the United States lapse into the Canadian model, which has far too few depository and lending institutions for its size. There is a strong need for independents to keep the chain banks competitive and in check.

The key to survival will be product development combined with merchandising and marketing. It will not be sufficient simply to have location or longevity or good standing within the community. Joining forces with mass merchandisers like Sears, J.C. Penney, Wards, Venture, K Mart, or others may be a solution for some. A small booth or counter space in the store might feature "blue light" specials on certificates of deposit, car loans, mortgages, or credit cards. Some may say that this isn't sufficiently dignified for banking, but they miss the point. I am talking about product distribution centers in the retailing chains. The brand name on the product will reflect the dignity of a bank's friendly home office. Admittedly, there is a certain solemnity and hallowed image associated with banking institutions as storehouses of value. That is why the first coinage came from the religious temples where people worshiped, and the coins often carried religious symbols on their faces. Banking remains a dignified business where integrity must be without compromise. Therein lies the challenge, to build a differentiated brand identity while simultaneously utilizing all the modern delivery systems for effective, convenient distribution.

Don Perkins, the former chairman of Jewel Companies, used to tell me that the Jewel supermarkets in Illinois were the largest check cashing facilities in the state. He said that nearly half their assets were checks in the process of collection. He, as much as anyone, was interested in the establishment of a cash disbursement network like Cash Station. Today, there is even greater opportunity to utilize the electronic media as a delivery system, as well as the telephone and personal computers. This presents an opportunity for banks and thrifts. Produce product, establish the brand, get distribution points, and then market with skill and imagination.

FOURTEEN

Trust Banking

Trust banking is a prestige business, at the opposite pole from retail banking. Trust is compatible with the culture of some institutions, and not so compatible with the culture of others. To be successful in the trust business, a bank has to communicate a certain attitude internally and externally. It is a style, an image, a certain gentility that attaches to the institution and generates confidence and respect. In Chicago, the Northern Trust has it more than Continental Illinois, and the Harris Trust has it more than First Chicago.

One of my long-range priorities when I was chief executive of First Chicago was to improve our position in the trust market. Unlike retail, trust is not a business that lends itself to aggressive turnaround through innovative new products and heavy mass promotion. Quite the contrary, it is like the refurbishing of a fine, old restaurant that has fallen on hard times. It requires a quiet upgrading of existing product, the introduction of high-quality, modern products, and, above all, word-of-mouth advertising by satisfied customers.

Trust is a business of caring for people, their families, and their treasured possessions with love and tenderness. It requires its own identity and separate premises that exude stability and tradition. Oak paneled walls, leather chairs, and traditional oil portraits of 18th and 19th century curmudgeons aren't bad. Exquisite modern furniture with teak floors, liberally laced with fine, sturdy antiques and high-quality traditional art is okay. Unfortunately, at First Chicago I inherited functional, nondescript furniture in a modern glass-and-granite skyscraper, where the decor featured a budding collection of modern art. It was good art very capably assembled by a top professional, Katharine Kuh, and it constituted an excellent investment for First Chicago. But, somehow, it just didn't enhance the spirit of the trust environment.

To improve our trust capabilities, I turned to Charles Woodford, whom I had hired from American National Bank before its merger with First Chicago. Chuck was a traditionalist and believed, as I did, in personal service. Today, he is chairman and chief executive of Trust Services of America, Inc., California Federal's trust subsidiary.

What I lacked was a chief investment officer to succeed Waid Vanderpoel, the chief financial officer, then nearing retirement. Waid was largely responsible for building the surplus in First Chicago's pension fund, a surplus that was taken into First Chicago earnings in 1986. It is the chief investment officer who prepares the list of approved securities from which trust officers make their investment selections for the individual accounts they manage. The chief investment officer also establishes the investment philosophy of the institution and makes judgments as to market timing and the condition of the relevant economies around the world. All these activities are done with the advice, counsel, and ratification of the Trust Investment Committee, a group of insiders and/or outsiders selected for their knowledge and judgment of markets and industries. The undertaking is not inconsequential. First Chicago oversaw some $30 billion in trust assets.

The chief investment officer we retained was Gary Brinson, whom Chuck Woodford discovered at Travelers Insurance. The management at Travelers was furious about losing Gary. Chuck and I went to Hartford to mollify the Travelers management (Travelers is an important customer of First Chicago) and we both pledged that Gary would have a long and rewarding career as an officer at the bank. Today, he is president of First Chicago Investment Management, a wholly-owned investment advisory company of First Chicago.

Other key functions in a trust department are legal and operations. Both were well staffed in my day and, to my knowledge, are today. Legal is important because of the fiduciary responsibilities peculiar to the trust business. Trustees are often sued by beneficiaries for losing money in the portfolio, for paying the wrong beneficiary, or for failing to distribute income. Operations is important because of the millions of daily transactions that take place around the world in a big trust operation.

What has not continued at First Chicago, I believe, is my commitment to a separate, stand-alone Trust Department with an identity of its own and a reputation for refined, individual, personal service and excellence in every category of performance. I viewed the Trust Department as a core business unit, both within the United States and abroad, serving middle-income to high-net-worth individuals. The opportunity to serve non-U.S. residents was particularly attractive, and, with that thought in mind, we built First Chicago's Swiss offices in Zurich and Geneva.

Today, many banking companies reject such a commitment to the trust business as old fashioned. They have chosen to merge their trust operations with retail operations, creating one integrated "individual banking" business. I suppose the theory is to cross-sell products from one area to another. It is a theory that has yet to be proven successful over time. I personally believe that the trust and retail functions are inherently different, the legal accountabilities are different, and the culture and training of the personnel must of necessity be different.

Trust, as a concept in the Anglo-American legal tradition, stems from the Statute of Uses passed in England in 1536. Simply stated, the statute converted beneficial ownership of property to an actual right of ownership, that could be protected legally, even though the legal title was in someone else's name. The law protected the rights of lords and barons and knights to enjoy the benefits of land that the king permitted them to use, while actual title to the land remained with the king.

From this sprang an entire body of law setting forth a trustee's duties and obligations to his principal, known as the trustor. The trustor entrusts something of value to another person, the trustee, to manage. Under common law and now by actual legislation, a trustee cannot be in conflict with or compete with his or her principal. Trustees owe the principals a duty of care, and they cannot take advantage of their position to reap personal gain at the expense of their principals.

This is why the trust business is different from retail banking or personal banking or even special "private banking" for high-net-worth individuals. In regular banking, the institution provides a service with a simple duty of care. By contrast, trust banking involves management and stewardship and a duty that is more demanding than mere care. It involves a relationship of trust.

Banks and thrifts that combine personal or retail banking with their trust activities are blurring this important distinction. At some point, lawsuits will attempt to reestablish the differences in accountability to the customer based on the type of service performed. It could mean trouble for the banks. It could even lead to legislation mandating that there be a separate company with its own capital to perform trust services.

This type of separation could make sense because of the highly personal services promised over long periods of time. It can take two or three generations or more before the obligations of a trust are fulfilled and the trust is terminated. Such a lengthy period of obligation is inconsistent with the theory of letting mismanaged banks fail and go out of business. A trustee cannot be allowed to gamble or put in jeopardy the capital that supports his or her obligations of duty and care for generations to come. A trustee must have different standards and accountabilities than an entrepreneurially oriented banker or thrift executive.

There are several types of trust activities serving individuals and corporations.

The personal trust business is very big and potentially very profitable. This is where an individual gives money or other assets to a bank or a thrift to manage for a specified time: for a lifetime, until the children reach a certain age, or, in the case of charities, perhaps forever. Personal trusts are also created in wills. For example, a will might name First Chicago as executor of an estate, a procedure called *naming a corporate executor*. After probate and the closing of the estate, the will might direct First Chicago to establish a trust to direct predetermined amounts of income, and sometimes principal as well, to be paid out to the deceased person's family, perhaps into future generations as well. Proceeds from insurance policies may also be used to fund such trusts. These are called insurance trusts.

For this service, the banks or qualified thrifts charge a fee. The service includes investment of the money in the trust in accordance with the criteria established by the person who set up the trust. If no investment standard is specified, then the trustee must be guided by the so called "prudent man" rule, which states, in effect, that the trustee may only make investments of the type that a careful person investing his or her own money might make.

The service also includes timely collection of interest and dividends, timely presentation of securities for cash calls or tenders, or any action required to keep the assets fully invested and managed prudently. Accounting and preparation of tax returns are also part of the service.

Sometimes unique assets are included in the trust, and the trustee is directed to care for these assets. Such items might include pets, artwork, real estate, museums, sports teams—almost anything the mind can imagine.

Overall, trust is a unique and special relationship, lasting long after people's deaths and requiring banks to do what they would do if they were alive to do it. It is people's loved ones that they are placing in a financial institution's care.

The trust business also includes the management of what we used to call at First Chicago "the closely held unit," or a business that was owned by the trust customer when he or she died. The customer may have willed the business to the trust to be managed, or to be managed and sold, or to be managed and liquidated, or whatever. These businesses often have unique needs as they include such various enterprises as professional sports franchises, resorts, gambling casinos, private zoos, factories, or farms. When presented with such a challenge, the trustee must hire a manager, supervise his or her activities, and then execute the instructions contained in the trust. For a banker, assignment to trust department service is both interesting and personally rewarding because of the variety and unpredictability of the challenges to be met. At one time, the Northern Trust had a team of agricultural experts just to manage the farm properties in its overall trust portfolio.

Trust departments also provide escrow services. An escrow service is sometimes needed when two or more parties are fulfilling the terms of a contract. A buyer of a home or a building might say, "I'll leave the money in a special account at the bank and instruct the bank to pay you the money when you have delivered clear title and all the documents needed to complete the sale." When the seller accepts, a bank or thrift is selected to set up the escrow account. Generally, provision is made to invest the funds, and instructions are provided in the escrow document as to delivery of the interest or gain, if any, and who is to bear the loss, if any.

Any number of transactions require escrow arrangements, for example, the sale of a business, the purchase of a race horse, or damages for matters in litigation or arbitration. This is an important service that works only because both sides trust the integrity and security of the escrow holder.

Then, there are trust services performed for corporations. These include serving as registrar or transfer agent for the stocks issued by a corporation to its shareholders. Whenever you buy a share of stock, the certificate issued for your account must be registered. And, if you sell the share of stock, the certificate you send in to the broker must be transferred over to the new owner. These functions are performed by bank trust departments for a fee. The annual reports of publicly held corporations usually list the names of the registrar and the transfer agent.

Corporate trust also includes serving as trustee on public issues of bonds or debentures. And the service is not limited to corporate securities but extends as well to issues of bonds and debt instruments by states, municipalities, school districts, or public housing authorities and public transportation agencies. The duty of the trustee is to monitor the progress of the borrower, be it a corporation or government agency, and to protect bondholders by declaring a default whenever the covenants made in the indenture (the loan agreement) are not met. Such defaults might occur when revenues are insufficient to cover payment of interest or principal, when restricted assets are pledged to some other lender, when the money is used for a prohibited purpose, in the event of catastrophe such as a fire or casualty loss, if agreements are breached with other lenders, or when a borrower declares bankruptcy.

Trust banking is not riskless business. In fact, for a lending institution, there are subtle dangers. A 1930s legal decision, in the Dabney case, ruled that, if an institution were both a lender and a trustee, and if the credit went bad, then the loan would automatically be subordinated to the bond issue. In other words, the bond obligation would be repaid before the loan.

Consider the consequences for a bank that makes a short-term working capital loan to a transportation authority to meet its payroll. At the same time the bank serves as trustee on one of its bond issues. Assume that, for whatever reason, the authority is lacking in funds and defaults on one of the loan covenants in the bond indenture. The working capital loan may then become subordinated, or junior, to the rights of the bondholders.

Or, consider the case of a public utility. Bond trusteeships are routinely solicited by lending institutions, the same institutions that are typically lead commercial lenders to the same utility. Imagine the impact on the lending institution in a situation such as that of Washington State Public Power Supply System, WPPSS, which declared bankruptcy and defaulted on its debt. It is a predicament to be avoided.

When I was at First Chicago, approval to take on a trusteeship where the bank was already a senior lender had to be approved by one of the top three officers. The last thing we wanted was to find ourselves in a situation where we believed we were protected as senior creditors, only to find ourselves at the "bottom of the totem pole," junior to the bondholders.

Another corporate trust activity is the compilation and recordkeeping of all of a corporation's investments in pension and profit sharing accounts. This is called "master trust." Some banks, for example The Northern Trust of Chicago, do it very well. Essentially, it involves recordkeeping and making sure the securities are all accounted for and in hand. Corporations like to have different investment managers invest portions of the overall pension or profit sharing fund in order to stimulate competition in maximizing performance. However, it would be chaos if the individual managers kept their own records and were responsible for the physical holding of securities. So, a system has been developed where one bank is the keeper of all the records and the securities, provides a monthly report, prepares performance analyses, and executes purchases and sales under orders from the various investment managers. It is a good, fee-based business for those of good reputation able to generate enough business volume to pay for the sophisticated electronics necessary to make the business profitable.

Trust departments are also major corporate money managers. Under the guidance of the chief investment officer, a team of portfolio managers invests money for corporate, union, or public authority pension funds and profit-sharing plans. The amount of money locked up in pension and profit-sharing accounts is in the $100 billion-plus range. These funds are the true owners of America's corporations and real estate. They have large portfolios of bonds, equities, real estate holdings, and foreign securities.

Generally, boards of directors or trustees of unions or public authorities are not equipped to invest these large sums on a day-to-day basis. Typically a Fortune 500 or Forbes 500 company might have $100 million to one billion dollars or more in pension and profit sharing accounts. These are big sums, requiring a fiduciary duty of care because the money belongs to the employees and offers protection for their old age. So, managements and boards of directors, union officers or public authority trustees select a professional money manager to handle all or part of the account.

The professional money manager may be an individual or a corporation set up for that purpose, or a bank trust department. The amounts allocated to an individual manager by a large corporation or union may range from five million dollars to $500 million. The fee to the investment manager may be 0.5 percent to one percent of the amount under management (or less in the case of a bond fund manager). This is very desirable business because it requires virtually no capital. It does require talent—people who have the judgment, knowledge and decisiveness to outperform the market on a consistent basis. In essence, it is a form of informed gambling, but so is every type of investment activity. The key is to be successful in comparison with other money managers. A report from the master trust bank measures the investment performance, and corporate directors and union officers decide whether to keep or change investment managers based on the performance record.

Sometimes, instead of managing a portfolio of publicly traded bonds and equities (stocks), investment managers may establish a fund in which they issue "participation certificates." For example, one certificate may be worth one percent of the fund. To place these certificates, the investment manager must describe the nature of the fund in a report called a *prospectus*. There is no limit to the nature and variety of these funds. Some of the more popular ones have been formed to invest in real estate and foreign stocks and bonds. The Japanese and London stock markets are particular favorites.

To handle all the various kinds of trust transactions, a trading desk is a necessity. Much like a trading desk in a brokerage house, it buys and sells securities on any and all of the exchanges around the world. Because it is generally not a member of the exchange, it places orders through established brokers who are members. The sheer volume of the business is attractive to brokers, so trust departments get the most favorable fee available. In addition, trust departments get investment advice from the brokers. They pay for it with "soft dollars"—the continuing heavy flow of orders to buy and sell stocks and bonds. The bank or thrift can also offer its customers discount brokerage services; that is, customers who place buy or sell orders through the bank or thrift get the benefit of the low price that a broker charges the institution. By charging a small markup to the borrowing customer, the discount brokerage business becomes a profit center.

In most trust department activities, questions of conflict and duty are always present. For example, if the trading desk chooses to place more volume with a broker who charges slightly more but who gives better investment advice than a competitor, is it entitled to pass along the full brokerage commission to the individual accounts for which the trades are made? Or, if there is discretionary investment authority in a personal trust account, and if the beneficiary of that account is also a borrower in the personal banking department, should investments be made to increase current income to service the loan? Or should the investment be in securities that are more likely to increase in long-term value so that the heirs will get more when the life beneficiary dies?

Conflict questions like these must be answered every day of every week by those responsible for trust banking.

There are no hard and fast rules. Confidence in the decision-making process comes from putting professionals of undisputed integrity in charge. As in all banking matters, strong, recognizable leadership is all important in setting the standards. With trust activities in particular, the leader should be a person of reputation and stature.

FIFTEEN

Operations

Operations is the least publicized but the most important aspect of banking. It is the support system upon which every other activity depends. There is no such thing as a good bank or a good thrift without a good operations department as its foundation. One of the top three officers in any depository or financial services organization should be an operations officer, and every trainee in the management development program should serve a tour of duty in operations.

Operations consists of keeping the books and records, but it is also much, much more. It is administration, premises, insurance, communications, security, auditing, loan and asset review, management information systems, product development, customer service, labor relations, housekeeping and appearance, care and feeding, medical and first aid, and the list could go on and on. Operations is a business in itself.

Keeping the books and records is no small feat. The number of transactions to be tracked ranges from hundreds per day in a small depository to hundreds of thousands, if not millions, in a big bank or thrift. Remember, we are talking about facilities around the world, operating seven days a week, 24 hours a day. They are dealing with checks written and deposited, foreign exchange bought and sold, bonds and securities traded, loans made and repaid, interest and dividends paid and received, escrows, guarantees, accommodations to travelers, support systems for stock and commodity exchanges—transactions galore on every continent, in every country, and in every community throughout the world. The books of the world's banks are, in the aggregate, a global financial EKG that is remarkable and wondrous to contemplate and interpret.

The money and banking system comes into play whether we are harvesting and selling crops, or manufacturing or selling product, or traveling to some resort, or taking out insurance, or restructuring our investment portfolios, or just buying an article of clothing or art or household utensil. Our bank accounts go up or down, the cash in our pockets circulates faster or slower to one economic sector or another, and all of this is recorded by the operations departments of banks and thrift institutions. The statistics come together on the books of individual institutions and are forwarded to the local Federal Reserve Bank or Federal Home Loan Bank for consolidation into the national figures. Government agencies use the national figures to compile economic reports. The national figures then go to the International Monetary Fund for compilation in the world figures.

At each institution, this process of recording, compiling, and balancing requires efficient and careful administrative practices. Individual units and departments perform designated functions like selling travelers checks, taking deposits, or making loans. Each must have the right number of people to handle the business, the proper supervision to oversee the work, and detailed policies and procedures specifying how the work is to be done. Training and professional education must go on continuously and everyone must be conditioned to work closely with the auditors, who conduct their audits on a regular but unscheduled basis.

The auditing department is a key ingredient of proper operations. Some banks and thrifts use the auditing department as a training ground for future managers. Some banks have a special group of traveling auditors who visit business borrowers to determine if the information they provide the bank is accurate, if collateral is being maintained as promised, and if the housekeeping and management are up to agreed standards. These traveling auditors can pay for themselves many times over by keeping the bank out of trouble both before and after a loan is made. First Chicago was spared considerable agony in the famous "Salad Oil" scandal, when bank loans were being secured by a supposed cache of salad oil. First Chicago's auditors checked before the loan was disbursed and could not locate the oil.

In the Billie Sol Estes scandal, loans were being obtained from banks against computer print-outs of mobile liquid fertilizer tanks. Again, the loan officer was sufficiently knowledgeable to dissuade his superior from proceeding, and First Chicago did not make the loan.

Auditors also travel to branches, subsidiaries, and anywhere the institution has an installation in the United States and abroad. Their job is to check the flow of work, the morale and attitude of the staff, and the books and records to determine if all is being handled in accordance with prescribed policy. Sometimes, there is tension between the staff conducting regular operations and the auditors. The staff considers them a burden to be suffered. However, the auditors always find little slippages, and a well functioning organization will welcome them as a help in maintaining and improving the efficiency of its departments.

Good auditors purposely program false balances in collection accounts and deviations in the operating system. As the books and records track through the bank, two and two don't always add up to four, by design. The purpose is to set traps for anyone trying to falsify or "cook" the books. The misbalances or "traps" are changed irregularly, and their nature and presence are closely guarded secrets. So also are the codes to authorize money transfers and movements of negotiable instruments and other valuables.

The head auditor is a very important senior member of the management hierarchy. Normally, he or she reports directly to the board of directors, by-passing all intermediate management. At least once a year, he or she should make a special report to the full board of directors, giving the audit department's opinion of the value of each category of asset on the balance sheet and assuring the board that the liabilities are as recorded. There should also be a special report on the extent and nature of the contingent liabilities, with an estimate of the likelihood that these contingent liabilities will become actual liabilities.

The head auditor not only must be experienced and capable, but also must have a total knowledge of the institution. Credibility and integrity are paramount. Whenever a head auditor resigns or takes early retirement, the board should insist on a full-scale inquiry as a precaution. The head auditor is a key component of the institution's overall security system.

Security in a depository institution is a big responsibility, beginning with the security of the physical premises worldwide. Unfortunately, robberies and attempted robberies are still a way of life. At one time, First Chicago had the third largest police force in the State of Illinois, behind only the State of Illinois and the City of Chicago. It was a highly professional force whose members not only safeguarded the premises but also aided customers with knowledgeable answers to their questions, directions to the location of various services, and one-on-one assistance to the elderly or handicapped. The security force was often the first contact between the customer and the bank. Its appearance and demeanor were important. To maintain an alert, service-oriented tone, I encouraged the force to excel in competitive activities, not the least of which was their participation in the drill team. It won several championships and always had a high ranking in the national standings. I asked it to perform at correspondent conferences, and other bank events. I viewed it as psychic recognition for a first-rate group whose sharpness and competitive excellence were important ingredients in the overall operation of the bank. For the same reason I encouraged other mens' and womens' teams to foster pride, tradition and a spirit of belonging throughout the rank and file.

The drill team's record of excellence carried over to its guard and other duties. I do not remember one successful armed robbery, although there were frequent attempts. Almost all who tried were caught and physically overpowered, which attests to the training and coordination with the teller staff. There were also some humorous incidents.

I remember one case where a would-be robber approached a teller counter at 8:30 a.m. and slipped a note to the woman behind the window. The woman read the note, which said, "This is a stick-up, give me all your money." The woman looked up at the man and said, "I can't do that, I'm the auditor. You will have to come back at 9:00 a.m." The man said, "Oh, I'm sorry. Can I please have my note back?" The note was returned and the man left.

Sure enough, at 9:00 a.m., the man returned and presented the same note to the teller serving the same counter. The bank police, having been alerted by the auditor, were waiting for him.

Of course, there are always serious armed robbery attempts. In addition, there are attempts to pass counterfeit money, travelers checks, and forged checks and passbooks. There are also the more sophisticated frauds, such as forged or counterfeit securities used as collateral, or penetration of the wire network to transfer money fraudulently. I was always fearful that someone would find a way to transfer unauthorized money to a place such as Brazil or the Philippines, where the United States had no extradition treaties. Fortunately, I never had to confront such a situation, although there have been reported cases of illegal transfers at other banks.

I did face one frustrating dilemma which puzzles me even to this day.

One weekend in 1977, I attended a conference of business and media leaders sponsored by Fred Friendly, a Columbia University professor and dean of the media establishment. Toward the end of the conference, I was called by the head auditor and informed that exactly one million dollars in U.S. currency was missing from the main vault. I did not become overly concerned, figuring that the missing million dollars was nothing more than an accounting error. Such an error would not be all that unusual where different denominations of bills have to be counted, sub-totaled and then totaled. The fact that it was an even one million dollars made this conclusion possible.

When I returned to Chicago, I found that our bank police force, the head auditor, the senior operations officer, and the Chicago Police Department were convinced that the money had disap-peared over the weekend. We frequently had a special shift work over the weekend when the race tracks were open to prepare cur-rency for delivery to the race tracks and to receive money from them. We always assigned a trusted employee of long tenure to supervise this effort. Every precaution seemed to have been taken, and every operating procedure appears to have been followed. Chicago police detectives to this day are convinced they know how it was done and that it was professionally planned and ex-ecuted. The Chicago newspapers covered the story as an intrig-uing mystery. The bank, of course, cooperated fully with the federal, state, and city officials who investigated the matter, and the bank's self-insurance policy covered the loss. Yet, there was never sufficient evidence to bring an indictment.

I was told that the robbery was planned and ordered by profes-sional criminals and that ties were established to an employee through family connections. Apparently, these connections could not have been discovered by our security personnel because of some special arrangement with the FBI to hide the identity. It all sounded mysterious and fanciful to me until I read Ron Koziol's story in the *Chicago Tribune* which reported the following:

> Twenty-three $100 bills taken in the unsolved theft of one million dollars from the First National Bank of Chicago dur-ing the Columbus Day weekend of 1977 have turned up as part of a suspected narcotics payoff in Savannah, GA.
>
> It is the first time any money from that theft has been reco-vered by law enforcement authorities. Officers said the

condition of the bills indicated that they had been buried for some time. They also had holes 'like tiny acid burns,' investigators said.

FBI sources said the agency would try to determine whether Brooks, who never worked for the Chicago bank, had any connection with a key suspect in the 1977 theft, a west suburban employee who refused to take a lie-detector test after the theft and was fired.[12]

The story simply illustrates that, even with the best of procedures and precautions, there is still room for mysterious disappearance. When it comes to security, there is never room for relaxation or complacency.

I seriously doubt whether our system of crime prevention and enforcement is adequate for the challenge. Look at the burden and expense imposed on society because of terrorism. The airport security systems alone cost the consuming public billions of dollars a year. Visas are now required by nations such as France that heretofore did not require such precautions. Public places, parking garages, storage warehouses, financial institutions, and even our own homes require special security measures. I wonder whether our system of punishment and deterrence is sufficient for the task at hand, and this goes for white-collar crime as well.

I do not envy judges who have the responsibility of meting out sentences. The judge is, first and foremost, a lawyer. He or she is an expert in administering the trial or the appellate process. But, what makes judges experts on the current temper of societal needs? I would bet that, if sentencing decisions were entrusted to the juries (even if only advisory to the judge), the overall crime rate would drop considerably. Certainly something needs to be done, because the present system is not working and the financial system, like other units of society, is therefore vulnerable.

Part of a bank's security function is to provide for offsite record storage in case of a major disaster that could demolish primary

---

[12]Ron Koziol, "First National Loot Found in Savannah" *Chicago Tribune*, 5 May 1981.

facilities and all the records they house. Major regional operations centers, with all their computers, disc drives and stored memories, need to have disaster plans. There must be daily transfers of data to secure underground facilities so that if a natural or man-made disaster strikes, the necessary information can be reconstructed promptly.

First Chicago had just such an incident back in 1871 during the Chicago fire. It destroyed most of the city, including the new bank building. The story goes that the cashier, the officer in charge of the records, visited the charred ruins to see what could be salvaged. As he was surveying the charred wreckage in deep contemplation, a customer approached the cashier and asked for his money. The story says that he was quickly repaid and his account closed.

Another customer approached and asked if the bank was okay. Assured that it was, the customer wished the cashier good luck and, thereafter, was always accorded the status of a valued account.

A third customer approached and asked what he could do to help the bank. He was elected a director.

Obviously, the goodwill and loyalty of the customer base is paramount to the success of any depository institution. But so also is good housekeeping. Good housekeeping means the ability to compile and maintain accurate records and the ability to reconstruct these records in the event of emergency or disaster. Someday we will probably store duplicate records on satellites in space as still another precaution.

Banking is 50 percent the efficient, timely and accurate management of records and information, and 50 percent everything else. Just imagine the work involved, considering the millions and millions of daily transactions, in compiling routine reports such as annual and quarterly reports, 10K and 10Q forms, tax returns, reserve requirement reports, daily position sheets for trading departments, spread analysis reports, profit center reports, daily liquidity reports, monthly customer statements, trust department reports, trust customer statements, customer tax returns for trust accounts, loan review and classification reports, just to name a few. If all the reports prepared during the course of a year by a major money market bank were listed in a single-spaced column of titles, the index would probably be as large as a good-sized telephone book. To know and understand each of these reports is the function of the chief auditor. First Chicago had two of the best in Charlie Meyer and Marion English. The people they trained are countless in number, including me.

One of the areas in which both Charlie Meyer and Marion English took particular pride was loan review and classification. This function is often labeled "difficult to manage" because it requires coordination and cooperation by four different disciplines: the Operations Department, which houses the discount or loan disbursement function; the Controller's Department, which tabulates the books and records; the Law Department, which handles the documentation; and the Audit Department, which reviews the process to determine if everything is being done the way it is supposed to be done in accordance with prescribed rules and procedures. Loan review and classification is where Continental Illinois reportedly ran into difficulty. Yet, it is the guts of any depository and banking institution. The key is discipline and the priority accorded to the maintenance of discipline.

I instituted a procedure whereby the loan officer, upon making a loan, rates the quality of the business at the time the loan is made. Subsequently, the loan review people rate the files using four separate classifications on a scale of one through five. The classifications were: 1) creditworthiness; 2) pricing; 3) documentation; and 4) legal sufficiency for enforcement. As each loan file was received, the scores would be entered into the computer so that our management would have a continuous running index of the quality of the portfolio. The program was just getting underway when I left. It was probably discontinued after my departure. Nonetheless, it is a good system and I would heartily recommend its adoption to all bank managements and particularly to outside audit committees of boards of directors.

Testimony in the 1987 trial of the case brought by the FDIC against Ernst & Whinney, Continental Illinois Corporation's auditors, revealed a fatal breakdown in procedures.

Outside directors are at the mercy of the internal management information system, and the adequacy of the internal management information system is primarily a reflection of the organization's internal culture. The internal culture is determined by the chief executive officer and the senior management and the degree to which they feel accountable to priorities established by the directors. Thus, the process is circular. If the boss thinks a particular activity is important because he believes the board will hold him accountable, then that activity will be conducted properly and the necessary information will flow upward. Conversely, if he or she does not feel accountable or if neither the CEO nor the board deems an activity important, then it will receive short shrift.

The problem with the Continental Bank, at least as it appeared to an outsider and a direct competitor, was that internal controls and loan classifications were not accorded high priority. In fact, the whole process was regarded as "back-room stuff." The princes of the organization were the new-business loan officers, and the lower echelons of this cadre were the business school graduates who matriculated in the late 1960s and 1970s. This was the era of "grand hauteur" when operations, memo writing, and "number crunching" were considered demeaning—duties to be relegated to other, lower-paid people. In fact, up against such an attitude, the so-called "back-office people" don't stand a chance. When they complain to the loan officers that proper documentation or spread sheets have not been received, they are often told to disburse funds anyway upon authority of the loan officer or risk reprimand for interfering with an important customer relationship. In such a climate, the operations officer generally backs off, and the results are what happened to Continental.

The culture of an organization is what the chief executive and the board of directors mandate it to be. If the audit controls, the asset classification procedures, and management information systems are inadequate, it's because the chief executive and the board of directors allowed this to happen.

And the danger is not just with tardy or nonexistent loan classifications. It is with every activity in which the bank is engaged, including trading activities, trust services, and retail banking. This is particularly critical for the very large retail banks with wide-ranging subsidiary and branch systems. The margins are very narrow and the overhead per transaction is generally high because it is a people-intensive business. You need lots of people with their salaries and benefits to handle many small, low-profit transactions. So cost control, efficiency, management of capital expenditures, maintenance of margins, and mechanization are critical. This is where the operations department becomes the best asset a bank or savings and loan can have to maintain an aggressive position in the market with good, sound, safe, and profitable business.

Operations is a science that translates into a marketing asset or a marketing liability, depending on how well it is managed. It is not, as some loan officers sometimes view it, a back-office clerical activity that is nothing more than a support system for the more glamorous new-business activities. Any financial institution that fosters this attitude will eventually face difficulties. Operations is like engineering in a manufacturing facility. The sales department can sell the product, but if the engineering department can't build it or can't maintain quality control, then the business will suffer.

Continuous contact with the operations department, its requirements, capabilities, and limitations, is a paramount responsibility of each board member. This is why it is important that one of the top three officers of the institution have an operations background and that this person be a member of the board of directors.

SIXTEEN

Commercial Banking

Commercial banking always has been, is now, and ever will be the core business for commercial banks. Moreover, it will soon become the same for the savings institutions that adjust successfully to deregulated markets.

As the name implies, *commercial banking* is the business of serving commerce, whether it be handling checks, making payments, advancing loans, issuing letters of credit or guarantees, buying and selling foreign money, handling real estate transactions, providing information and financing for foreign trade, managing pension funds, and serving the employees of business customers. If the heartbeat of America is business and jobs, and I believe it is, then the lungs of America are the commercial banks and thrifts, because these vehicles provide business with the oxygen for vigor and growth.

Business is not just large corporations, although they play a significant role. Business is commerce in all forms and sizes. It is the corner drug store, the local real estate agent, the butcher, the baker, the contractor, the grocer, the tailor, the dressmaker, the farmer, the seed merchant, the farm supply store, the cartage company, the printer, the publisher. It is every conceivable service, manufacturing, agricultural, and retailing activity. It is sales and advertising, news gathering and broadcasting, and health care. It is everything that absorbs our everyday labors and activities.

Business is, of course, also General Motors, General Electric, Westinghouse, IBM, and the oil companies. It is what makes America tick. When business is good, America is good. When business is bad, America is in trouble. And the squire of business, the necessary support system, is commercial banking.

No business, no matter how small or simple, can operate without a bank, if for no other reason than to accept deposits and clear checks. When I use the word *bank,* I do so in a generic sense, because it is no longer possible for savings and loans and thrifts to stay out of this business and still thrive and prosper. I contend this having served as a director of a large money center bank, a director of a much smaller regional bank, and a director of a savings and loan association. Savings institutions are going to have to accept the fact that they must either serve business as well as homeowners or find themselves absorbed by institutions that are broader in function and scope.

I know this thinking runs contrary to that of many savings and loan executives. But it is a fact of life and those executives had better lead, follow, or get out of the way. America needs the savings of its communities put to work, and for the foreseeable future, the pressing need is for jobs. To create jobs, we need to encourage, serve and stimulate business. No financial institution which is granted a precious charter, such as the right to collect and invest the savings from its market territory, should be permitted to say, "I am a savings and loan and I won't participate because I haven't done so historically, I don't know how, and I don't feel comfortable." To thrift executives who persist in this attitude, I can only say, "Learn, baby learn."

One major difference between commercial banking and investment banking is that commercial banking depends for profitability on an overall relationship that endures over a long time span. Investment banking is more transaction oriented. The value added is the willingness to serve as an intermediary between the borrower and the lender. This role of an intermediary, or go-between, is paid for in fees when the transaction is completed.

Commercial banking, on the other hand, generally does not involve being a broker or intermediary. It is normally a one-on-one relationship whereby the bank grants the borrower a line of credit that the borrower can use in whole or in part as the business situation dictates. The bank derives its profits by handling all the transactions required by the individual business. It provides a support system for the business customer on a day-to-day basis.

The secret of successful commercial banking is to have a strong balance sheet and, therefore, to be able to attract money at lower cost than a competitor because you are viewed as safe and risk-less. It stands to reason that, if you pay less than anyone else for money, you can afford to lend at lower cost to the borrower. And by being the low-cost supplier of funds, you can require the strictest credit standards and make the safest loans.

This strategy was the one I chose to adopt. It meant a major policy reversal because I perceived a cyclical shift in profitability from wholesale commercial lending to retail lending. First Chicago began its reorientation in that direction when I took over in 1975, only to reverse again after my departure in 1980.

I perceived major risk in the credit quality standards being applied, particularly by our principal competitor, Continental Illinois, and decided that the prudent course of action was to wait until conditions were more favorable to build the kind of commercial loan portfolio that would conform to my overall strategy.

This approach is not necessarily right for everyone. In fact, it would be a sorry market if everyone chose the same course of action. That is the danger of nationalized banking. There would tend to be a conformity of credit standards that would dominate and suffocate the marketplace. America would not want this. We need diversity. And risk lenders are as important to the commercial marketplace as conservative lenders. In fact, there is a certain pride and *esprit* that attaches to the risk lenders, which is not generally found among the stolid, conservative lenders. Some of the great names in banking were extraordinarily able risk lenders, such as Serge Semenenko of the First National Bank of Boston and Walter Heymann of First Chicago. These bankers knew people, bet on people, and were far more often right than wrong.

The important thing is to know where you want to be on the risk spectrum and then to build a corporate culture capable of excelling with the chosen strategy. This cannot be accomplished overnight. It takes years of consistent application.

As noted, I chose the most conservative end of the spectrum for three reasons. First, we were coming off a period when the loan portfolio had almost capsized the institution. Second, the lending climate and the credit standards being applied were fraught with danger. Third, I wanted to redress an imbalance in the balance sheet by building the retail network in order to lower our dependency on purchased money.

If we were going to take risks, we would do so in deposits taken and placed where the danger might be an interest-rate squeeze for one or two quarters. There would be no risk of loss of principal. The mismatch could hardly last longer than two quarters since deposits taken and placed are seldom for more than 90 or 180 days.

Additionally, I wanted to increase the limits that foreign financial institutions had for total outstandings to First Chicago. These limits had been contracted in the 1974 to 1977 period, and it was important that they be restored and expanded, particularly if we faced another liquidity crunch like the one in 1974.

All of this succeeded, although I permitted it to go to excess in late 1979 and early 1980, when First Chicago had one billion dollars more of fixed-rate assets than fixed-rate liabilities, primarily because long-term fixed-rate deposits used to fund the fixed-rate loans were maturing and could not be renewed in the prevailing frenzied climate of rapidly rising interest rates. The deposits were replaced by short-term variable rate money purchased in the eurocurrency markets. In an institution of nearly $30 billion, this doesn't appear to be much of a mismatch by today's standards. But, at the time, interest rates were getting up close to the 20 percent level and, for the two quarters while this condition prevailed, the cost was visible and painful. I would do the same thing today faced with a comparable situation. I was prepared to trade profitability for safety. I was willing to forgo earnings to make certain I had liquidity by buying deposits at whatever price the market dictated and always broadening the sources. I would urge all bankers to do the same. A reduction in potential profits—not losses, but a reduction in profits—is an inexpensive insurance premium to pay for liquidity. When the asset portfolio gets out of kilter on rate (quality is an entirely different situation) whether on bonds or loans, bite the bullet quickly, purchase ample funds at any price for an extended period in order to have the necessary time and flexibility to bring the rate structure back into balance. Don't delay in the hopes that interest rates will come back your way.

Of course, in those days, we did not have interest-rate swaps or interest-rate hedges to the extent they are available today.

First Chicago was experimenting, and one of our talented lending officers prepared a magnificent report on how the futures market might be used to hedge interest rates and render fixed-rate assets less painful in a rising-interest-rate climate. This was leading-edge technology at the time, and I remember making a speech about it to the National Futures Association in Florida during the winter of 1980. My exhortation to the banking industry at the time was to perfect the technique and to use the futures market more extensively.

Essential to commercial banking is knowing your own strengths and weaknesses, having a view of the market, aiming for the distant horizon, and, most important, leaning against the wind. The last attribute, to lean against the wind, is perhaps the most difficult course for bankers to adopt. It goes against the old Wall Street adage, "The trend is your friend." In other words, you may be wrong, but if you are doing what everyone else is doing, you won't lose your job. This attitude is a cancer in the system.

It would have been easy to follow this adage in the late 1970s. The Continental Illinois Bank was leading the pack in growing commercial loans at a compound rate of 15 percent or more per annum. They were lauded and honored. It was volume at any cost. Credit standards and controls did not serve as a deterrent.

I knew they were headed for trouble because I had just been through a massive workout in our own institution. Money was being thrown at borrowers, domestic and international. Inflation was heating up, making that a particularly bad time to build a commercial loan portfolio. The monetary authorities would soon have to take decisive action to curb inflation, just as they did in 1974. The credit tightening by the monetary authorities would curb the inflation and soon thereafter bring interest rates down just as they did in 1976.

That was my view of the market in 1978 and 1979.

First Chicago was going to build a commercial loan portfolio of top-quality credits by offering the lowest rates in town and by offering credit in bad times as well as good to high-quality customers. The bank would be able to occupy this niche in the marketplace because its loan writeoffs would be minimal and because it would have the strongest balance-sheet among its peers and, therefore, be able to attract deposits at less cost. The retail thrust was a key ingredient in this overall balance sheet strategy.

It was a long-term strategy that required patience and courage to buck the trend. But, once implemented, it would give First Chicago a powerful identity as the quality lender in its territory. The bank would be viewed as strong and as solid as the granite that framed its towering headquarters. It would develop a lending product, set aside money to fund it, and then stay with it. The product selected was fixed-rate loans.

First Chicago's corporate customers in 1978 were worried about both rising interest rates and the availability of credit, as well they should have been. By offering fixed-rate loans, we could develop a strong group of top-quality customers, overcoming the stigma we had encountered by imposing the earlier facility fee and the 15 percent and five percent deposit requirements imposed for liquidity purposes in 1975.

We couldn't go overboard because there was a likelihood that these loans would be "under water" for a short period, so we had to limit the amount to be allocated to this activity and control the quality and type of borrower. I remembered the experience of Continental Illinois in the early 1970s when George Baker had put a lot of fixed-rate loans on the books and the cost was painful for a short period. It did, however, establish Continental as a differentiated lender and, in retrospect, appeared to accomplish its objective.

Under our system in 1978, Ed Yeo, as chairman of the Asset and Liability Management Committee, was in charge of pricing the fixed-rate loans. The responsibility was his because First Chicago's strategy involved matching these loans with fixed-rate deposits, if not for the full term, at least for a substantial part of their term. Ed did a fine job. I then made the mistake of assigning the responsibility for monitoring the volume and pricing of the fixed-rate loans to First Chicago's president, at his insistence, and over Ed Yeo's objections. The volume was allowed to exceed the established limits. Ed Yeo's objections had been appropriate. I sorely regret my decision not to let Ed remain in charge. He would have continued to implement the strategy as I had intended. It was a good sound strategy which I allowed to be executed badly by my decision to switch control officers.

It wasn't a catastrophe, but it did mean that the funding of the fixed-rate loan portfolio during the coming period of escalating interest rates would be more costly. We would, of course, make up for some of it when rates started back down, as they in fact did in May 1980, but we wouldn't capture all the negative spread (the difference between the stated rate on the loan and the marginal cost of purchased money) because some corporations and businesses would refinance when rates came down and pay back the higher-rate, fixed-rate loans. They would refinance even though there were agreements not to do so. In practice, the bank would relent in the interest of preserving the relationship.

In any event, this was the main mission of the whole program: to build lasting relationships with high-quality borrowing customers by lending in both bad times and good times and on advantageous terms and conditions. With this reputation, we could then demand the very best in quality and credit protection.

By December 1979, interest rates were climbing precipitously and First Chicago's earnings were down from the previous string of record results because of the negative spread on the fixed-rate loans, particularly since the volume had been allowed to rise above the preestablished limits.

As for blame, I repeated for any and all who would listen that the fixed-rate loan program was my strategy. Any fault in execution was mine. Ed Yeo counseled against it (this was circulated in memo form signed by me), and if there was a temporary impact on earnings, so be it, because it was part of a longer-range commercial banking strategy that, by May of 1980, was working. The strategy of high-quality credits and advantageous rates, during good times and bad, requires the strongest possible balance sheet to execute. It requires a superb retail banking capability to generate core deposits. It also requires patience during the build-up period and steadfast credit controls. It is a sound strategy. If I had to do it today, assuming the same interest rate forecast, I'd adopt the very same program, again with the *caveat* that it isn't necessarily good for everyone.

Barry Sullivan, my successor at First Chicago, was not sold on the program. In retrospect, this was too bad because interest rates dipped sharply, as expected, in the summer of 1980 (in fact, First Chicago purchased $400 million of fixed-rate time deposits at advantageous rates in August 1980), rose briefly and then trended down and remained down. A portfolio of these loans would have been good business and established a favorable identity for First Chicago. Moreover, the time to build a portfolio of such loans is at the end of a rising-rate cycle and before the downward turn. First Chicago's timing in 1980 could not have been better to build a fixed-rate loan portfolio, with top quality credit-worthy commercial customers. The appetite for such loans by the right kinds of customers would be short lived and needed to be exploited decisively and with conviction. But in the March 1981 issue of *Euromoney* Magazine, Barry Sullivan was quoted to say:

> My preference would be not to do any fixed-rate commercial lending, but you cannot drop completely out of the marketplace when a customer has a real genuine need. Right now, there sure as hell isn't much demand for fixed-rate loans, so it isn't really a problem.[13]

I had taken a position against the trend. I wanted to hold back on commercial lending except for the very top quality credits. Barry was not convinced. So First Chicago reversed course and joined the trend. The timing was unfortunate. Worse yet, the trumpet to begin the charge was sounded for all to hear. Mr. Sullivan said he wanted First Chicago's loans to grow faster than the average of the top 10 commercial banks, then running at about 10 percent a year over a four-year period while First Chicago's commercial loan portfolio had been rising 2.7 percent a year. The article said that loan approval procedures were speeded up, the loan approval committee was abolished, and loan officers had been given authority to approve credit by themselves.[14]

By late 1983, it became clear that the combination of rapid growth in commercial loans pursuant to Mr. Sullivan's objective, the relaxation of internal controls, and abysmal timing with respect to the economy had produced a very serious portfolio problem.

It wasn't Barry Sullivan alone who missed the economic signals leading to the 1981-1982 downturn. Ben Heineman, his dominant director and the person who hired him, started having earnings problems with his own company, Northwest Indus-

---

[13]Derek Bamber, "First Chicago: Under Sullivan, After Abboud," 51.
[14]Susie Gharib Nazem, "The Hard Road Back at First Chicago," *Fortune*, 14 December 1981.

tries, in the first quarter of 1980. The earnings reportedly were hit hard by high interest rates on $700 million of debt. Then, in an August 5, 1982 *Chicago Tribune* article by Terry Atlas, Mr. Heineman was taken to task for being late in recognizing the impact of the downturn in domestic oil drilling on Lone Star Steel, a Northwest Industries subsidiary. It was said he made consistently bullish projections, which turned out to be wrong, about the outlook for Lone Star Steel.

There were, at the time, four First Chicago directors on the Northwest Industries board. So, it is little wonder that First Chicago was in a full-scale offense when it should have been exercising prudence. The course of the economy was simply misjudged. Because of the misjudgment, the aggressive lending program produced sour loans. To address the situation of the deteriorating loan portfolio, a study team was put together to see what could be done to upgrade the quality of new business.

The *Wall Street Journal* of November 20, 1984, detailed the implementation of the study team's recommendations to set up a committee, loan-monitoring structure that "looks like something out of a business-school textbook on the thoroughly modern bank." There were an industry analysis unit for business forecasting, a credit-process review unit for revamping internal procedures, and a top-level credit strategy committee to review and adjust the bank's lending to various industries.

> 'Barry is a guy who really believes in the power of the process,' a planning officer told the *Wall Street Journal*. 'And much of that process involves a collegial, task force approach to problem solving. He has brought organizational discipline and marketing focus to an organization that seemed to lack both.'[15]

Well, "the collegial, task-force approach" apparently produced the results you might expect of anything run by a committee. In

---

[15]Jeff Bailey, "First Chicago's Losses Diminish its Luster as Management Model," *Wall Street Journal*, 20 November 1984.

the third quarter of 1984, First Chicago reported an after-tax loss of $71.8 million, the first quarterly loss in my memory, reflecting a $279 million problem loan write-off.

In a July 21, 1985 *New York Times* feature on First Chicago and Bank of America, Robert A. Bennett wrote:

> When asked, during an interview last week, what he believed his greatest mistake at the bank had been, Mr. Sullivan immediately answered that CRESCO (the Credit Strategy Committee) should have been started a year earlier. 'We would have missed a lot of mistakes and would have avoided the big third quarter write-offs,' he said. But Mr. Sullivan stressed that recent problems would not propel him to revert to the conservatism of his predecessor.[16]

Six months later, despite assurances to investors that the 1984 third quarter reflected an unfortunate coincidence of one-time problems, the disaster of a Brazilian partnership of private individuals, Denasa Desenvolvimento Nacional S.A. Participacoes, began to unfold. First Chicago was forced to write off $131 million on an initial investment of $15.8 million.

Then, in April 1987, First Chicago reported that it placed loans to Ecuador and some loans to Brazil on nonaccrual status. The total of nonperforming loans jumped to $1.34 billion, or 5.4 percent of total loans and real estate owned, more than triple the dollar level when I left the bank. And all of this was by contrast to Mr. Sullivan's announced objective to get the nonperforming loans below two percent.

What are the lessons from all of this? The answers will come from future students of banking. But one observation appears inescapable. In the two decades since the late 1960s, Chicago banking has provided enough textbook material to challenge professors and students for years to come.

---

[16]Robert A. Bennett, "The Humbling of Two Banking Stars," *New York Times*, 21 July 1985.

To me, the central lesson is that, no matter how much training you provide individual lending officers, and no matter how many smart young business school graduates you have in staff capacities churning out studies in three-ring binders, the commercial banking thrust will succeed or fail or limp along based on leadership from the top. Whatever the boss wants, the organization will rationalize a way to get it done. And that goes for everything from credit analysis to documentation to administration, and ultimately to portfolio management and collection.

Commercial banking is unique because the numbers per transaction can be very large and the gestation period for determining success or failure is long. It generally takes two to three years between the time a big loan goes on the books, often accompanied by celebratory pomp and ceremony, and the day it is written off with all the attendant remorse. In the meantime, the figures can look good. Loans are up, accrued earnings are up, customer relations are cordial, and everyone feels good. Then reality hits home. The loan is deemed to be in trouble or uncollectible. Loans go down as writeoffs begin, accrued interest is reversed, customer relations sour, and the finger-pointing starts.

Leadership from the top is the single most important element in commercial bank administration. The leader must determine the present point of the business cycle, the strengths and weaknesses of the organization, the overall strategy and positioning of the organization in the market, and the timing and speed required to reach the desired point on the horizon. Above all, the leader must be a strategist with firm convictions. More often than not, the successful leader must lean against the wind. Bernard Baruch, the fabled investment banker, put it succinctly when he said, "I made money by always selling too soon." He made money by leading, not following. For those who follow, the best they can hope to attain is average performance. More likely they will go over the cliff with the other lemmings.

A leader views an organization in terms of its maximum ultimate potential as he or she perceives it, not the way he or she finds it upon taking over. A leader also stamps the organization with his or her standards and then affixes and implants those standards with intensity and commitment. If the leader views the standards as frills or nothing more than boilerplate, then the organization will respond in kind. But, if the leader is deeply committed to a vision and strategy, the organization will soon become equally committed.

Americans of all ages, in all walks of life, believe in standards and respect those who manifest sincere belief in standards, whether they agree with the specific standards or not. The challenge is to obtain a consensus as to the standards to be applied.

In contrast to a leader, a follower is one who seeks to rank well with and gain approval from peers. The goal is always to rank in the upper half or even the upper quartile of the peer group, as in, "We want to be in the upper half of the top 10 in our size category." Unfortunately this is common in the banking industry. It means putting up the antenna and extending the sensors to determine what everyone else is doing. This is what "binder set" (the staff group who prepare the studies based on market data) are good at doing. I don't disparage this function. Every big organization needs it, and the leader also needs it as one of many data inputs. The difference with the follower is that he or she believes that the data compiled by the "binder set" are like revelations from the mountaintop on tablets of stone. "I have divined the way the industry is going," he or she might say, "and I am going to be in the forefront of that pilgrimage."

The leader, on the other hand, will say, "I, too, have divined the way the industry is going. Because of the industry's traditional lemming instincts, the field will soon be overcrowded and abuses are sure to creep in, with an accompanying adulteration of standards. I will chart a new course and, soon, the industry will be following me." The best I have met in the banking industry who typifies this brand of leadership is Walter Wriston, the retired chairman of Citicorp. In my judgment, he has to be rated one of the greatest commercial bankers in U.S. banking history. Needless to say, by definition, there are very few true leaders and very many genuine followers.

Looking at the recent history of Chicago banking, first, we had the respected and popular Homer Livingston, Sr., chairman of First Chicago, a conservative banker of the late 1960s and disciple of the great Edward Eagle Brown. He left Gale Freeman a strong, squeaky clean, heavily capitalized bank.

Then, we had David Kennedy, chairman of Continental Illinois and later secretary of the treasury, who started Continental's "go-go" era and who left some clean-up functions for the interim chairman, Don Graham. Don Graham deserves more credit than he has received for the task he accomplished.

Then, we had Gaylord Freeman, a charming, consummate leader and chairman of First Chicago. He charted new courses and then looked back at the pack to see if they were following him. Gale Freeman was no follower. He had a view of the landscape, pointed First Chicago in the direction he wanted and applied the spurs to propel First Chicago at full gallop.

Then came Roger Anderson, who succeeded Don Graham as chairman of Continental Illinois. Roger, too, was a leader. He had a vision for Continental Illinois to become the premier commercial bank and wholesale lender (making loans to big corporations) in the world. Yes, Roger had no small dreams. He blessed George Baker as his informal heir apparent and regarded the hard charging, hard driving Baker as his George Patton on the commercial banking front. It was a spectacle to behold. Continental's credo was the one made famous by Satchel Page, "Don't look back, someone may be following you." Apparent success bred more success, and more hubris, and more frenzied lending to keep the game going. This was Roger Anderson, the leader, all the way. Make no mistake about it.

Robert A. Bennett, in a September 28, 1981 *New York Times* feature story on Continental, wrote, "If the past is any example, the changes will be effected with cold, colorless determination. Under Mr. Anderson's stern leadership, these changes can be expected to be carried out with a lot of thought and little fanfare."[17]

---

[1]Robert A. Bennett, "Shaping Chicago's Top Bank," New York Times, 28 September 1981.

When I read the record in the September and October 1984 Congressional hearings in the aftermath of the Continental Illinois collapse, I had to smile with amusement at the excuses used by Continental Bank officers citing peer group analogies and peer group pressures. For those of us who were on the firing line at the time, this is pure, unmitigated balderdash. Continental Illinois wasn't driven by peer pressure. It was so far out in front that there was no peer against which to measure it. In driving Continental Illinois to such a point, Roger Anderson attracted the admiration of most. He was listed as the highest-paid U.S. banker in 1980, and John Perkins, president of Continental Illinois, was fifth. Ben Heineman, my director, would opine to us that Roger Anderson was considered the best banker in the United States.

I, on the other hand, was viewed as proficient in retail and balance-sheet administration and commendable in my commitment to fixing the bad loans, but a laggard in competing for growth in commercial loans, and, in particular, a laggard in competing with "the greatest banker in the United States," Roger Anderson. My policy of holding back on commercial loan growth because the market standards were too risky, concentrating on the highest-quality customers with senior indebtedness at advantageous rates, and building the liability side of the balance sheet through retail banking, had no sex appeal to some of my businessman directors. They were feeling the peer pressure. Ben Heineman said to me, "How can you be right and the whole rest of the world be wrong?"

Ben wanted to go with the pack, in fact, to lead the pack like Continental. I wanted to lean against the wind. Here were two banks in the same city, competing in the same world market, and one was leading in one direction and one was leading in the other direction. Remarkable and unusual? You bet. Not since the days of General Robert Wood at Sears Roebuck and Sewell Avery at Montgomery Ward had two competitors veered off in completely opposite directions. Everyone familiar with that history was betting on the hare versus the turtle.

Was it conceivable that either leader, Anderson or Abboud, would blink and moderate his course? Not a chance! Anderson and Abboud had been head to head in direct competition for 20 years. I knew his moves and he knew mine. We both started in the late 1950s as assistant cashiers (first-level officers) in our respective international banking departments. We both headed international banking during the growth years. And, if I am permitted to say so, I think I beat his socks off. I pursued a strategy of wholly owned branches. He pursued a more "glitzy" strategy of joint ventures, and First Chicago emerged as the international network of greater substance.

As chief executive, I was confident I was right again, and I think by 1980 Roger knew it. I was delayed in meeting him head to head because we had the portfolio of bad loans to repair first. Moreover, my strategy called for a strong balance sheet, high quality loans, and a reliable base of core retail deposits. Retail loans were going to be the most profitable in the 1980s and I wanted to build the portfolio when no other bank in town was interested in such business, just as Edward Eagle Brown did with savings deposits in the 1930s. Continental Illinois, on the other hand, from 1974 forward under Roger Anderson, was charging ahead at full gallop, taking on new business anywhere and everywhere apparently without regard to balance sheet constraints.

The fact is that the Comptroller's Office in 1976 had told the Continental Bank to slow down its rapid growth. Continental's capital was rated a clear and emphatic "inadequate" based on the ratios at the time. I might add parenthetically that Continental's ratios, as cited, were considerably better than those of First Chicago. So you can imagine how First Chicago's capital adequacy was rated.

In any event, Continental's capital in 1976 was "inadequate." This conforms with the message I had received from Chairman of the Federal Reserve, Arthur Burns, who said, "You two banks in Chicago, stop it." He was referring to our respective rates of loan growth in 1974. Jim Smith as Comptroller of the Currency had set the tone. Capital was inadequate. Get the balance sheet in shape.

After the Carter Administration came into power, John Heimann became Comptroller of the Currency. What Jim Smith considered inadequate, John Heimann no longer considered inadequate. Ironically, the new Democratic administration was looser than the Republicans on regulatory standards. Growth, profitability, and subjective assessments of management became the criteria.

In the Continental Illinois hearings, Rep. Jim Leach of Iowa noted that, by 1982, when performance ratios at Continental had worsened measurably since 1976, Continental's capital was described in the then current examination report as "presently considered adequate" by the regulators. It was, purely and simply, regulatory failure of the first order. The Comptroller's Office was basically converted from objective, hard-numbers-oriented standards under Jim Smith to subjective standards under John Heimann. "Good guys" were permitted more latitude than "bad guys." John Heimann's subjective judgment on the situation in Chicago was just plain wrong. He and I had been on opposite sides of the fence on the Bert Lance loan controversy. That made me a "bad guy" and Roger Anderson a "good guy."

I might digress at this moment to comment on the loan to Bert Lance, who was President Carter's budget director, because it received so much publicity. Bert was recommended to me by a prominent businessman and old customer of the Bank. The Bert Lance loan was reviewed for collateral sufficiency and legality by the appropriate departments in the bank. The loan request had initially been turned down by one of the big New York banks, so we restructured it and obtained more collateral. The general counsel, Don Yellon, told me the loan met our standards in all particulars, but he advised against making it because it was being made to a public official. Don was a superb general counsel and I respected his judgment. So I pondered the matter. The issue, it seemed to me, was threefold. First, do public officials have the same rights as everyone else? I knew of no law that said otherwise.

Second, was the loan being granted to curry political favor with the Administration? That was unthinkable. A tie with the new Carter Administration, which was unpopular with the business community, was no particular asset. It was a fair question, but it still rankled me because of the implicit suggestion that I would use bank assets to buy favor. And since I tend to lean against the wind, this, probably more than anything else, gave me the resolve to go ahead.

Third, assuming the credit was good, was there going to be disclosure to the Senate committee approving Bert Lance's confirmation before we disbursed the funds? I was assured such would be the case. It was so disclosed, the disclosure was reported in the national press, and I approved disbursement. The loan was handled meticulously during its term and was paid off in full with interest in accordance with its terms. I wish I could say the same about all our loans.

Much later, well after Bert's confirmation as director of the Office of Management and Budget, and after the affair began to attract national attention, Mr. Heimann sent in examiners to review everything about the loan, and he repeated this on more than one occasion. The first time, the loan passed muster with national bank examiners in Chicago, with the only comment being its notoriety. The Comptroller then sent special examiners from Washington to look again. Their judgment was to lower the classification to substandard. There was no justification for a lowered classification. I believed then, and I believe now, that the real issue was who was going to be the economic spokesperson for the Carter Administration, the Treasury Department or Lance at the White House. The "ethics weapon," as a 1987 *Wall Street Journal* editorial by that title suggests, can be exploited as a "political weapon" with a "double standard," depending upon who is being accused ("Ethics Weapon," *Wall Street Journal*, 24 April 1987).

First Chicago and other banks and thrifts across the United States have always conducted a full range of banking business with people in political office. This is particularly true of people who move from the private sector into a political position. The public policy aspects of these dealings have been well and long established.

The reality of the Lance loan was not creditworthiness since the creditworthiness of our loan was beyond criticism as the subsequent payment record demonstrated, but the political spotlight and the fact that it all fell squarely upon John Heimann, a well-connected New York Democrat, the former New York State banking regulator, who is now an investment banker with Merrill Lynch. Bert Lance was the main attraction. Regular business such as capital adequacy, balance sheet ratios, documentation, and dependence on purchased money appeared to take a back seat in the determination of good bankers and bad bankers. In any event, the facts noted in the Congressional Record by Congressman Leach about the interpretation of capital adequacy and capital inadequacy speak for themselves.

On a similar note, much has been written about my involvement with Lockheed during the early to mid-1970s. Lockheed, of course, is a major aerospace and defense contractor. The management decided to diversify by building commercial aircraft and the Lockheed 1011 became the major thrust in this area. As it turned out, the company was late in getting the 1011 introduced and delivered compared to the Douglas DC 10, the principal competitor for the 1011. Meanwhile, the losses from the 1011 program were mounting, the remainder of the company was being drained of needed cash and all of the losses were being financed by drawings on the bank lines of credit. It was a bottomless pit. There seemed to be no end in sight. The multi-bank line of credit was in default. A new loan agreement was in the process of negotiation. And right in the middle of these negotiations the story broke that the senior management of the company had permitted illegal payments to be made to officials in Saudi Arabia to achieve sales of the 1011.

Clearly, the program had to be curtailed to save the company and to save the bank loans. I took the position that an agreement should be obtained from management that the 1011 program would be curtailed as a condition of the loan restructure. Management was adamant that it would not do so. Therefore, I took the position that First Chicago would not go along with the restructure until management agreed. The net result was that management resigned. A new management committed to the 1011 curtailment was installed, the multi-bank credit was restructured, and the company promptly proceeded to recover as the losses from the 1011 program diminished and eventually disappeared.

When the Reagan Administration took command of the Comptroller's Office in 1981, the orientation shifted back to quantitative determinations of balance sheet ratios and capital adequacy and the crackdowns began. At first, there was criticism of the hard-numbers approach, but it was right. Capital adequacy is fundamental. The banking system, following the capital deterioration of the Heimann years, is now rebuilding its capital base.

There are those who argue that capital adequacy is a non-issue, that banks have too much capital for the risks they might reasonably encounter, and that too heavy a capital requirement encourages banks to take on less creditworthy business in the quest for profitability. I could not disagree more strongly. If there was ever a time we needed to strengthen the balance sheets of our financial institutions, it is now.

There is still a long way to go to restore a truly adequate capital position. The industry's ratio of non-performing loans to total loans is still too high. The agricultural loans in the farm belt and the big banks' loans to developing countries continue to be major concerns. And, now there is a new menace called off-balance-sheet risk such as loan commitments and "contingent liabilities," which do not immediately show up on balance sheets.

The off-balance-sheet liabilities alone are not to be regarded lightly. The aggregate rises above the trillion-dollar level. The amount of each bank's liability is recorded in a required report called Schedule L.

The January 1986 cover story of *Institutional Investor* described the magnitude of off-balance-sheet risks:

> Many banks have amounts far in excess of their total assets theoretically pledged through these commitments. As of last June, for instance, Bankers Trust Co. had clocked in with the equivalent of nearly 300 percent of its assets in contingencies and commitments, Citibank with 230 percent, Chemical Bank with 201 percent and Morgan Guaranty Trust Co. with 168 percent. It's easy to see why the banks have embraced these shadow liabilities so eagerly; they generate much-needed fee income — and they don't tie up precious capital. At the same time, banks have been increasing their trading activities, deepening their involvement in the futures and forward markets.[18]

The same magazine quoted past-Federal Reserve Chairman Paul Volcker's remarks to the American Bankers Association: "Has the attention paid to simple capital-asset ratios driven risk off the balance sheet — and is off balance sheet also out of mind?"

I agree with Walter Wriston that the publishing of volume numbers is misleading and has confused the issue. There is double counting and triple counting and quadruple counting. That is precisely the danger, as I see it. One institution's liability is another institution's asset. It is a chain. The unanswered question is what happens if one link of the chain is broken? Is the damage contained right there, or is there a domino effect? If a domino effect, does this mean that the regulatory authorities will have to step in to save the system? That is the greatest danger, in my judgment, because such actions ultimately will lead to nationalized banking. I also agree with Walter Wriston that the marketplace is the best evaluator of risk. I simply want the marketplace to have more access to information on a timely basis in order to evaluate the risk properly.

---

[18]Suzanne Andrews and Henry Sender, "Off Balance Sheet Risk—Where Is It Leading the Bank?" *Institutional Investor*, January 1986.

There are those who apparently feel otherwise. John Heimann, for example, sticks to his case-by-case, subjective view of regulatory administration with the ultimate savior being government intervention of one form or another.

In the previously mentioned January 1986 issue of *International Investor*, Mr. Heimann was quoted as follows:

'On a case-by-case basis, I'm pretty confident,' says John Heimann, vice chairman of Merrill Lynch Capital Markets and former U.S. comptroller of the currency. 'But if the world goes to hell, the only question is, What will the Federal Reserve do?' To create real turmoil in the banking system, Heimann suggests, 'you have to predict a whole bunch of horrors, including a serious recession — worse than 1981-1982 — and a laissez-faire, hands-off policy by the Fed.'[19]

John Heimann looks to the Fed, just as Gale Freeman in the early 1970s looked to the Fed, to provide liquidity rather than looking to each individual bank's resources. How many Continental Illinois Banks will it take? Continental started down its extreme path during Mr. Heimann's watch. So did Penn Square, Seattle First, and other near disasters.

A "good old boy," laissez-faire regulatory attitude is a prelude to disaster. There must be objective standards. There must be public education, and there must be far more public disclosure of information in a timely fashion. By all means, let's establish a consensus that responsibility and accountability for the safety and solvency of each institution rests squarely and solely with its management and its board of directors. If they fail, then let the shareholders and creditors pay the price in a forced recapitalization or bank closure. It is not the taxpayers' problem, no matter how big the institution. Moreover, let's give the shareholders more practical means to change the boards of these institutions if they are not performing in accordance with shareholder wishes.

---

[19]Andrews and Sender, "Off Balance Sheet Risk—Where Is It Leading the Bank?"

Apparently, John Heimann continues to believe that "big brother" should establish and be the arbiter of acceptable codes of behavior and the "government fix" should be applied to "harmonize" the rules for financial intermediaries on a global basis.

In a speech entitled, "Global Deregulation, An American Perspective," that he delivered in Tokyo on April 9, 1987, Mr. Heimann called for worldwide regulatory standards, with financial authorities able to respond quickly and decisively when a situation warrants.

I totally disagree. I don't want legislated uniformity. It suffocates creativity and stifles innovation. The implications of such a regime, if adopted, would be examiners as global policemen enforcing codified rules. Or, alternatively, they would permit subjective exceptions or deviations from the codified standard based on some currently popular perception. I don't want depository institutions run by government examiners exercising some central authority's notion of sound banking practices. The only rules needed are investment criteria for insured deposits. That is the area of legitimate government concern and surveillance. Beyond that, the task of examination is impossible, prohibitively expensive, and futile. Controls don't work. When will we ever learn that lesson?

I want the responsibility for sound banking practices placed where it belongs, on each institution's management and board of directors. I want to encourage leadership, creativity, and market responsiveness through bold new initiatives. And, most of all, I want the marketplace to be the disciplinarian and not the government, whether ours or someone else's. If an institution fails, let it fail as far as the management and directors are concerned, force it to recapitalize, and place the economic penalties where they belong, on the stockholders and the subordinated or holding company creditors. I don't want to leave room for excuses as used by Continental Illinois executives in Congressional testimony to the effect that, "we complied with all the rules and we were given the okay by the examiners."

Each institution must determine its own tolerance for risk. There are good high-risk lenders, there are good medium-risk lenders, and there are good low-risk lenders. The adopted strategy must fit the overall balance sheet. The institution that has a great deal of capital can afford to take more risk.

The rate of return or interest earned on the loans will vary directly with the amount of risk. Some loans are so risky that, for all practical purposes, they are viewed as substitute capital. These will have equity kickers, which give lenders a chance to convert the loans into stock. Kickers may be options to buy or convert into the borrower's common stock, or a right to participate in the company's cash flow or earnings, or warrants to buy stock, or privileges to trade the principal balance of the loan for all or part of specific assets belonging to the borrower. The range of possibilities in structuring these arrangements is limited only by a banker's creativity.

When I describe an institution as a low-risk or a high-risk lender, I am not talking about all of its activities. I am merely describing the main body of its loan portfolio. When I adopted a low-risk commercial banking strategy for First Chicago, I did not include all the lending activities, only the mainstream corporate banking department. For example, as mentioned, First Chicago was the first commercial bank to lend to Kohlberg, Kravis, and Roberts and to participate in their early leveraged buyout deals. We later were replaced in this relationship by Bankers Trust. Bob Judson, who initiated this business for First Chicago with our participation in the Vapor Corporation credit, tells me that we were slow to respond on one or two deals. I truly regret that because this was an excellent specialty business that complemented our overall strategy. Kohlberg, Kravis, and Roberts were the talented investment bankers who left Bear, Stearns and formed their own company to do leveraged buyouts. If they didn't invent the leveraged buyout, they at least made it fashionable by making it immensely profitable.

First Chicago's very creative venture capital subsidiary, First Capital, has been profitable year in and year out. It was in on the ground floor of such notable success stories as Federal Express and MCI. I remember working out the MCI credit in the mid-1970s and speaking with Bill Brown, then president of the First National Bank of Boston. Bill wanted out of the credit and did not want to go along with the restructure. I told him that we, First Chicago, would take over their position if he insisted, but we would also take over the warrants to buy stock that went with the loan. We subsequently made a lot of money for First Capital. First Capital also made good money on its position in Federal Express. And the situation has been the same with one company after another, year in and year out.

This type of lending, or venture capital investment, is risky. However, it is contained in a separate, well-capitalized subsidiary that has much lower borrowings per dollar of capital than the bank. It is managed differently, and, as it makes profits, it builds the capital base to do more and bigger deals. This activity is kept separate, managed independently, and in no way influences the standards applied in the main lending functions.

Another specialized activity is lending to small and medium-sized businesses. This requires real skill and, when properly performed, is immensely profitable. For some small and medium-sized banks, this type of lending is all they do. Some are good at it and some are not so good. The successful commercial officers that handle this business are real bankers who know their customers, know the businesses their customers operate, and know the communities served by these businesses. There is probably more personal satisfaction in this aspect of commercial banking than in any other.

Walking the factory floor of a borrowing customer and watching product move down the assembly line is, frankly, a lot more fun than meeting in the oak paneled boardroom of a big corporate customer. This is not to say that bankers don't derive considerable psychic income when meeting with the movers and shakers of the *Fortune* or *Forbes 500* companies, but it still feels good to get on the firing line of a good mid-sized company's factory floor. And, tremendous loyalty arises between banker and customer when the relationship is sound. The loyalty goes both ways, in good times and difficult times.

First Chicago's acquisition of American National Bank enabled it to move into the middle and smaller-business market successfully. This was an excellent acquisition by Barry Sullivan because American National Bank carved out a position as a bank for that type of business. First Chicago was smart to leave it alone and to let American National's own management team operate it, and the rewards have been handsome. I truly believe that this is the only way a big money center bank or savings and loan can effectively enter and prosper in the small-business market. It requires its own culture and cannot coexist with big wholesale, retail, agricultural, or real estate banking.

Not only is middle-market business the most profitable, the most enduring, and the most rewarding for lending institutions generally, but also it is the most important business segment for the health of the U.S. economy. The industrial giants are always slimming down, restructuring and eliminating jobs. It is the middle-market businesses that expand, hire new employees, provide all around training, and invest in new local facilities. They readily introduce new products and services, seek out new markets abroad for exports, and become active in local community affairs. This is a market segment that needs the advice, counsel, and support of its bankers. It is not a market where banking officers should be changed frequently. It is not a training ground for young hot shots on their way up to serve the big industrial giants. I give the advice about being serious about serving the middle-market, knowing how hard it is to implement. I wish I had found a way to do better in this regard myself. It isn't easy.

Banking officers serving the middle-market generally do not get paid as much as those who have what are perceived to be more visible and glamorous jobs in capital markets, real estate, venture capital, or large corporate banking. Yet, the middle-market business is the bedrock of any lending institution's commercial banking activities. It spawns a whole range of other types of banking business. According to account analyses of middle-market customers, they are always the most profitable.

The big commercial accounts—the giants of retailing, manufacturing, natural resources, entertainment, pharmaceuticals, health care, transportation, publishing and agribusiness—are important to have on the roster, and it is nice to be able to boast of their support and allegiance. But the days when the giants kept large, interest-free demand deposits on account are gone forever. When I was a young bank officer and Marion English was an assistant controller, he would open the general ledgers, which at the time were kept by hand, and point with pride to a list he maintained of the 25 largest deposit accounts that accounted for 80% of the bank's profits. They were all the names you might suspect. But, no more! These large multinational giants, with their sophisticated treasury departments, are commercial banks in their own right. They have captive finance companies and mortgage banking subsidiaries. They raise money in the professional money markets like banks. They do bond and securities transactions like banks. They buy and sell foreign exchange and take positions in the futures markets like banks. Many of them have, sadly enough for the banking industry, higher credit ratings than the banks that grant them lines of credit. This irony implies, quite correctly, that it becomes hard for a bank to make a profit on the spread between what it pays for money in the professional markets and what it charges a customer to borrow. The business has become fiercely cut-throat and competitive as a result.

So, how do lending institutions compete? They extend huge lines of credit to finance mergers and acquisitions. This is how the big lenders make money, through big-dollar commitments, with attractive front-end fees, and premium margins to compensate them for risking large sums of money in deals containing abnormal leverage or risk.

A noted author once asked me, "Why do you support the merger mania now taking place; isn't it like the mating of the dinosaurs?" I said, "Yes, it is. But, once mated, the dinosaurs have babies, and these babies are the future generations of middle-market businesses."

I meant that when the giant corporations merge or get taken over in leveraged buyouts, they almost invariably must sell off divisions or subsidiaries to pay off their enormous borrowings. Everyone does it. When Occidental Petroleum bought Cities Service, we sold off 43 companies in the short space of 13 months to pay down billions of dollars of loans.

These so-called spin-offs are the "babies." They are sometimes bought by the managements of the individual companies, sometimes by small investor groups, and sometimes they go public by selling stock to shareholders. This is where the bank replenishes its middle-market lending base and establishes new, long-lasting, comprehensive relationships. It is all part of the revitalization process, and legislation that seeks to prohibit the absorption or takeover of large corporations and the rebirth of their offspring is, in my judgment, ill conceived.

If there is to be legislation, let it be to hold managements and boards of directors more accountable to the shareholders for performance. The notion that individual shareholders have a voice in selecting the boards of directors or influencing the managements of large, publicly held corporations is a myth. Usually the majority of the stock is held by other large institutions in their pension or profit sharing accounts, by fund managers, or by Employee Stock Ownership Programs (ESOPs). Managements either directly control or can influence the vote of the stock in the ESOP or profit sharing account. Institutional holders and fund managers almost invariably vote with management or sell their stock. Very seldom do institutions or fund managers vote with dissidents or sponsors of proxy fights, and bank trust departments almost never do. The result is that managements and boards of directors become increasingly entrenched and self-perpetuating, and the only effective remedy to date has been the hostile takeover.

I maintain that such takeovers, or at least the credible threat of takeovers, has done more to promote accountability to shareholders than any SEC rule, editorial challenge, public policy pronouncement, or legislation. It is the market at work. Once again, the market, if allowed to operate freely, finds remedies to right the wrongs. I believe that such market remedies do more to maintain jobs and create new jobs and preserve the vigor and vitality of the economy than any legislative remedy yet proposed.

I understand the motivation that drives the quest for legislation. More than a few are making lots of money from the process. The so-called raiders are making money because they are buying poorly managed, undervalued assets and reselling them at huge profits. Managements, who were responsible for the undervaluation of the assets, make money through their "golden parachute" contracts, which pay them in the event the company is taken over and they lose their jobs. Predators make considerable money by purchasing blocks of stock in public companies and frightening managements and boards of directors into believing that they are about to be gobbled up. When the managements and directors buy out the predator at a profit, this is called "greenmail." Arbitrageurs and speculators (investors who take positions in stocks of companies they believe are about to be taken over) make money by gambling on winners and losers in the takeover game. Investment bankers make a lot of money by defending the companies targeted as takeover candidates, usually at the expense of the public shareholders of the targeted company. Accountants and lawyers make a lot of money by representing all sides in the takeover fight. Now commercial bankers are making a lot of money by initiating takeovers, charging investment banking commissions, and investing in the securities of the takeover or leveraged buyout candidate. With the big fees and commissions, senior officers in the commercial banks are being awarded big raises and bonuses to keep pace with their subordinates who engineer the buyouts. It is a win, win, win game. And let us not forget that the public shareholders of the company taken over, virtually disenfranchised by the system, finally get a share of their just values when the raider buys them out at a premium. Otherwise, they would be stuck with a low-priced stock and no realistic way to throw out the management or the board.

The fundamental malady of undervaluation was so extensive that the value added by the remedy has brought billions and billions of dollars of profits, distributed to a limited class of participants. The competitive nature of executives stimulated flagrant examples of greed, and these examples became highly publicized.

No one should object to generous compensation for the singular executives who provide higher earnings, higher dividends, and higher market value for their shareholders. But now, it isn't just the few singular performers who are participating but a broader group including average and below-average performers as well. The notion of incentives has given way to an attitude of "keeping up with the Joneses."

There is a real danger that this quest of greed may take on a life of its own, losing all sense of proportion or connection with the market condition that caused it, namely entrenched management and the resulting undervaluation. There is also the danger that the rich will get richer and the poor will get poorer and the middle class will continue to wither as a percentage of the total. This will happen if we don't do something about the rust belt and the farm belt and the pockets of unemployment created by the economic woes of major industries. The temptation to management in takeover situations is to trigger their bonuses not by expansion and market penetration, but by contraction and by reducing reserves or reversing benefits. All of this creates unemployment, and nothing will destroy the middle class faster than prolonged periods of unemployment, causing prideful men and women to lose confidence in themselves, their abilities, and their commitment to self-help and self-reliance.

Should that occur, the political landscape will be dramatically altered. The rich and those who aspire to be rich will become targets. Avenues of opportunity will be curtailed for future generations. The free market philosophy will be endangered. This is what managements and boards of directors who abuse this system should fear the most. Their excesses endanger all of us because the excesses endanger the market system.

Takeovers and mergers should have the positive result of spin-offs and restructurings that create jobs.

One director of a major financial institution asked me, "What can we do? Have you seen what kind of money the kids are getting these days? Do you know what the investment bankers are making? We don't want our senior executives to lag behind." These questions reflected no concern about the potential danger to the financial system and no desire to arrest the trend by leaning against the wind.

It is precisely the temptation to be like high-flying investment bankers that executives of banks and savings and loans must resist. They must exercise moral leadership, both by word and through self-discipline, within their own organizations. Bankers or thrift executives are the intermediaries between the capitalist entrepreneur and the saver. They are different from investment bankers who are themselves entrepreneurs, traditionally risking their own and their partners' capital. Commercial and thrift banks require the trust of the community to do their job. They cannot be viewed as avaricious or greedy. They need the moral authority of the clergy. Like the priests of ancient times, who were the first bankers, they are entrusted with the community's savings. Their job is to protect them.

More than that, they must work with medium-size and small businesses to mold them, and modify them, and help them grow and prosper. They must nurture the "babies" that emanate from the "marriages of the dinosaurs." They must work to build the communities they serve by attracting business, providing resources for repair and modernization, and providing moral leadership as well.

Consider the role of the banker or savings and loan executive in the midwest farm belt. Farmers are hard pressed. They may have overspent and overinvested during the good times of the late 1970s and early 1980s when commodity prices were high. But, it wasn't entirely their fault. All of us, including those who made U.S. official policy, share blame.

Agriculture is a demanding business that requires advance planning, much financing, and time for implementation. Land must be purchased, equipment ordered, and the necessary preparations made. If the land is to be used for planting, then the soil must be graded, and the watershed and drainage, or irrigation, as the case may be, must be put in place. The out-buildings must be ordered and erected and facilities acquired for harvest and storage. If the land is to be used for processing—such as feed lots, slaughtering, canning, or freezing—then equipment must be ordered, contracts for construction arranged, and the facilities built. All of this must be accompanied by support facilities, such as trucks and barges for cartage, grain elevators, port facilities to handle exports and imports (yes, imports for such essentials as ammonia, which is used as fertilizer), and warehousing facilities for dry and cold storage.

It is sometimes thought that developing countries produce food and developed countries make television sets and fabricate manufactured products. In fact, the reverse is true. Developing countries assemble electronics and manufacture labor-intensive products, and developed countries produce food. Agriculture is a capital-intensive business. I saw one study in the 1970s which concluded that, in the aggregate, there is more capital invested on the farms in the United States than in all of our factories. A successful agricultural economy is a capital-intensive economy, what we usually think of as an industrial economy.

In short, agriculture is not something that can be turned on and off at will. It is a culture, a way of life that takes on a momentum of its own. We have always been proud of the fact that the United States has been the food basket for the world. Agricultural exports account for a good part of our export earnings, and, if the United States is ever to correct the deficit in its balance of trade, then agriculture will have to be a key component in that effort.

It has long been national policy to encourage farmers to achieve higher production and higher efficiency. We have always been proud of our capacity to produce hybrid seed, more efficient fertilizers and pesticides, mechanized planting, cultivating, and harvesting equipment, and, at the end of the process, to witness the bounty in our markets and to view ships laden with food-stuffs leaving our ports, destined for other markets around the world.

The support system for all of this includes banks, thrifts, and specialized farm credit and financial services businesses. Where else do farmers get the loans they need to buy that adjoining sec-tion of land from the farm down the road that is being broken up? And how can one not buy it when it becomes available since the opportunity may not exist again, particularly if it becomes a shopping center? Where else can the cooperative borrow to build the fertilizer plant, or to supply cartage or storage? Where else does the processing company go to finance the construction of a grain elevator or a new, modern slaughter facility? And let us not forget, such new facilities are technologically state-of-the-art in terms of electronics, robotics, and automation.

The financial institutions in the farm belts of the United States were caught up in all of this. At one point, when soybeans were six dollars a bushel, Iowa farm land sold for as much as $3,000 an acre. Today, that same land is for sale at less than half the price. Tractors and combines cost as much as $100,000 or more a unit. Today, that machinery is lying idle, and sales at bargain prices are plentiful as banks and thrifts try to liquidate their past-due loans by putting land and equipment on the auction block.

Such a situation is intolerable! The world population is grow-ing, people are starving around the globe, available agricultural lands are being absorbed for development, the supply of such es-sentials as fresh water has limitations, and, in the face of all this, we permit the most efficient food production system the world has ever known to come apart at the seams. Bad, bad policy! We should be opening up foreign markets, promoting more export earnings, and encouraging our farmers to produce all they can, as fast as they can, and efficiently enough to make money at mar-ket prices. The overall supply-demand situation is clear. There is more global demand for the food, in terms of hungry people, than there is food. The argument is made that they cannot pay for it. True enough. Starving people, now existing on subsistence rations, cannot pay hard currency to buy new supplies of food. But the rest of the world can pay, and must pay, in order to get these people on their feet, relocated if necessary, and trained to produce enough to care for themselves. The need is present, the demand is present, and given an adequate payment mechanism and distribution system, enough food can be supplied to meet the aggregate demand. We need to put our farmers back to work.

To do this, we need the Federal Reserve banks to rediscount five-year paper for the banks in the farm belt at concessionary rates of interest. The Federal Reserve is empowered, and in fact was originally set up, to do just that. We need the Federal Home Loan Bank to do the same on land loans made by the thrifts it supervises. We need to refinance the Farm Credit System, which has gone broke. It holds one-third of the nation's farm debt and is losing money—$2.7 billion in 1985, $1.9 billion in 1986, an estimated $1.4 billion in 1987. Several of the regional land banks are virtually insolvent. The crisis in the farm credit system, and the reported unwillingness of its more healthy components to help the land banks in need, is reminiscent of the disagreement in the savings and loan community regarding funding for the Federal Savings and Loan Insurance Corporation. The stronger, sounder institutions don't want to pay for the mistakes of the institutions experiencing difficulty. I can't say that I blame them. It is really the system, its regulatory structure, and its lack of disclosure that are at fault. But, fault or no fault, the fact is that the system is broke and needs to be fixed with "can do" programs.

Lest anyone infer from this that I have abandoned my free market orientation, let me hasten to add that nothing could be further from the truth. The marketplace and the free market must be the central arbiter. That is a principle I will not abandon, for farmers or for financial institutions. We must have good management and efficiency. If it makes more economic sense to farm for catfish than to plant land crops, and in many places it does because the dollar yield per acre is better, then so be it. Let the farmer who produces catfish prosper, and the farmer who fails to evolve with the market fail and sell out. I do not advocate that the farmer be guaranteed anything but a market at a world price which is fairly established. I simply challenge our leaders to mobilize the money and distribution systems around the world to make certain that all the food produced is purchased at freely established open-market prices between a willing buyer and a willing seller in a legitimate commercial transaction. No agricultural system can withstand distress prices brought on by "dumping." Prices must be realistic and legitimately reflect value in the marketplace. Beyond that, it is the farmers who take a risk to make a profit within this pricing constraint or sell out to someone else who can.

In that context, I challenge our leaders to marshal the resources to purchase all the food produced and to distribute this food to the people who need it to survive, provided they work for it by learning to make do for themselves. I also challenge our banks and thrifts and the Farm Credit Administration to provide bridge financing to get us through these tough times. Such financing is possible if we accept that it is the government's responsibility to provide a market for the food produced, at market-determined prices.

It is not inconsistent with a free market philosophy to help those who are down to get back on their feet. I don't mean a "bailout." I mean credit and access to markets. And, it is not inconsistent with a free market philosophy to spend money to develop new markets by investing in poor people around the globe who are willing to learn and to work and to relocate and to do whatever may be necessary to survive. This isn't charity. It is insuring our own long-term survival. It is an investment we make in our own future.

I am not discouraged by the wagging heads and the nay sayers. If it were easy, it would have been done long ago. It is not easy, but it is a challenge we must conquer.

The same can be said about our energy industry. Unlike the farmer, energy producers always had an end market for their products. They may have disliked the price, but they had a market. The mistakes made were pure and simple human error, spurred by greed and ambition, compounded by bad market timing and carelessness, including carelessness by the regulators. The Washington State Public Power Supply System, the nuclear power facility in the Northwest, is a prime example.

Like agriculture, energy is a critical industry, essential for our national survival and independence. Without energy sufficiency, we are not politically independent. To become energy independent, we need to deregulate totally. We also need higher prices, which can be accomplished in a free market context. Whether that should be accomplished by an import tax on oil and gas coming in from abroad or total deregulation or some form of incentives is a policy to be debated and established. Special consideration should be accorded to oil and gas from this hemisphere to encourage regional development for mutual security.

Domestically, however, the system of state and federal controls must be dismantled and replaced by deregulation. Can you imagine the anomalies and contradictions created by regulation? Under the mandated price structure prevailing in the early 1980s, natural gas produced from the Hugoton field in Kansas and Oklahoma could not be sold, in some cases, for more than 32 cents per thousand cubic feet or even less, yet the exact same natural gas was trading on the free market for as much as $5 per thousand cubic feet. Obviously, this is no way to encourage exploration and development.

I love the energy business. It is operated by a rare breed of individuals who pursue impossible challenges and who accept great risks all over the world. I say this from the vantage point of years as a primary lender to the energy industry and then as chief operating officer of a major energy conglomerate.

The challenge of exploration, in some cases, reaches three miles below the earth's surface, drilling in thousands of feet of ocean, braving wind, storms and icebergs, combatting jungles and deserts. Building facilities for production and transportation over the most hostile, impassable terrain in the world is true adventure.

And this is to say nothing about handling explosive materials under great pressures, dealing with toxic waste and corrosion, and producing product that is clean and safe. I am not just talking about liquid hydrocarbons, such as oil and gas. I am also talking about coal and nuclear and synthetics such as solar, gasahol, geothermal, wind, bagasse, orimulsion and the like.

The coal industry fuels a large part of the world's population. The capital investment in mines, transportation, and storage facilities is enormous. It is reported that Exxon's Columbian coal facility cost more than the Panama Canal. The new coal mine at Ping Shou in Shanxi Province in the People's Republic of China, a joint venture between Occidental Petroleum and the Chinese Coal Ministry, is a $600 million sight to behold. A new town had to be built and a river diverted to create one of the largest open pits in the world.

The same is true of nuclear power. This industry is essential to our future competitiveness. When the world supply of economical oil and gas runs dry, as surely it must in the centuries ahead, then an important substitute will be hydrogen created from seawater, using vast quantities of electricity. We will also create fresh water the same way. How can we do this without nuclear power? The right course is not to stop its development but to make it safe and clean.

A whole range of other industries—from retailing to mining to entertainment and communications—are as dramatic and exciting and full of challenge as the agriculture and energy industries I have just discussed. Commercial banks are crucial to all of them as lenders, as investors and joint venturers, and as suppliers of many related services. This is why commercial banking is so hard to manage. The diversity of its activities is almost infinite. It is also why strong leadership is so important to keep each financial institution hewing tightly to the course chosen.

If the person in charge is a "me too" follower, does not develop the institution's strengths based on the needs of the particular communities served, and strives to do what everyone else does but faster and in more volume than others in his or her own market area, the institution is probably on the road to future trouble. The market is too efficient and other bankers are too smart to allow one member to outperform them noticeably on the standard and universal business in which they all participate. To be competitively strong and still safe, each institution must exude its own distinct personality and a style that is deeply rooted in its own unique skills, history and traditions. The successful banker must set standards and zealously guard these standards through efficient, unyielding administration. The banking leader must be strong and resolute, ever vigilant and unyielding in terms of basic principles. Watch out when a banker admits, as John Stavropoulos of First Chicago did when losses started mounting, to the sin of "We've been wimps."

SEVENTEEN

Asset and Liability Management

Asset and liability management is the platform supported by the four legs of banking. These four legs are assets, liabilities, capital, and earnings.

ALCO (the Asset-Liability Management Committee) is the committee that monitors all the activities of the institution on a daily basis for soundness of asset distribution, liquidity, and profitability. Each bank goes about asset and liability management in its own way, aimed at keeping the institution profitable and able to meet its obligations in the context of general economic conditions.

In 1973, I was chairman of the Asset and Liability Management Committee at First Chicago. On May 10th of that year, I gave a report to the board of directors which put forth a disturbing conclusion: "The large banks of the United States do not have within their own asset mix adequate liquidity to meet a large withdrawal of deposits." I went on to explain the basics of banking, including a cautionary look back at the crisis of the 1930s. My historical discussion read as follows:

Banks hold themselves out to the public as depositories and lenders. We accept deposits payable on demand, or short notice, and invest those deposits in loans or investments on the assumption that the deposits will not all be withdrawn at once, although inevitably some large amounts of deposits will be withdrawn daily. This gives rise to the two basic precepts of banking—liquidity and capital.

Liquidity—To be able to meet deposit withdrawals and fund asset growth, we must have access to adequate cash, either through the sale of marketable assets or through the creation of other liabilities.

Capital—To be able to absorb losses on our loans and investments, we must have adequate capital (stockholders' money).

The liquidity of banks has seldom been adequate to cover large-scale withdrawal of deposits. (Borrowing short and lending long is the nature of the banking business.) Nor has a large capital position proved effective as a substitute for liquidity. At the close of 1929, for example, equity capital totaling 25.7 percent of loans appeared more than adequate. However, the deepening depression during the following years resulted in a deterioration in the value of both the loan and investment portfolios.

Banks, unable to convert their assets into cash, except at disastrous discounts, were not able to meet the large-scale withdrawal of deposits at the depth of the depression and were forced to close, even though many had had what in normal times seemed to be adequate amounts of capital. Their inability to convert loans and investments into cash or to borrow money by issuing liabilities was due to two causes:

The value of bank assets, marketable in "normal" times, fell sharply because all banks (and corporations and individuals) were trying to convert assets into cash even at excessive losses. This was true even of the best-quality marketable bonds. (See Figure 17.1)

FIGURE 17.1: AVERAGE PRICES OF LONG-TERM BONDS (1927–1933)

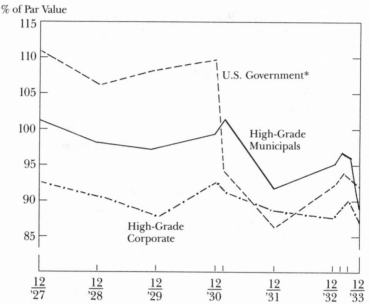

% of Par Value

*Derived from yields on partially tax-exempt bonds through 1930 and fully taxable bonds thereafter.

Bank loans were even more illiquid because borrowers could not pay when there was no other lender willing to refund the loans.

The Federal Reserve provided some liquidity, but it was woefully inadequate compared with the needs of banking, finance, and industry. Prompt, dramatic, and massive infusions of funds and liquidity through large-scale purchases of financial assets by the Federal Reserve might have arrested the decline.

However, the Federal Reserve, overwhelmed by the severity of the depression, failed to provide the liquidity; and the continuing decline in prices and the economy further weakened the financial position of both banks and businesses alike.

In February 1933, the dam broke with the failure of the Union Guardian Trust Company in Detroit—one of the largest banks in Michigan, with close ties to many other banks. The panic spread quickly across the nation, causing massive withdrawals of gold and currency from the banks. By March 4, every state in the Union had declared bank holidays, so President Roosevelt's decree of a four-day, nationwide banking holiday, beginning March 6, only recognized the actual situation.

Of the 4,000 banks that closed during 1933 (22.5 percent of the total), less than 1,300 were members of the Federal Reserve System, and over 2,700 were nonmembers which did not have access to Federal Reserve borrowings.

Based upon size, only seven banks had loans and investments of more than $50 million while more than 3,300 had loan and investment totals of less than one million dollars. Thus, it was mainly the small banks which were unable to survive the financial storm.

Survival in a financial storm, and no storm was worse than the Great Depression, depends upon sound asset distribution. The soundness of asset distribution is the degree to which the institution approaches the model ratios established by the management and the board of directors. It is the availability of adequate cash and cash equivalents in all currencies around the globe. It is the monitoring of the ratio of bonds to total loans to all other assets. Other assets might include real estate owned. It is the further monitoring of subdivisions within the bond portfolio; for example, the quality, amount, and ready marketability of government bonds, long- and short-term municipal bonds, and corporate bonds. It is the monitoring of the quality and maturity of the loan portfolio. And it is the monitoring of the marketability and liquidity of the other assets.

When I use the word *monitoring*, I mean pro-active surveillance with pro-active participation in the inner workings of the system, including taking the necessary corrective action, when the proportions and ratios and quality classifications get out of kilter. This is the safety dimension.

Liquidity means having ready cash resources in all currencies to pay the bills, to fund the drawdowns of loan commitments, to meet depositor withdrawals, to honor cash calls on foreign exchange contracts and guarantees, and to meet reserve requirements in the United States and around the world. Our system of reserve requirements permits banks and thrifts to invest most of the money they receive as deposits. Our whole economy is geared to this reinvestment by the banking system. A liquidity ratio (cash to total assets) of 20 percent is high. The other 80 percent is invested in bonds, loans, and other assets.

How, then, can a financial institution be certain that it will always be able to meet its financial obligations? It does so principally by maintaining the confidence of the community it serves, so that depositors are always putting more money into the institution than they take out. It also does so by maintaining the quality and marketability of its loan portfolio, so that other peer group institutions would always like to buy its loans at par value or better. And, it does so by maintaining the quality and discountability (with the Federal Reserve or the Federal Home Loan Bank) of its loans and other assets, so that these institutions would readily accept them as collateral. In other words, everything on the asset side of the balance sheet should be marketable at par or better in the spot market. Any shortfall in this standard has to be covered by capital. The earnings obtained from creating such a shortfall must compensate for the risk built into the portfolio and provide an adequate profit return to the shareholders.

This is the objective of proper assset and liability management.

It is important to view capital in its proper context. Capital is not there just to absorb losses. Obviously, the capital must be adquate to cover such losses, based on generally accepted accounting principles. It must also cover the shortfall between the values of the bank's assets as recorded on the books and the amount they would bring in a liquidation sale on the spot market.

Management that keeps all its assets in cash basically needs no capital.

Management that keeps all its assets in cash and short-term government bonds needs very little capital.

Management that keeps its assets in speculative, high-risk, and illiquid assets needs a great deal of capital because the valuation of these assets on the spot market is likely to be discounted substantially from the figures recorded in the published financial statements.

It follows, therefore, that continuous monitoring and classification of the asset portfolio, to establish the premium or discount from par, is critical to determine *capital adequacy*. This is the responsibility of the Asset-Liability Management Committee. It is also the test regulators should make when examining the institutions they administer.

Some will argue that bank loans and investments are long term, intended to be held until maturity. Therefore, valuations on a current-market basis are misleading.

It is true that many assets are of a long-term nature and the intent is to hold such assets until maturity. However, if such assets are priced properly and the quality is good, they can be sold readily at par or even at a premium.

If the assets in total are valued on a spot sale basis at less than par, then management has deliberately created this *open* or *risk* position. There is nothing wrong with such portfolio management as long as the open position is within guidelines approved by the board of directors, is adequately covered by capital funds, and produces a rate of return commensurate with the risks incurred. To test the extent of this open position, I believe the regulators should take a small random sample of an institution's loan and investment portfolio and require that it be sold. In this way, there will be validation of "realizable values" in the free market.

At First Chicago, I viewed several realizable values as supplementary capital: unrealized profit at the various real estate holdings used as bank premises, First National One, Two, and Three and the London branch building; the overfunded portion of the pension fund; unrealized capital gains in the venture capital subsidiary, First Capital Corporation; as well as the value of the franchise in Chicago and the licenses to do business around the world. This supplementary capital provided First Chicago with great hidden strength. Some of these "capital cushions" have since been cashed in, notably the excess funding in the pension plan, the real estate of First National Two and the London branch building, and some of the unrealized appreciation in the venture capital unit. But, these have been replaced by the unrealized gain on the American National Bank acquisition, and, I assume, more unrealized gain in First Capital. Furthermore, the unrealized gain on First National One and Three remains intact. So also does the value of the franchise in Chicago and around the world.

All of these items must concern the chairman of the ALCO committee, and each institution has different intangible and unrealized assets. They need to be catalogued and factored into the overall safety equation.

Very often, asset-liability management committees forego the function of asset classification and concentrate solely on funding, i.e., getting enough deposits and borrowings to pay the bills and support the growth. Funding is, indeed, a critical function. No financial institution should outrun its ability to fund itself.

The most obvious source of funds, of course, is deposits. But, the word *deposits* covers a broad spectrum of activity from the everyday passbook savings accounts to overnight borrowings in the London interbank market, called Eurodollar deposits.

No listing of the ways a depository institution obtains funds to finance its loans and investments could ever be complete or up-to-date because the imagination and creativity employed to access the market is virtually infinite. Some of the more traditional deposit and money raising activities include the following.

We all know about checking accounts. These include big corporate checking accounts, personal checking accounts, and NOW accounts (Negotiable Orders of Withdrawal, a kind of *payable through* item). The payable through item was originally used by insurance companies and railroads, among others, in order to avoid keeping idle credit balances in the banks, balances that did not earn interest. The payable through item, a draft much like a check, was only paid when the draft was actually presented to a bank for payment. This practice gave rise to the *zero balance account,* a cash management service made famous in the halcyon days of "go-go" banking, which allowed corporations to write checks before putting the money into the account. It also gave rise to the *consolidation account* that, at the end of each day, offsets the negative balances in accounts used to pay bills with credit balances in accounts used to receive and record deposits.

Then there are the savings deposits. These include the traditional passbook savings account, the retail savings certificate (a fixed time period at a fixed rate of interest), the individual retirement accounts (IRAs), the Christmas club account, the vacation club account, the savings bond account, all the "super saver" accounts one could imagine, the combination "saver-investment" account, and the bullion savings passbook for gold, silver, or other precious metals or gems.

There are retail money market deposit accounts and money market certificates of deposit whose interest rates rise or fall with the money market.

A big source of money is *float.* Float is the free money the institution can use to finance loans and investments because it has not yet credited your account with the funds it has collected on checks that you deposited. Commercial banks used to obtain significant funds from checking accounts maintained by corporations, called *corporate float,* i.e., proceeds from checks that corporations would submit for deposits in their *cash letters* (bundles of checks for deposit with notification letter attached). But corporate treasurers discovered they could capture these funds and invest them to make a profit for their own accounts. This was called *cash management* and became, in its application, a form of art or a mystical science. Corporations in Oregon would open an account with a bank in North Carolina so the checks they gave suppliers would take the longest possible time to clear. Corporations in the East would open accounts with banks in remote communities of North Dakota. Corporate float within banks became a relic of the past. So financial institutions turned to individuals. Lists of *availability dates* were published, letting depositors know how long it would take for checks to clear.

These availability schedules allowed the institution to use the funds for a day or two (i.e., *float*) before the depositor could draw down the funds.

Float is not just available on checking accounts. It is also available on credit card balances, trust department deposits, proceeds from discount brokerage operations, proceeds received and disbursed on municipal, corporate, and government bond transactions, disbursements on loans, escrow accounts, collections on drafts, letter-of-credit transactions, and the full range of trust services. The Swiss branches of the big multinational international banks do a big business in collecting coupons on securities managed for customers. The proceeds from these coupon collections must be converted into the right currencies and deposited into the appropriate accounts based on published availability schedules. The potential opportunities for float are considerable.

The most obvious sources of float are services that are purchased in advance, such as the security deposits on letters of credit, or consumer purchases of travelers checks, where the money is put up when the checks are issued and no interest is paid while the checks are outstanding. Travelers checks produce enormous amounts of usable float balances. This is why American Express, Citicorp, and the VISA and MasterCard issuers push them.

Another mechanism for raising money is the so called *repurchase agreement*. This is where the institution sells an asset, usually a bond, for a specified price and agrees to buy it back at a negotiated higher price on a specified date. The purchaser pays the selling institution "good funds" and is compensated for the use of those funds by the profit, which is the difference between the price charged by the institution when it sold the securities and the price paid by the institution when it repurchased them.

The securities most often used for such transactions are U.S. Government bonds. But, theoretically at least, any asset is eligible.

Bankers acceptances are also useful vehicles to raise money. Specifically provided for in federal banking legislation, a bankers acceptance is the forerunner of the *collateralized mortgage obligation* (CMO) that became popular in the period of high interest rates prevailing in the late 1970s. Like the CMO, the bankers acceptance allows a financial institution to finance its loan portfolio through a sale of a certificate which uses the assets financed by the loan as collateral. Federal legislation specifies the criteria for *eligible acceptances* which qualify for rediscount or purchase by the Federal Reserve bank. They are, therefore, prime paper and can be issued at the lowest possible rate of interest. To qualify for financing by eligible acceptances, the drafts which the institution would accept must cover loan advances to finance "goods in international commerce," goods in transit covered by bills of lading, or goods in a public warehouse covered by public warehouse receipts.

Like the eligible acceptance, the *ineligible acceptance* or *finance acceptance* is generally three-name paper (i.e., the drawer of the draft, the drawee, and the accepting bank). Because they are not covered in the enabling legislation permitting the Federal Reserve bank to purchase them, ineligible or finance acceptances usually carry an interest rate of higher than eligible acceptances by 0.25 to 0.50 percent.

Significant monies are also raised by foreign exchange *swap* transactions. If I have excess deposits of deutsche marks or can borrow deutsche marks but need dollars now, I can sell you deutsche marks for dollars now (i.e., *spot*) and buy back those same deutsche marks for dollars at an agreed upon price on some specified future date (i.e., *forward*). This gives me the use of the dollars in the interim at a cost represented by the difference between the selling price and the repurchase price. Such a transaction can be accomplished in any combination of currencies to produce credit balances in the currency needed at the moment. The so-called swap is the interplay of the spot with the future transaction.

Credit balances are also created by marketing *escrow* transactions. People putting up deposits to purchase real estate, or parties in litigation who choose to leave the amount in dispute with a neutral party, or people making bids at auctions on general merchandise or on art works, or parties contracting with each other and wishing to demonstrate their good faith or credibility, all use escrows to accomplish their goals. Certain institutions excel at these kinds of transactions and raise considerable money in the process to finance their loans and investments.

Deposits on commercial transactions are a regular part of a financial institution's business. For example, the mortgage department often requires deposits to be maintained to cover repairs or insurance or real estate taxes. In the aggregate, the deposits so generated may amount to a tidy sum.

And, then there are bill paying services for utilities or local merchants. The pay-by-phone product is one such service. Customers can call into the depository institution's computer at any time of the day or night and use a touch-tone telephone to key in the proper instructions. These transactions create additional opportunities for deposits and float.

Big institutions also seek to provide services to the U.S. Government, such as issuing and servicing U.S. Savings Bonds for the public. The institutions are paid through a U.S. Treasury tax and loan account, where corporations deposit their quarterly tax payments and the U.S. Treasury decides, institution-by-institution, how long it will leave any or all of those funds on deposit. Similarly, banks help states and municipalities to sell their bonds or obtain other financings. Banks provide other services such as direct payroll deposits, collection services for taxes, parking tickets, or other receivables; and, in return, the states and municipalities reward the institutions by leaving deposits with them. This is usually the responsibility of the city or state treasurer and/or controller to negotiate and administer.

Big institutions raise large sums of money in the *Federal funds* market. Fed funds are excess reserves available overnight to large and small banks alike, or excess liquidity at savings and loans, which work through banks to invest this excess in the Fed funds market. Most big institutions have a money market desk to trade Fed funds actively and, typically, the larger institutions are net takers of such funds. It is a danger sign when an institution is a net taker all the time, as was the case with the Continental Illinois during the period just prior to its collapse.

The major activity for the money market desk, however, is the marketing and servicing of professional money market instruments, such as the *jumbo certificates of deposit* among others. These jumbo CDs can be hundreds of thousands or millions of dollars in size. Making a market for these instruments is big business. With billions of dollars in volume, each 0.01 percent makes a big difference in profitability to a big institution. It is also in this area that financial institutions have been known to use brokers and investment bankers to help them place and make a market for their certificates. This is another danger area. It means the institution does not have the capacity to place the paper on its own, and buyers of the paper should be cautious. It is also cause for the investment bankers and brokers who market the paper to be certain of their own responsibilities in ascertaining the soundness of the paper they are marketing and that proper disclosure has been made.

Another big source of funds is the Euromoney market. There are *Eurodollars, Eurosterling, Euroyen, Euromarks, Eurofrancs,* and so forth. Akin to the Fed funds market in the United States, it is where international financial institutions invest their excess liquidity for terms ranging from overnight to five years. The terms and conditions of each transaction are individually negotiated by trading desks in bank branches and subsidiaries around the world. Because of its flexibility and ease of entry, this is a market fraught with danger. It is particularly vulnerable because there is no effective regulatory surveillance and no meaningful reserve requirements to govern velocity or the multiplier.

Funds can also be raised by selling assets. A traditional mechanism for selling assets has been the *syndicated loan* where an agent bank negotiates a large loan with a borrower and then sells participations in that loan to other lending institutions, usually charging an *origination fee* and a *management fee*. But loan syndications aren't the only way. There is also the mechanism of placing mortgages or other loans into a pool administered by a trustee and then selling participation certificates in that pool of assets for some percentage, say 80 percent, of the value of the assets in the pool. This is a modern development which is accelerating rapidly. The advantage is that it helps to fortify liquidity, but there is also a risk of loss.

As I have indicated before, I like the idea of a free market test to value assets. In another sense, however, I believe that the practice of selling off assets in collateralized pools supporting trust certificates (i.e., securitized loans) should require additional primary capital. This would offset the pledge of excess assets that are committed to support the credit of each pool.

A good retail institution has the culture and capability to adapt and package all of these money gathering facilities and instruments for general distribution to the public. What is good for the "big guy" can also be packaged for the "little guy." An institution that can successfully merchandise its money gathering product to the broadly based retail public is a safer and sounder institution than one that relies heavily on professional brokers or intermediaries to get its paper into the marketplace. There are, of course, special situations like Morgan Guaranty, which is not retail oriented but which holds a commanding position in the large corporate and international markets, particularly with foreign central banks. Only a very few can successfully pursue the Morgan Guaranty strategy. The vast majority of other financial institutions must build a broadly based money gathering system among loyal customers in the communities they serve.

Bank holding companies can borrow directly from the marketplace. One common form of direct borrowing is the issuance of commercial paper. In addition, there are the so-called "Citicorp auctions," so named because they were invented by Citicorp. They auction blocks of commercial paper to investment bankers. The advantage of such bidding is to move large blocks of paper all at once without depressing the market, which might be the consequence if the holding company tried to distribute a little at a time over a long period.

Another form of direct borrowing is to use the discount facilities provided by the Federal Reserve System to commercial banks and by the Federal Home Loan Bank System to savings and loans. Assets eligible for rediscount must meet criteria set by the boards of directors of the Federal Reserve banks and the Federal Home Loan banks. All require eligible collateral as security. This is why it is important for the audit departments of each institution to keep the management and board of directors continually informed as to what proportion of the institution's assets qualify for rediscount and at what rate of interest. There is more than one rediscount rate depending upon the eligibility of the assets put up as collateral. The *discount rate* is a prime bellweather rate for other money market instruments.

Bank and savings and loan holding companies also raise capital by selling securities in the public markets. These sales include subordinated debentures, capital notes, preferred stock, and common stock. Bank holding companies are no different from any other public corporation in this regard. The objective is to raise term money or permanent capital at a price that will permit profitable reinvestment. Until recently, the risk inherent in holding company securities has not been adequately perceived by the investing public. The advent of holding company failures and forced recapitalizations caused investors to lose money and thus identified such risks.

With respect to profits, ALCO must monitor the interest spread and its bottom-line impact, along with its other accountabilities of safety and liquidity. Profitability is a balancing act, weighing risk versus safety and average life of loans and investments versus liquidity. Most big financial institutions make their money by borrowing short-term and lending somewhat longer. The art of prudent management is knowing how much is too much, and the degree of optimum *gapping* (short versus long, fixed-rate versus variable-rate, liquid versus illiquid assets) in the context of the current and expected future economic environment.

ALCO strategy is only as good as its ability to forecast economic conditions several years into the future. That's how long it takes for loans and investments to mature and be repaid. In 1979 and 1980, my view of the future was directly contrary to the views of Roger Anderson and Continental Illinois. That is why our policies were diametrically opposite. I was pursuing a retail banking thrust and emphasizing quality loans at fixed rates on a restricted basis in First Chicago's commercial banking. In retrospect, my view of the future in 1979 and 1980 and my policies of holding back on "go-go" commercial growth was right and Roger Anderson's opposite tack was wrong.

Forecasting is not a calendar quarter-by-calendar quarter exercise. It is an insightful examination of underlying strategy to be measured and evaluated over a full business cycle. It does not imply running with the herd. On the contrary, the best strategies sometimes require courage to lean against the wind.

The inventor and "patron saint" of asset and liability management is my friend and senior colleague, Edward L. Palmer, formerly chairman of the Executive Committee of Citicorp, and inventor of the "Citicorp auction" of commercial paper. On February 6, 1971 at Citicorp's annual correspondent bank forum, Ed Palmer introduced all of us to the management science of asset and liability management. This landmark address had a great influence on us at First Chicago and indeed on the entire U.S. banking industry. Because it remains relevant after all these years, I will quote from it at length as follows:

> By any standard, 1970 was one of the wildest years the banking system has seen since the '30s. We all learned some lessons, and hopefully, we came out of the experience a little wiser. I would like to share with you some of our thoughts on the long-range implications of 1970, for the events of the past year are bound to have significant impact on the way

we manage our banks, our views on liquidity, and finally, our planning for the future.

By any criterion, 1970 was an eventful year, one which re-affirmed two important realities — that political and social occurrences have more impact than ever upon the general health of our economy, and that change is occurring so rapidly that these events are increasingly difficult to anticipate.

These realities have significant implications for our banking system. Interest rates are the pulse of the economy and movements in interest rates have a substantial effect upon bank profitability. The sensitivity of our own earnings to such changes has accelerated dramatically during the last five years as we come to depend increasingly upon purchased money to fund our new loans. During 1970, a change of only five basis points in the cost of our purchased funds over the year cost one million dollars in net operating earnings. A change of less than four basis points in our average loan yield had the same effect.

All indications suggest the stakes will be even higher tomorrow. In our last five-year plan, we forecast that only one-third of the new funds we will require over the next five years will be supplied through the normal growth in demand deposits, savings accounts, and additions to capital. The remainder, or two-thirds of our new funds needs, will have to be purchased from various money market sources. By the end of 1975, we expect that 41 percent of our total domestic liabilities will be represented by interest-sensitive purchased funds, CDs, commercial paper, etc.

Improving our interest-rate forecasting, therefore, is one of the highest priority items we have. Whether you go through the formal exercise or not, rate forecasting is at the core of the asset and liability management problem, and it doesn't make any difference whether you're dealing in billions, hundreds of millions, or millions, the relative impact on your P&L is likely to be the same. Regardless of how well our projections compared to others, they lacked the accuracy we needed. In fact, our forecasts were off enough to threaten the credibility of our entire budgeting and planning process.

We worked on the rate forecasting problem all year through the mechanism of a monthly projection of key money market instruments prepared by five forecasters within the bank. Each of these forecasters supplied us with independent estimates for each of the following six months and the two subsequent quarters. We then attempted to reach agreement on these rate forecasts for use in establishing our asset and liability management strategy for the month.

These rate forecasts are used for another purpose, probably peculiar to our own bank. Several years ago, we adopted a marginal cost of funds approach in valuing pool funds transferred between our profit centers as well as for valuing deposits of customers in the analysis of the profitability of their accounts. Our objective was to develop a mechanism that would describe to our account managers the effect of their pricing decisions on the bank's income statement.

In essence, our system assumes that every new deposit is worth the marginal cost of funds the bank is purchasing at that time from the money market. The same principle holds true for evaluating the cost of making a loan. For example, during much of 1970 our new loans were funded by purchasing Eurodollars which cost us up to 12 percent. The bottom-line effect of the transaction was the difference between the yield on the loan and the cost of the funds we were purchasing in the Eurodollar market. Today, the negotiable CD rate is the basis for calculating the transfer pool, but we also use holding company commercial paper or foreign central bank time deposits or whatever instrument that represents the principal source of our marginal funds. Since our management information system traces these transactions back to the profit centers, individual account officers are motivated to price their loan transactions at a high enough level to recover the marginal cost of funds to the banks. Although the theory is not without its limitations, we have found marginal costing to be highly preferable to an approach where our decisions are based on an average cost of funds or the allocation of assets to specific liabilities.

I don't intend to dwell on our internal management information systems. The point I do want to emphasize is that our decisions are closely tied to our rate forecasts, for the profitability of an investment depends as much on future interest rates as on the marginal costs of funds today. Although the marginal value of money is only one of many criteria we use in assessing a new loan, the concept does place a greater premium upon forecasting as a guide to our account officers who must buy and price our deposits and assets. The future, therefore, will find us strongly committed to solving the forecasting problem.

Although more precise rate projections are key to effective asset and liability management, the experience of last year has indicated that we can't rely exclusively on better forecasting *per se*. Better management techniques must ultimately deal with uncertainty. One method is to develop a range of forecasts and test alternative strategies or policies against each projection. In the drafting of our five-year plans this year, our Economics Department supplied us with two scenarios based essentially on two monetary policy options open to the Fed. One scenario was an economic forecast under an inflationary environment and the other, under a noninflationary environment. Given these alternate interest-rate climates, it is then possible to test a number of optional strategies against each rate environment for their cost or profit and liquidity implications.

The next level of sophistication is to assign probabilities to the assumptions and proceed from there with hedging techniques, the net product of which is a strategy which theoretically minimizes your risks and maximizes your potential gain. It goes without saying when you move from one simple forecast to the analytical technique of varying assumptions I have just described, your equipment includes a computer and someone who understands your management problem and computerized analytical techniques. What this all adds up to is that we're in the middle of an R & D effort which every member of senior management is behind, and I'll report back to you next year on whether we deliver any of our promises.

We also made good progress last year on improving the coordination and administration of our asset and liability management. By forming the Asset and Liability Committee, ALCO for short, we set up a new mechanism to coordinate our general strategies and policies. Our major lending groups, the chairman of our Credit Policy Committee, the head of our Money Market Division, and the head of our Planning and Management Information Division, are represented on the Committee.

In a broad sense, ALCO functions as a corporate overseer in our search for an asset and liability mix that will maximize Citibank's earnings. Of equal concern is the *liquidity position* of the bank, a word that, to us, includes the quality of our loans and investments as well as the most appropriate liability structure to support our earning assets. Since earnings and liquidity must often be balanced off against each other, the committee is made up of those individuals who have a direct interest in at least one side of the earnings-liquidity equation. For example, Reuben Richards and Al Costanzo represent the principal users of funds through the lending operations of the Corporate Banking Group and the International Banking Group in New York. On the other hand, Al Costanzo is also the manager of liabilities through foreign central bank time deposits and Eurodollars taken in London, Nassau, Tokyo, the Virgin Islands, and elsewhere. This is further complicated by his use of Eurodollars in loans, redeposits (placements with other banks), and swaps for foreign currencies for foreign branches that need them. This is where George Scott comes in to worry about liquidity as it affects us globally; he worries about that and quality as well. John Larkin is concerned with the long-term investment portfolio and our dealer operations, and Joe Fleiss has to come up with the shortfall by finding a home for CDs and commercial paper as well as managing our daily money position, which includes running to the Fed with a note when the other fellows overdraw our account.

In addition to its general supervisory role, ALCO has specific responsibility for establishing Citibank's liability position, both long and short run. Key to this assignment is the integration of interest-rate forecasts into the decision process. Each week the committee assesses these rate projections in light of the expected requirement for funds and then gives the money desk instructions as to the most appropriate purchased funds and short-term government position to assume for the week.

Two immediate benefits of ALCO have been greater continuity and efficiency in the asset and liabilities management process. The committee, which meets weekly, has replaced five special-purpose committees, one of which met on a daily basis.

These, then are some of the managerial problems we wrestled with last year. Next, I want to think out loud with you on the subject of liquidity. We came through 1969-70 with a better understanding of liquidity. Some concepts were validated, but many others near and dear to our hearts were made obsolete by the changing nature of our business.

First, 1970 reinforced our conviction that liquidity itself is not obsolete. The banker must still protect his customers and stockholders against unexpected reductions in deposits, a rise in the cost of purchased money, or sudden surges in loan demand. However, it seems clear that the way to achieve liquidity and the way to measure liquidity have changed. Many notions and concepts about liquidity have been built up over the years upon the idea of a liability structure dominated by demand deposits. One can still argue that for a bank relying exclusively on demand deposits as its source of funds, the most appropriate way to achieve liquidity is through a highly liquid short-term investment portfolio and that the way to measure liquidity is through the loan-to-deposit or risk asset-to-deposit ratios. That may still apply to some of you lucky fellows.

Most of us, however, have come a long way from the days when we relied exclusively on demand deposits. As I mentioned earlier, our funds growth over the foreseeable future will come through aggressive bidding for interest-bearing money. As we all know, the nature of our assets is also changing, with term loans and installment notes becoming more and more common to bank balance sheets. It's clear the nature of the liquidity problem of a bank with these characteristics is different from that of the bank trying to protect itself against unexpected demand deposit withdrawals. In some cases, the differences are more obvious than others and in some respects, more subtle.

In spite of some favorable developments, liquidity still poses a major problem. While the search for more perfect forecasting models and management techniques goes on, much of the solution will ultimately lie with the development of new liquidity instruments.

On October 6, 1971, in an address to those attending the First Citicorp Investor Relations Dinner, Mr. Palmer elaborated on asset and liability management as follows:

> But mathematical techniques are not the sole answer to managing the interest differential portion of our business profitability. Continual assessment of expected loan demand and the effect of various pricing policies are also important. Each month we ask each of our lending areas to develop loan targets, sales targets if you will, for the remaining months of the year. After estimating the expected demand for credit, we can then test the appropriateness of several liability strategies. Also, various loan pricing policies can be examined.

> Later this month, we are bringing on stream a fully automated system to back up our commercial lending decisions. Built into this system is the capability of simulating the revenue that would result over the next 12 months from various pricing policies. This system also gives us a means of liquidity management. The runoff of loans presently on our books is one of our major sources of funds. Our loan system shows us exactly what this will be over the life of the loans. It also allows us to see the substantial positive earnings effect of the replacement of loans we made at low fixed rates in the mid-1960s, which are now maturing and being replaced at today's prices.

> In addition to its general supervisory role, ALCO has specific responsibility for establishing Citibank's liability position, both long and short run. Key to this assignment is the integration of interest-rate forecasts into the decision process. Each week the committee assesses these rate projections in light of the expected requirement for funds and then gives the money desk instructions as to the most appropriate purchased funds and short-term government position to assume for the week.

Note the interaction of ALCO management with the money desk and the bond trading operations.

The bond department traditionally had been the provider of primary liquidity by purchasing and holding readily marketable short-term government bonds. This role was subsequently expanded to include trading government obligations of all maturities, trading and investments in all maturities of state and municipal obligations, and trading and investments in corporate commercial paper and corporate bonds (recorded on the balance sheet as the *Other Bonds* account).

The volumes in these bond trading activities are very large, and so the potential dangers are also large. Merrill Lynch recently recorded a $250 million loss in its bond trading operations because a trader devised a scheme to sell the revenue from the bonds but required Merrill Lynch to keep the risk of principal loss. While this program was in operation, the traders made a lot of commission income. No one focused on the potential vulnerability until it was too late.

The same vulnerabilities are present when bonds are purchased on margin, or swapped for maturities, or used as vehicles for interest-rate hedging operations. These volumes are enormous, and trades are triggered by computer programmed models. The potential for mistakes or misplaced zeal in executing some scheme, as in the Merrill Lynch situation, is always present.

Bond traders and money market traders, like foreign exchange traders, are largely independent businesspeople running their own positions. They make dozens, if not hundreds, of trades per day and feed the information into the computer for follow-up by the operations department. Some of the more sophisticated trading operations record the telephone conversations of the traders to guard against inadvertent mistakes or misunderstandings. And the principal safeguard is the timely issuance and receipt of confirmations.

Despite all the safeguards, it is a business susceptible to considerable risks—of market loss, of trading losses, of underwriting losses when large blocks are bought from the U.S. Treasury or other Government agencies. Other losses can result from arbitrage transactions (i.e., finding differences in rates among securities of similar quality and maturity), new-product inventions or trading schemes, operational mistakes caused by a breakdown of control or "back room" support, and fraud.

In some institutions, including First Chicago, the heads of the various bond trading operations as well as the money market personnel report to the chairman of ALCO. Thus, the chairman of ALCO plays a key role in the senior management structure. His or her judgment will determine the institution's ability to foresee market conditions and shape a loan and investment strategy to take advantage of those changes. It is, of course, the responsibility of the chief executive officer and the board of directors to monitor and approve the strategies and performance of ALCO.

EIGHTEEN

The Economy Is Flunking

Overall Grade: D

Budgets	D	for Deficit
Trade Balance	D	for Deficit
Balance of Payments	D	for Deficit
Net Worth	D	for Deficit

Just as in ancient times, today we require credible forms of payment for commerce to prosper. We need money that has value in its own right and will be universally accepted. After many debacles and money crises, the United States formed the Federal Reserve System to issue credible money. The system provided for the paper to be backed by, and in some cases redeemed in, gold or silver. That backing eroded in part after the 1929 crash and the ensuing bank holiday. The 1933 legislation called in the "yellow backs" and banned the public from owning gold coins. Immediately after World War II, however, we returned to a position of strength relative to the rest of the world. We had the vast preponderance of the world's gold reserves and the only functioning macro economy. The Bretton Woods agreement of 1944 was the starting point for the monetary era in which we now find ourselves.

Under the Bretton Woods accord, the dollar was the fulcrum on which everything else turned. The assumption was that the dollar was, and would remain, as good as gold. The price of gold was pegged at 35 U.S. dollars per ounce. The problem was that, from 1944 to the present, we didn't keep it that way. Far from it, we allowed the price of gold to climb as high as $800 an ounce. Even at over $400 an ounce, the price prevailing in 1987, gold was more than 10 times the price of 1944. Obviously, the system came apart. The dollar did not stay as good as gold. Relative to gold, the dollar took a nose dive. It is appropriate to ask why.

Beginning in the 1960s, we took away the Federal Reserve System's exclusive franchise to print money and we accorded that concession to two other players: the commercial banking system and the U.S. Treasury.

That is why it has become imperative for all of us to understand reserve requirements and CDs, and demand deposits, and money supply. The fractional reserve system allows banks to lend more money than they accept in cash deposits or keep in their capital accounts. The new deposits created by these extra loans are classified as money. In the 1960s, the Federal Reserve System's mechanisms for controlling bank reserves were emasculated as the growth-and-profit motive took over. By leveraging their balance sheets exponentially, the banks increased the money supply exponentially. The tidal wave of liquidity began to chase hard assets such as minerals, commodities, and real estate; and we set the stage for the volatility of the 1970s.

The other player printing money in the 1960s was the U.S. Treasury, as it tried to finance a war in Vietnam, rapidly expanding welfare programs at home, and major foreign capital investment programs to refloat the European, Latin American, and Japanese economies. All were noble efforts, but they led to massive current account deficits and runs on the dollar because we refused to cut spending, to raise taxes, to increase revenues.

The first post-war run on the dollar occurred in the early 1960s. As the United States ran up its current account deficits, foreigners accumulated quantities of dollars they did not want and did not need. It was a reversal from the 1940s and 1950s when foreigners needed and wanted dollars.

In the 1960s, foreigners changed their tune completely. It was said that, because of the Bretton Woods agreement on exchange rates, the United States was requiring nations such as Germany, Switzerland, and Japan to buy dollars in the open market. That would serve to maintain the dollar at its gold parity while the United States was doing everything possible at home to depreciate the value of the dollar. The foreigners argued that the artificially high dollar coupled with the requirement to maintain its value under Bretton Woods meant that we were exporting our inflation to them. It was an appropriate argument and factually correct.

However, we were strong, the military shield of the free world, and so we listened but did little to remedy the situation. We had our own priorities.

Robert V. Roosa, who was undersecretary of the Treasury under President Kennedy, did try to alleviate the situation. He devised a scheme whereby foreign governments with surplus reserves of dollars could invest these dollars with the U.S. Treasury and receive interest. These were labeled "Roosa Bonds," a clever stop-gap but by no means a solution to the basic malady, that is, too much outgo and too little intake. The justification repeatedly advanced to our foreign critics was that our trade balance was positive and this positive trade balance, over time, would redress the deficiencies in the current account.

Basically, the government printed money to pay our foreign debts. The United States had exported unwanted dollars abroad. The holders of those dollars said they had enough. They threatened to redeem the dollars for gold at the official price, or to freeze them against collateral at a value commensurate with the official price, which everyone recognized was inflated. The United States said, "No, we can't do that, but we'll give you an IOU." This is like writing a check with no resources in the bank to back it up. However, since it worked, we continued to do it throughout the 1960s, printing money for any foreign government wishing to exchange its surplus dollars. The dollars received in return for the Roosa bonds were used to finance our domestic deficits, thereby keeping pressure off the domestic bond markets and keeping interest rates artificially low.

The government's Ponzi scheme could not last forever, and by 1970 the downward pressure on the dollar became extreme. By then, even the trade balance had weakened and started to go negative. Thus, the United States was faced with continued red figures in the current balance-of-payments account, the beginning of red figures in the trade account, and a commitment to redeem dollars at $45 per ounce of gold (the $35 figure had been adjusted upward). Foreign creditors demanded that we intervene to buy dollars with the foreign currencies they would lend us under prearranged swap agreements. If we refused, they threatened to exercise their right to present their dollars for payment in gold in order to force a default, just as Edward Eagle Brown did in the 1930s with the Federal Reserve Bank of Chicago. In that instance, confronted with the threat of having to redeem "yellow backs" for gold, the Federal Reserve backed down and did not ship the gold to New York as previously ordered.

It was in the 1970s that the concept of freely floating exchange rates began to gain a following. It was the easy way out. It was considered preferable to making long-term commitments to borrow foreign currencies as a way of intervening in the exchange markets. This practice previously had been woefully unsuccessful and served only to enrich the speculators. U.S. Treasury officials decided that the only solution was to abrogate the link to gold, terminate the Bretton Woods agreement, and let the dollar float freely at whatever rate the market might dictate. Everyone was happy. The foreign creditors breathed a sigh of relief, because they would no longer be required to intervene to buy more dollars they did not want. Moreover, they would be able to sell their excess dollars and at least get something for them. The Treasury was happy because the solution protected the gold reserves at Fort Knox and removed a persistent source of political irritation. The large banks active in the foreign exchange markets were happy because they had universally taken positions against the dollar. Now the dollar was not only in a free fall but the free market for foreign exchange meant expanded opportunities for a lucrative business. I was one of a very small minority to argue against the new exchange-rate policy.

I remember visits to Paul Volcker in his office at the Treasury to argue for adjustments in the pegged rates of the Bretton Woods system and for continued maintenance of the Bretton Woods system of parities. I also argued for a tie to gold in some form as a discipline against overcreation of dollars. In fact, I visited with Secretary Volcker on the gold question just before the gold window was closed. Subsequently, I testified before the joint Congressional committee on fixed rates versus floating rates, again suggesting that freely floating rates would not work and would introduce undue instability among trading partners. I was afraid that a cheap dollar would bring on virulent inflation, and the loss of any peg to gold or some other fixed standard would permit money to be printed without limit.

The United States had started with virtually 100 percent gold cover for its currency in 1944, modified that to 50 percent in the 1950s, reduced that by announced policy to 25 percent in the 1960s, and here we were in the 1970s with no cover at all.

The sponsorship for floating rates was powerful and influential. The political community, bankers, foreign dignitaries and, the academic community, all espoused freely floating exchange rates and a total break with gold or any fixed standard. The reasoning was that a depreciated dollar would stimulate exports and provide jobs, which, of course, was true. It is also true, of course, that inflation eventually catches up with the exporters and all the advantages disappear. The only time that devaluation works is when it is coupled with tight credit and comprehensive domestic deflationary policies, all of which are painful and politically un-popular, if not suicidal, for the regime that adopts them. These truths were overlooked and euphoria took hold.

It was argued that gold and silver as backing for the currency was a relic of the past, to be viewed in the same light as supersti-tion or witchcraft. The real strength of a currency, it was said, was the strength of the economy backing it, and there was no stronger economy in the world than that of the United States. The point that was lost in all of the ideological discussion was that no government in history had been strong enough to resist the temptation to debase its currency when there was no exter-nal standard or discipline to keep it in check. There was little prospect that the United States Government, which had demon-strated little monetary discipline in the 1960s and 1970s, would break the pattern. Also lost were lessons of the past regarding the insidious damage caused to long-term trade and investment arrangements by erratic exchange-rate behavior.

For the impact of floating exchange rates on the U.S. economy in the 1970s, let's look at the dismal record. We had the greatest sustained inflation ever recorded in the United States. Our na-tional debt grew more in that decade than it had from the found-ing of the Republic to 1970, from $400 billion to just over $800 billion. It more than doubled again from 1980 to 1985 to over $1.8 trillion, and there is no sign of slowing. (See Figure 18.1.) Federal spending increased from a normal 20 percent of GNP in 1981 to a whopping 24.5 percent of GNP in 1985, and the tax cuts of 1981 reduced the tax revenues that otherwise reduced the deficit.

Our position in foreign trade has continued to erode. Trade deficits have never been larger, over $100 billion annually, and if it weren't for the heavy inflow of foreign investment money, the pressures on interest rates would be noticeable. As it is, these pressures are just being postponed. And our debts, both foreign and domestic have continued to swell so that today we are, for the first time in our modern history, a debtor nation. That means that foreigners have more investments in the United States than

Figure 18.1: Public Debt Ceiling
As Set by Congress

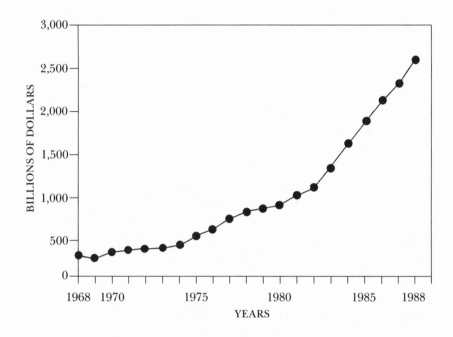

Americans have abroad. It is the first time this has occurred in more than 50 years and the erosion during the past year has been startling, a swing of more than $300 billion from net creditor to net debtor.

These are big numbers and they are mounting up on the wrong side of the ledger. Our percentage of world exports has declined, and our annual percentage of world imports has increased by 150 percent in 10 years. We are surviving because foreigners are pouring money into the United States, and we are not investing abroad commensurately. Our federal deficits are unsustainably large and seemingly out of control, a shocking record of fiscal irresponsibility.

Where will all of this lead? It will lead inevitably to inflation and a cheapened currency. I am sure of it because the pattern has occurred and reoccurred throughout history. We are merely following the classical pattern, a pattern that happens over and over again. The cycle varies in length but it generally follows this progression. Because of a nation's dominant political position relative to its trading partners, the progressive weakening of the currency is tolerated to excess in order to finance the country's political or military objectives. For a recent example, we need only look to England during the 19th century. If you want to go back much further, look at the Roman Empire. The story is always the same.

A cheapened currency provides the stimulus for booming domestic activity, and everyone has a happy feeling of well-being. As the booming domestic activity produces inflation, there is a flight to commodities. The inflation becomes an oppressive burden on the populace and its financial institutions, and measures are put in place to contain and reduce the inflation. These measures include high interest rates, budget balancing mechanisms, and cutbacks in sovereign spending.

All of this, in turn, cripples domestic manufacturing and agriculture. Because of dampened domestic activity, the currency begins to strengthen which, in itself, enhances the deflationary measures. With the weakened manufacturing and agricultural economy and the progressively strengthening currency, exports decline, imports increase, and the trade balance deteriorates.

To compensate for the structural weakness in the domestic economy, taxes are cut to stimulate consumption, tax shelter schemes abound as a result of seemingly "directed" tax incentives. Those most able to pay the taxes take advantage of the tax shelters. Consider in the present circumstances the big corporations that make profits but pay no taxes, the "safe harbor" leasing schemes, real estate shelters, and similar escapes from taxation, all properly motivated to provide stimulus, but all ending up in the hands of those most able to pay their taxes. As a consequence, the government's annual cash revenue declines from what it otherwise would have been. Simultaneously, the sovereign itself steps up spending to compensate for lower direct investment by the manufacturing and agricultural sectors. Military spending and transfer payments such as social security, health, education, welfare, all continue to escalate on a programmatic basis.

The renewed escalation of budget deficits combines with trade deficits because, with the domestic economy depressed but with money available for consumption, imports greatly increase.

To combat the trade imbalance and to stimulate domestic recovery, determined efforts are made to cheapen the currency. Eventually the process starts all over again with inflation, then a rush to commodities, followed by inflation-fighting measures, and the whole cycle repeats.

Each cycle will generally be more pronounced in its intensity than the last because the numbers are larger. The capacity of the sovereign to dampen the impact is lessened because there is more currency in circulation and the national financial statements are weakened by the carryforward effect of combatting previous cycles. The Latin American economies are modern cases in point.

Yes, nations, like individuals, have income statements and balance sheets. A sovereign's income statement is the combination of 1) the annual budget; 2) the balance of trade; and 3) the current account, i.e. the movement of money in and out of the country.

A sovereign's balance sheet is the combination of 1) its assets; 2) its liabilities, including accrued pension, retirement, and disability plans for military personnel, civilian employees, social security, veterans compensation, federal employees' compensation, other pension plans, guarantees and other obligations (This does not even consider the implicit guarantees for such critical confidence keepers as FDIC and FSLIC); and 3) its net worth, which, in the case of the United States, is negative.

If the U.S. Government were a private company, without the power to tax or the power to print money, we'd be broke.

The statements of the U.S. Government clearly indicate where we find ourselves on the classic cycle. The spending and excessive currency-cheapening policies of the 1960s were followed by the removal of the gold standard and freely floating exchange rates. Inflation and commodity speculation, including investment in hard assets such as real estate, followed in the early 1970s. The impact on financial institutions and the financial system was overly stimulative, and measures were taken to curb the resulting inflation which occurred in the mid-to-late 1970s. These measures took hold in the 1980s and the result was lowered inflation, a strengthened dollar, and depression in the nonmilitary manufacturing and agricultural sectors.

To stimulate activity again, tax cuts were adopted and military spending grew, while transfer payments such as social security and welfare continued to increase. Predictably, our trade balance deteriorated, while the current account remained heavily in our favor as foreigners sought to invest in a militarily strong and politically safe haven.

All of this is preparatory to movement to the next phase: cheapening the currency to reinvigorate the manufacturing and agricultural sectors and to pay off the enormous deficits and explicit and implicit contractual liabilities incurred by the Federal Government. The result will be renewed inflation, a rush to commodities and real property and the cycle will complete its predictable revolution.

At this point, there appears to be no alternative except to inflate. The national debt, increased by recent deficits, is approaching the point of becoming unmanageably large, now over $2 trillion. The accrued liabilities for retired military personnel are nearly one half trillion dollars (the City of New York retirement program of half pay for life after 20 years of service nearly bankrupted that city). The accrued liability for social security is nearly two trillion dollars. The accrued liability for federal civilian employees is upward of a half trillion dollars. Future contract obligations to international agencies and contractors are unquantifiable. The implicit backing for FDIC and FSLIC, the guarantors of the safety of our money in banks and savings and loans, is also unquantifiable. The FDIC, however, is now soundly funded and will remain so if commercial bankers fully appreciate their accountabilities and responsibilities and adhere to the necessary disciplines.

How will the nation meet all of these obligations? Present assets are obviously insufficient, and the national net worth is in the red by nearly four trillion dollars. There are only three broad options available:

1. Muddle through and push the burden off to our children, starting them out deep in the red with little choice except to repudiate the debts we have contracted;

2. Sell assets, shrink the economy, raise taxes, and reduce the standard of living dramatically to pay for our past excesses;

3. Cheapen the currency and pay off our debts with a heavily depreciated currency.

I wish there were brighter alternatives. If there are such alternatives, we should devote every resource to discover and implement them. But I'm afraid the old adage is true: There is no free lunch. Our classic cycle of economic and fiscal policies brought us to this point, and now we have to pay the price. It is no different than the Pharaohs of ancient Egypt wasting resources to build the Pyramids, or the medieval monarchs investing in military build-ups for their foreign campaigns. It has happened in the developing nations in modern times with their attempts to construct big infrastructure programs, unfortunately, in many cases, encouraged and aided by our own nation and the World Bank.

The data on our government's assets and liabilities and income come from a publication called *Consolidated Financial Statements of the United States Government, Fiscal Year 1984—Prototype*, compiled by the Financial Management Service of the Department of the Treasury. They revealed the following financial position. (See Figure 18.2.)

FIGURE 18.2: UNITED STATES GOVERNMENT CONSOLIDATED STATEMENT OF FINANCIAL POSITION
as of September 30, 1984 (in billions)

Assets

Cash and monetary reserves		$72.8
Receivables (accounts, loans, etc. net of allowances)		301.4
Inventories (goods, materials, supplies, etc. at cost)		151.4
Property and equipment (at cost)		
Land	10.3	
Buildings, structures and facilities	137.0	
Military hardware	330.2	
Equipment	88.6	
Other	45.5	
Accumulated Depreciation	(299.5)	
	312.1	
Deferred charges and other assets		99.6
Total		$937.3

Liabilities

Accounts payable		$161.5
Unearned revenue		31.8
Borrowing from the public		1,299.5
Accrued pension, retirement and disability plans		
Military personnel	476.1	
Civilian employees	542.7	
Social security	1,911.8	
Veterans compensation	221.8	
Federal employees compensation	11.2	
Other pension plans	18.2	
	3,181.8	
Contingent liabilities		3.5
Other liabilities		58.5
Total		$4,736.6

Financial Position

Net Worth (deficit)	($3,799.3)

The report has a preface written by the Comptroller General of the United States. In this preface, the Comptroller writes as follows:

This consolidated financial report provides useful information about the financial condition and operations of the Federal Government as a whole that is not available elsewhere: It is supplementary to information contained in the budget documents. The consolidated statements disclose the magnitude of the government's assets and future claims on resources not fully disclosed in the budget, such as the government's inventories and fixed assets as well as its pension and social security liabilities, and public debt.

Although this report is a prototype, it demonstrates a goal we strongly support—the annual publication of formal audited consolidated financial statements of the United States Government. Achieving this goal will be a significant milestone towards building strong viable financial management systems that will serve the needs of government and the public in the last decade of the 20th century and beyond.

That is also a goal of this book. Governments will always go to excess and run out of control unless the people at large understand what they are doing and apply the necessary restraints. When the financial system is corrupted by expediencies or excesses, everyone is ultimately corrupted. A nation that lacks the will to keep a close watch on its purse strings, is doomed to lose its purse. A democracy that lacks the enterprise to learn about banking and finance, is doomed to be betrayed by it.

NINETEEN

Leaning Against the Wind

This book ends as it started, with an insider's look at the workings of financial institutions and at some issues and problems that merit discussion and, in some cases, corrective policy changes.

There is no time to lose because the challenges we face with the economy, the trade balance, the current-account payments balance, and the national deficit are enormous. To address these challenges properly, the money and banking system must be made strong and kept that way because there is no such thing as a healthy economy without a healthy banking system. We cannot survive if we are condemned to move from financial crisis to crisis without a larger vision of how to achieve stability, continuity, and orderly economic growth.

Both the causes and solutions to our problems are ourselves. We cause the crises ourselves and we do it over and over again. We do it because we entrust our savings and our financial institutions to ordinary men and women and we don't take the time or trouble to understand what they are doing and, thereby, to assure ourselves that they are keeping the money and banking system healthy and safe.

We have seen that the temptations of ambition and greed, the lust for position and power, the arrogance of self-delusion, and false conviction can engulf even the most pro-establishment leaders. The only constant wisdom in a democracy is the collective wisdom of the voting public. A humorist once told me, "I would rather be governed by 1,000 names picked at random from the telephone book, any telephone book, than the 1,000 renowned scholars identified by the nation's major universities." I happen to agree. I don't believe in governance by the so-called "best and brightest" à la Aristotle's city state. Aristotle believed in the singular wisdom of the benevolent king. His second choice was an oligarchy, a few elite people with absolute power to implement their special wisdom, and after that, an aristocracy. Aristotle did not believe in democracy because he considered it unwieldy and capable of manipulation by demagogues who would radicalize a democracy into an irrational mob, which he called *anarchy*. He feared anarchy because he believed it would ultimately lead to tyranny.

With all due respect, I disagree with the great philosopher. I believe that democracy is the most noble and most stable system of government as long as the voting public is provided with adequate information and exposure. Aristotle, after all, had not experienced the marvels of modern-day communication or the singular power of television. Give the people information, and their collective, educated judgment will be correct.

The purpose of this book is, in this spirit, to inform. Information is essential to keep the money and banking system vigorous, expansive and safe.

With information, the public can be the guardian of the system, giving approval when conditions are to its liking and mandating changes when conditions are not.

Generally, it is not the system that causes problems but the people entrusted with the responsibility to operate it. Leaders will not often have the vision and courage to lean against the wind when the exceptional situation requires such action. On the contrary, when the wind is at their back, leaders will tend to hoist maximum sail. The worst violators, those who hoist the most sail at the most inopportune times, are honored by their peers and, worse yet, are followed. When a banking leader such as Continental Illinois hoisted full sail and moved in an errant direction, motivated by greed, ambition, and a quick profit, it was admired and followed by a large part of the industry. Unfortunately, the public was not sufficiently informed to judge the banks' collective wisdom, or prevent their folly.

Bankers, like almost any group in society, find undeniable excitement, comfort and, at times, solace, in standing shoulder-to-shoulder with their colleagues and peers and "being all in this together." Moreover, it is probably essential to the stability of any society that people think more or less alike and agree on what is good or bad, on what should be done and what should not be done. This is our tradition. As children, we learn how to do things by watching others. Our educational system, in large part, asks our young people to memorize and accept uncritically facts and ideas handed down by others. There is good reason for the socialization process. We would make no progress if each of us tried to reinvent the wheel every time we needed a vehicle to help us move. Doctors must treat illness consistent with current methods and trends—indeed, they take great risks if they vary from accepted practices. Judges are required by law to follow precedent in resolving disputes. We judge each other legally, morally, ethically, esthetically, and in other ways according to standards of the community.

However, the potential pitfall is obvious. We sometimes need course corrections, and we need balance. We need the invigoration of new ideas and the ability to change our heading before we get too far off course.

This is especially true when it comes to our economy. Our economy is an essential underpinning of a unique society predicated on balance. This balance includes an equitable distribution of wealth, a strong middle class, and self-regulating professions carrying out their responsibilities ethically. We rely on markets and money to regulate the production and allocation of goods and services. More important, we rely on a belief that sooner or later virtually everyone will recognize the chance to seize a beneficial opportunity when it is presented to him or her. We accept that seizing opportunities will be tempered by respect and recognition for doing the right thing and disgrace for doing the wrong thing.

Enter the entrepreneur. He or she is a person with the vision, the energy, and the courage to raise capital, to take risks, and to pursue an idea—often creating something for all of us that we did not have before to improve our lives. The entrepreneur is the primary engine of change in our economy, if not our society. And, as change and progress are glorified, so is the entrepreneur.

The success of the entrepreneur is judged by the fortune he or she amasses. Our confidence in the efficiency of the capitalist market system to run our economy (a confidence I share) leads us to believe that the significant wealth earned by some entrepreneurs arises out of a positive contribution to the economy. Certainly we need the invigoration of entrepreneurs to make our economy work, but the accumulation of wealth and profit is not a surrogate yardstick for right and wrong. Just as we do not accept uncritically the proposition that one is poor because one deserves to be poor, we must not accept uncritically the proposition that the maximization of profits and wealth is the sole, or even primary, purpose of our professions and institutions. While the current trend may be otherwise, we know that such things as health care and education cannot be merely rationed and sold to the highest bidders. We know instinctively that when our lawyers become motivated by money alone and forget their ethical obligations to their clients and our legal system, people will lose respect for the law and the fabric of our legal system will begin to unravel. Similarly, few would see a bright future for this country if we changed "one man, one vote" to "one dollar, one vote."

It is the same with our financial institutions. Yes, they should make money. But, more than that, they must be strong and safe. They must exude stability and integrity. The people who run them must not be viewed as predatory or avaricious, nor must the institutions be viewed as partial to one constituency. The banker or thrift executive is not an entrepreneur. The public will not trust its savings to an entrepreneur. That is why banking was invented: to serve as a buffer between the saver and the entrepreneur. The role of the banker was first performed by priests, who were trusted because no institution was more solid than the temple. Even today, there is an aura of respect when one visits a bank or a savings and loan.

Financial institutions have to be accountable to many constituencies: the community, the depositors, the borrowers, the employees, the shareholders, and the economy at large. Making money for shareholders is a legitimate objective for those who manage financial institutions. But it is only one objective. The banker must have the vision and responsibility to rank all the priorities and to balance them in the context of current conditions. The winds of popular opinion—current trends and peer pressure—blow hard. Most of the time we keep those winds at our back, keep our sails full, and enjoy the ride. But we also must remain vigilant. We must strain to see as far as possible ahead of us, and we must always be willing to turn dramatically, if necessary, to lean against the wind, and to maintain that difficult stance until the wind shifts and is once again at our backs. And then we must be ready to repeat the pattern all over again.

To help us succeed in this endeavor, we need leaders, genuine leaders who will steer a prudent course, realizing that the winds are ever changeable. Such leaders emerge only when the public accepts the need for such leadership and is willing to follow because it is sufficiently informed. The recognition for such leadership is *respect*, not money. The leader's reward is satisfaction that the public interest has been served.

Money is the appropriate reward for a successful entrepreneur, but money can make a leader corrupt. Respect goes along with good public service, and with respect goes power. This is the most heady payback of all. But, a leader without power is nothing. To lead effectively, he or she must have respect, and respect is power.

You may wonder why this discussion is relevant. It is relevant because we, as Americans, have difficult, politically charged challenges to overcome.

Our economy is flunking. The moral fiber of our leaders is being found wanting. We run the danger of becoming a nation of cynics, willing to tolerate and accept the baser instincts of humanity instead of establishing standards for truth and honor and charity. We run the risk of destroying the underpinnings of civilized society.

If we allow our standards to deteriorate in this fashion, we cannot hope to reverse the economic trends with which we are now bedeviled. We face increasing loss of mutual trust and public support for our economic system, a system that cannot recover without such support. The free market needs the free flow of accurate information in order to regulate the system and allocate resources. Without the rules of conduct so important to a properly functioning marketplace, the market itself will disappear.

The good news is that it doesn't have to be. There is nothing in the scriptures that ordains we must self-destruct as a society or as an economy. Destiny is ours to shape as we see fit.

The first requirement is to reach a consensus on a code of behavior that will be practiced voluntarily, as opposed to being enforced by prosecutors. Let us teach ethics in the business schools and establish a code of honor for dealings in the business community, the breach of which will result in commercial ostracism.

The second requirement is to establish the proper hierarchy of acknowledged success, where accumulation of money and wealth are not at the top of the list. Let us advance the proper recognition and tangible evidences of appreciation and respect for educators, government officials and their staffs, academicians, clergy, political leaders, bankers, scientists, social workers, and others in our society who cannot and must not be judged by their ability to accumulate and manifest wealth.

A third requirement is to have the courage to face reality, to prescribe and take corrective actions against our present ills, no matter how difficult these remedies might be.

If we must raise taxes to eliminate the deficit, then let's raise taxes. If we must work harder and longer, then let's work harder and longer. If we must have military conscription to maintain our national defense and still cut costs, then let's have national conscription. If we must save and invest more and consume less, then let's save and invest more and consume less. If we must raise energy prices to maintain the independence of our foreign policy, then let's raise energy prices. If we must export more to redress our balance of trade, then let's export more. If the big banks must restructure their loans to developing countries to permit those countries to rebuild their economies, then let's enforce proper interpretation of the securities laws and require the big banks to value their assets at market prices. Such a requirement, by itself, will accelerate the need to restructure. If we need to invent new financial structures and distribution systems to ensure that our farmers are producing to capacity and the food they produce is being fed to the hungry around the globe, then let's invent these new structures and distribution systems. If we must build roads, bridges, airports, and public transportation systems to alleviate overcrowding and traffic jams, then let's build them and charge user fees to pay the bills. If we need to tax ourselves to maintain the integrity of our social security system, our health care system, our veterans' programs and our educational systems, then let's do it.

How can we afford to do all of this?, you ask.

How can we afford not to do it? Unfortunately, we will have to do it the old-fashioned way, as the Smith Barney advertisement on television proclaims. "We will have to earn it." We can talk all we want about character and morality and courage and strength, but no society could ever claim to have excelled in maintaining these standards without having the simple decency to pay its own way.

Paying our own way must be the basic moral standard for each and every one of us individually if collectively we are to make progress as a nation or a global community. Plato wrote that the state is merely the "individual written large." Plato is right. Our nation is nothing more than the collection of us all. If each individual is strong, the state will be strong. If each individual is weak, the state will be weak. And how do we rate ourselves on this standard? Look at the record! It reads: big national debt, big deficits, big negative net worth. Plain, old-fashioned poor financial management. Worse, we evidence no "guts" even to make a commitment to start the corrective actions. The first corrective action is to put this nation back to work. Everyone able to work must be allowed to work, even required to work. The nation needs the labors of each and every one of us, just as it did in other periods of national emergency. Yes, the present is a time of national emergency: The emergency is financial. We can measure the depth of that emergency by assessing the stability of our currency, our financial statement, our debt levels. As a society, and as an economy, we don't measure up well to a prudent management standard. The value of our money in the bank is debased, and the solution to this plight can come only from us, acting as individuals, in an educated polity.

My father, to whom this book is dedicated, used to say, "Let there be a living standard below which no one in this great country can fall, and above that standard let everyone compete freely to the level of their talent and abilities." I didn't believe this approach practical or possible. Now I am not so sure. Perhaps if all of us who can work do work, we can afford a basic subsistence standard for those who need it, and perhaps we can do it in a practical, dignified way through a negative income tax.

Through academic brilliance in the public school system, my father bootstrapped himself out of the Syrian-Lebanese ghetto in Boston's South End to Massachusetts Institute of Technology, where he received a degree in mechanical engineering in 1922. He started his own company and, like so many people, was forced to close by the Great Depression in 1932 when a bank would not make him a loan to carry his receivables. It was at that point that he felt and witnessed first-hand the debilitation and despair that joblessness brings about. He saw the benefits of New Deal programs like the WPA and the CCC and the hope provided by the National Recovery Act. He saw the good work that the settlement houses in the big-city ghettos performed for youngsters and oldsters.

People cared, and the political leaders cared. My mother wrote to Betsy Cushing, then Jimmy Roosevelt's wife and a prominent Bostonian, requesting her help in finding a job for my father. It was a beautiful letter citing his education and qualifications and strength of character. Mrs. Roosevelt responded and arranged for my father to interview for the local Federal Home Loan Bank, where he won a position amidst tough competition. After that, he taught at Hampton Institute in Virginia and had a distinguished career in engineering until his retirement.

The point is that people ready, willing, and able to work need a helping hand on occasion. This is particularly appropriate when the government itself is the culprit in destroying the economic marketplace through bad policies and a lack of fiscal discipline. The "trickle down" economic theory is fine in good times. But even then, the "trickle" only permeates the upper reaches of the economy. It never benefits the less advantaged sectors which need special attention to promote growth, to harness the talents and labors of the people who feel trapped and sorely desire to be productive.

President Roosevelt in the 1930s said, "We have nothing to fear but fear itself." In the 1980s we are not plagued by fear. On the contrary, we probably have some degree of subtle, self-righteous complacency. The issue today is not fear but weakness of character and spirit. We seemingly don't have the "guts" to take the bull by the horns and set him charging down the road of competitive performance.

The fact is that our nation is blessed with great national resources. We also have the greatest economic system known to man: free markets and capitalism. Yet we can't seem to earn our way to solvency and prosperity because we lack resolve and discipline. The cliche says, "When the going gets tough, the tough get going." We'll soon find out how tough we are when we finally decide whether we can productively harness our talents and labors to the bountiful resources with which we are blessed.

The alternative is to continue to evolve into a pure service economy, increasing the range and breadth of financial instruments and seeking to place mortgages and liens on every tangible asset known to man. This puts us on the road to becoming a nation of paper shufflers. Our overly litigious society is producing lawyers, financiers, accountants, investigators, and tax collectors in great supply. Robert Reich, the economist at the John F. Kennedy School of Government at Harvard University calls them "paper entrepreneurs." Our society is not producing adequate numbers of engineers, artisans, craftsmen, and blue-collar workers. Nations are capable of falling into such a negative spiral. It is happening in the United Kingdom where the service economy in the south of England prospers while unemployment in the industrial midlands and the north wreaks havoc on the social structure. In those regions unemployment is destroying the middle class.

Can you imagine what such a condition would mean to our country, where the middle class forms the foundation of our democracy? Shrink the middle class, underemploy it, or overtax it, and then stand by for trouble. But call on the middle class to rise to the nation's defense or to work to restore the nation's fiscal integrity and, if history is any guide, you will see a tremendous response. Moreover, it will be a healthy, enthusiastic response, its success reflected in a secure financial system bolstered by the most important capital of all—public confidence. The level of that confidence, the true worth and safety of our money in the bank, is something for each one of us to ponder as participants in a democracy.

My own judgment is that the money and banking system in its broadest reach is a direct reflection of the society and economy that serves it. A strong society will have a strong economy, and a strong economy must, by definition, include a strong money and banking system. Conversely, a weak society and a weak economy cannot sustain a strong currency or a safe banking system.

The operative question, therefore, is "are we weak or strong" as a society and as an economy and can the present money and banking systems sustain us? I, personally, have no doubts about the answers to these questions.

Our American society, rooted in a strong democratic tradition, continues to be fundamentally sound. Consider the crises we have weathered in the rust belt, in the farm belt, and natural resource regions and poverty zones. The impact on pride and dignity has been severe. But families have stayed together, commitment to values has remained intact and dedication to our free enterprise, market driven system appears stronger than ever.

Our economy is also basically sound. Admittedly, it has suffered through a major readjustment but it survived because the market was allowed to work. Obviously, there were casualties and these hurt. But we are living in an artificial environment of overspending, underworking, overleveraging, too many get rich quick schemes through financial legerdemain and an unwillingness to pay our own way. The October 1987 stock market collapse (precipitated by a tightening of the money supply at the wrong time just as in 1929) changed all of that. It is now back to reality—hard work, realizable profit expectations and the requirement to maintain strong balance sheets and to pay steady and ever increasing common dividends. The fancy stock market manipulations are now largely behind us. It is back to basics. Market a good product or service at a fair price and above all do it efficiently and watch your pennies. All of this needs to be done in a sensible tax environment and some of the recent proposals on taxation have been far from sensible. For example, non-deductibility of interest, double taxation for dividends and capital gains taxes discourage capital formation.

Throughout this rigorous period of readjustment, the inherent strength of the money and banking regulatory system maintained public confidence. Despite record numbers of failures among thrift and banking depositories, the ability of the banking system to cope and keep depositors' money intact has kept the system viable. But this result was achieved largely because a dedicated, hard working group of regulators at federal and state levels found ways to solve problems of crisis proportions despite outdated and, in many cases, counterproductive laws and regulations that impeded rather than helped rescue operations. It is a tribute to these unknown and seldom recognized men and women that we have done as well as we have. There is no question that we need a regulatory overhaul of major proportions. I have, in this book, described the areas that I believe need attention and the principles that I believe should be our guide, including the notion of conservative financial orthodoxy.

In all events, it is a time to provoke discussion of these matters because they are too important to be left unattended. Understanding the system and its mechanics is one thing. Using that understanding to formulate policies and then to develop consensus for those policies is another.

As a nation, we are at a crossroad. We can continue to ignore our deficiencies and our deficits and allow them eventually to engulf us. Or we can look at ourselves in the mirror and begin to deal constructively with harsh realities, warts and all.

The answer to the question posed by this book lies in the wisdom of the great poet, Robert Burns, "Oh for the power to see ourselves as others see us."

Index